# THOSE WHO STAYED

# THOSE WHO STAYED

## A VIETNAM DIARY

**CLAUDIA KRICH**

UNIVERSITY OF VIRGINIA PRESS
*Charlottesville and London*

The University of Virginia Press is situated on the traditional lands of the Monacan Nation, and the Commonwealth of Virginia was and is home to many other Indigenous people. We pay our respect to all of them, past and present. We also honor the enslaved African and African American people who built the University of Virginia, and we recognize their descendants. We commit to fostering voices from these communities through our publications and to deepening our collective understanding of their histories and contributions.

University of Virginia Press
© 2025 by Claudia Krich
All rights reserved
Printed in the United States of America on acid-free paper

*First published 2025*

9 8 7 6 5 4 3 2 1

LIBRARY OF CONGRESS CATALOGING-IN-PUBLICATION DATA
Names: Krich, Claudia, author.
Title: Those who stayed : a Vietnam diary / Claudia Krich.
Description: Charlottesville : University of Virginia Press, 2025. | Includes bibliographical references and index.
Identifiers: LCCN 2024017782 (print) | LCCN 2024017783 (ebook) | ISBN 9780813952352 (hardback) | ISBN 9780813952376 (ebook)
Subjects: LCSH: Krich, Claudia, 1948– —Diaries. | American Friends Service Committee—Biography. | Humanitarian aid workers—Vietnam—Diaries. | Vietnam War, 1961–1975—Personal narratives, American. | Vietnam War, 1961–1975—Vietnam—Ho Chi Minh City. | Vietnam War, 1961–1975—Civilian relief. | Humanitarian assistance, American—Vietnam—History. | Vietnam War, 1961–1975—Women—United States—Biography. | Ho Chi Minh City (Vietnam)—History.
Classification: LCC DS559.63 .K75 2025 (print) | LCC DS559.63 (ebook) | DDC 959.704/31 [B]—dc23/eng/20240808
LC record available at https://lccn.loc.gov/2024017782
LC ebook record available at https://lccn.loc.gov/2024017783

*All photographs are from the author's personal collection unless otherwise noted.*

*Cover photo:* The author writing in her journal on a Sài Gòn street corner, 1975
*Cover design:* Kelley Galbreath

To my dear friend Chị Mai, whose whole name is Nguyễn Thị Mai, whose original name is Khưu Thị Hồng, who stepped on an American landmine and lost both her legs from the explosion.

To the memory of my dear friend and teammate Rick Thompson, who died in an airplane crash in Việt Nam. He was charming, energetic, fearless, smart, and dedicated to a better world.

They both struggled and sacrificed, like so many others, to bring peace to Việt Nam.

# CONTENTS

*Foreword by Gareth Porter* | ix
*List of Abbreviations* | xv
*Author's Note* | xvii

**Prologue: Before Sài Gòn** — 1
1. Increasing Tensions — 31
2. Fear and Panic — 40
3. Liberation, or the "Fall" of Việt Nam — 54
4. Sunrise — 61
5. The First Few Days — 68
6. Yến Is In Charge — 76
7. Getting Organized — 86
8. We Are Detained, and Other Events — 91
9. Changes, Changes — 102
10. Celebrations — 114
11. Interesting Characters — 120
12. Hồ Chí Minh's Birthday — 130
13. Day by Day — 139

## Contents

14. Tiger Cages and Politics — 150

15. Adjusting and Adapting — 158

16. Immunizations and Red Tape — 165

17. "Rockets" and News — 173

18. A Culture of Visiting — 183

19. Yes, I Am — 187

20. Chị Mai, Yến, and Dung — 192

21. The Future — 199

22. We're Leaving — 209

Epilogue — 217

Acknowledgments — 223

Appendix: Historical Context
    My Story, by Nguyễn Thị Mai (Khưu Thị Hồng) | 225
    Letter from Đà Nẵng, by Tom Hoskins, M.D. | 227
    How I Came to Live in America, by Phương-Hằng Phan | 228
    My Congressional Delegation Trip to Việt Nam, by
        Paul N. "Pete" McCloskey Jr. | 231
    I Helped Find the Tiger Cages, by Don Luce | 232
    I Was a Prisoner of War, by Bob Chenoweth | 233
    At a Demonstration Led by Buddhist Nuns, by Max Ediger | 235
    I Sailed on the *Phoenix*, by Beryl Nelson | 237
    Meeting General Giáp's Son, by Craig McNamara | 238
    Why So Many South Vietnamese Feared a Bloodbath,
        by Gareth Porter | 240
    War Crimes against Vietnamese Civilians, by Gareth Porter | 243
    Agent Orange and Birth Defects, by Gareth Porter | 246
    The Third Force, by Gareth Porter | 248
    Re-education Camps, by Gareth Porter | 251
    Việt Nam's Religions, by Gareth Porter | 252
    The Paris Peace Agreement, by Gareth Porter | 255

*Index* | 259

***Illustrations follow page 164***

# FOREWORD

For Americans who remember the end of the Việt Nam War, their most indelible image is probably of South Vietnamese frantically trying to board the last helicopter leaving the roof of the U.S. Embassy in Sài Gòn. This has provided the dramatic frame for the dominant American narrative of the end of the war.

The thousands of Vietnamese who tried so desperately to leave were panic-stricken because the South Vietnamese government had been telling them for years that those who had worked for or collaborated with the United States would face terrible reprisals if the Communists took over. The United States and the Sài Gòn government declared relentlessly that the North Vietnamese would carry out a terrible bloodbath of Sài Gòn government personnel and families, and cited alleged Communist "blood debt lists" with hundreds of thousands of names of South Vietnamese on them. It was a cruel and successful propaganda campaign. It should be no surprise that so many South Vietnamese believed their lives were in imminent danger and that some resorted to extreme actions, including risking their own and their families' lives to get out of the country. Almost all Americans similarly joined the exodus, anticipating scenes of chaos and violence in Sài Gòn as a result of the Communist takeover. That fact reflects the high degree of agreement among American officials and civilians, including the news media, that mass Communist reprisals against those who had been associated with the U.S. military or the Sài Gòn government would certainly take place after a victory by the forces controlled by the North Vietnamese Communists.

One reason those scenes of panic-stricken Vietnamese played out before the rest of the world in the final hours before the Communist-led troops entered Sài Gòn is that key officials of the U.S. government, including Secretary of State Henry Kissinger and Ambassador Graham Martin, had refused to carry out an orderly evacuation over the previous weeks. As CIA official Frank Snepp recounted in his book *Decent Interval*, they had been determined to obtain a face-saving coalition government within the legal structure of the existing South Vietnamese constitution that would preserve a facade of U.S. influence in the country. This fanciful notion at that point in the war was the basis for not beginning a large-scale evacuation sooner, on the ground that it would undermine the prospects for negotiating that hypothetical coalition.*

As the North Vietnamese forces began taking over provinces, and would soon take over the town and province of Quảng Ngãi, Claudia Krich and her American Friends Service Committee teammates fled from there to Sài Gòn. But when the same change was imminent in Sài Gòn and the American government was urging all Americans to leave the country, they decided to stay and not flee again, in order to witness for themselves the final outcome of the conflict between the U.S.-sponsored government and army and the revolutionary government under the leadership of Việt Nam's Communist Lao Động Party.

As a result of their decision to stay, Krich has assembled a vivid personal account of the final days of the Việt Nam War and its immediate aftermath that provides a needed counterpoint to the images of the war's end that have been so deeply engraved on the collective memory of Americans by photographs, news footage, and documentary films. Krich's account brings to the surface lively encounters between the Sài Gòn population and troops of the victorious army in the days that followed the entrance of the troops into Sài Gòn. The scenes she describes present a dramatically different sociopolitical reality from the stark terror that preceded the arrival of the troops. *Those*

---

* Frank Snepp, *Decent Interval* (New York: Random House, 1977), esp. 325, 331, and 398.

*Who Stayed* is drawn from her own diary and letters, and other original sources. It also includes a number of firsthand recollections of individuals with unusual stories to tell, which add depth and original content.

Instead of stereotypical images of a conquering army suspicious of and antagonistic toward the Saigonese, the vignettes in *Those Who Stayed* reflect the reality that veteran Vietnamese revolutionary troops, most of whom had apparently been far from home for years, were both highly disciplined in their behavior and extraordinarily relaxed and friendly toward ordinary Saigonese. Many even displayed naivete toward locals selling them items of doubtful authenticity at inflated prices. These vignettes contradict the image from U.S. and Sài Gòn war propaganda of hard-bitten and severe Việt Cộng and North Vietnamese troops.

Even more surprising and revealing are descriptions of encounters with civilian political cadres, National Liberation Front members who had long served the revolutionary cause, some of whom Krich and her colleagues had known previously as foreign language tutors and workers in education and health care. The profiles of those personalities in the book shed light on a little-known but arguably important element of the long Vietnamese revolutionary struggle, which is that large numbers of covert cadres had successfully cultivated long-term personal relationships with Sài Gòn government officials and with foreigners, while concealing their affiliation with the revolution. Their dedication and the subtlety of their work were among the many reasons why the struggle was ultimately successful.

Krich's accounts are not written from the detached perspective of a scholar but from the lived experiences of the author and her colleagues who had witnessed the worst aspects of the war for years. Quảng Ngãi City and Province, in the northern part of South Việt Nam, where their volunteer program's medical relief center was located, had some of the oldest and strongest local Vietnamese Communist Party organizations in all of Việt Nam, dating back decades. Because of the loyalty of those hamlets to the revolutionary cause, the U.S. Military Assistance Command Vietnam under General William Westmoreland adopted a policy of treating the populations living in the long-term Communist base areas of Quảng Ngãi not as civilians but as combatants.

That is why some of the worst U.S. violence against Vietnamese civilians during the entire war was in Quảng Ngãi Province. The U.S. Air Force carried out many of its heaviest airstrikes against hamlets in Quảng Ngãi. Those airstrikes, reported in excruciating detail in the book *The Military Half* by Jonathan Schell, were explicitly aimed at forcing the people to leave the Communist-organized hamlets for government-controlled refugee camps.

The loyalty of the hamlets to the revolutionary cause also explains why Mỹ Lai, which is in Quảng Ngãi Province, was the site of a deliberate U.S. massacre of civilians, and why South Korean troops paid for by the Lyndon Johnson administration, who were also fighting in Quảng Ngãi in 1968, committed at least two dozen atrocities involving deliberate killing of groups of women, children, and elderly men in a number of hamlets. Diane Jones and Michael Jones—members of the Quaker team—heard about those atrocities from Vietnamese contacts and later documented them through interviews with survivors.

Because of their location in Quảng Ngãi Province, and the Vietnamese they met and assisted, Claudia Krich and the other non-Vietnamese working at the Quaker medical center there, more than most other foreign civilians working in South Việt Nam, were constantly confronted with the terrible toll of the American war on Vietnamese civilians and with the perspectives of Vietnamese who were most directly affected. That experience certainly strengthened their commitment to peace and reconciliation. It didn't make them ex parte defenders of the revolutionary side or of the government in Hà Nội, but it did make them open to experiencing a different drama at the end of the Việt Nam War.

In the years that followed the revolutionary victory and the swift reunification of North and South Việt Nam, orthodox Communist policies toward political organization and economic management prevailed over more innovative policies advocated by officials in both Sài Gòn and Hà Nội. And security officials in the south prevailed over those officials who favored more innovative policies such as much shorter periods in re-education camps for some levels of former Sài Gòn government officials. But the government never carried out the revenge killings of its former enemies that the American war propaganda had predicted. Within a generation Việt Nam had become the most successful economy in the entire region. Although the verdict of history on the events surrounding the end of the war has been essentially avoided in subsequent discourse about the war, it is certainly aligned with the narrative that Claudia Krich gives us.

Gareth Porter

# ABBREVIATIONS

| | |
|---|---|
| AFSC | American Friends Service Committee, a non-governmental Quaker pacifist humanitarian relief organization founded in 1917, winner of the Nobel Peace Prize. AFSC began humanitarian work in Việt Nam in 1965, carrying on its custom of establishing programs for civilians in conflict zones. |
| ARVN | Army of the Republic of (South) Việt Nam, military arm of the GRVN, including ground and air forces |
| COR | Committee of Responsibility, a non-governmental American humanitarian organization formed in 1966 to help Vietnamese children by bringing them to the U.S. for medical treatment and rehabilitation |
| DRV | Democratic Republic of Việt Nam, the government of North Việt Nam until July 2, 1976 |
| GRVN | Government of the Republic of Việt Nam, the government of South Việt Nam until April 30, 1975 |
| MCC | Mennonite Central Committee, a non-governmental American humanitarian organization founded in 1920 |
| NLF | National Liberation Front, the military arm of the PRG. This included uniformed guerrillas and cadres in areas of South Việt Nam controlled by the PRG, and civilians who were secretly also with the NLF. |
| NVA | North Vietnamese Army, military arm of the DRV |
| PAVN | People's Army of Việt Nam, formal name of NVA. PAVN included both the regulars from the north and the southern armed contingent. |

| | | |
|---|---|---|
| PRG | | Provisional Revolutionary Government of the Republic of South Việt Nam, the unoffocial government, opposed to the South Vietnamese GRVN. The official government of South Việt Nam from April 30, 1975, to July 2, 1976. |
| RSVN | | The Republic of South Việt Nam, the official government of South Việt Nam from April 30, 1975, to July 2, 1976 |
| SRVN | | Socialist Republic of Việt Nam, government of Việt Nam. The PRG merged with the DRV government of North Việt Nam to become the Socialist Republic of Việt Nam on July 2, 1976. |
| Third Force | | Anti-war activists against the GRVN Nguyễn Văn Thiệu government of South Việt Nam, working for a compromise solution to the war |
| VC | | Việt Cộng, American slang for Communist |
| VNCS | | Viet-Nam Christian Service, a cooperative relief and service program of Church World Service, Lutheran World Relief, and the Mennonite Central Committee. It was established in 1965 and operated in wartime southern Việt Nam until 1975. MCC withdrew from VNCS in 1972 and continued its work separately. |

# AUTHOR'S NOTE

I have used Vietnamese spellings throughout. I have also used the real names of my colleagues and acquaintances, with a few exceptions to protect their privacy.

The material in the appendix—historical pieces as well as personal anecdotes—is intended as a supplement to my own record, offering broader context. I am very grateful to all those who shared their personal stories, adding valuable dimensions to this book. I am particularly grateful to the scholar and historian Gareth Porter, who contributed heavily to this effort with his introduction and annotations. He was the Sài Gòn bureau chief for Dispatch News Service during 1971 while completing his Ph.D. in Southeast Asian Studies at Cornell University. He was codirector of the Indochina Resource Center in Washington, D.C. He returned to Việt Nam several times after the war to research postwar Vietnamese foreign and economic policy. And he is an author and journalist who has written several books and many articles about the Việt Nam War, Vietnamese politics and policies, and—since 2004—about U.S. wars and conflicts in the Middle East.

# THOSE WHO STAYED

## PROLOGUE

# BEFORE SÀI GÒN

It wasn't smart to get pregnant in Việt Nam during the war. I lost the pregnancy at six months, in late December 1974. But our lives were surrounded by human tragedy, and I had to remember that this was just another one among many. Nothing made me special. Nothing protected me. Our daily lives were pretty much the same as everyone else's.

My husband, Keith Brinton, and I were the directors of the American Friends Service Committee program in Việt Nam from April 1973 until July 1975. We lived in Quảng Ngãi in the very poor rural province of the same name. Quảng Ngãi had once been a small town, but by 1967 there were over 200,000 refugees from the countryside living in mud-walled structures with corrugated metal roofs in camps on the outskirts of town, and in makeshift tin structures in town. Military operations and conflict in the province were constant, as some areas were controlled by the South Vietnamese Army and others by the National Liberation Front. Our city was controlled by the South Vietnamese Army, which in daytime also had control of nearby surrounding territory, but the Liberation Front had control at night. Many villagers lived under this dual government. We always had to be aware of the time and where we were, especially if we were returning patients to villages that weren't close to town.

The dilapidated Quảng Ngãi Province Hospital was overwhelmed and understaffed, and injured civilians were given initial treatment and then discharged as quickly as possible. Often patients were not ready to leave a medical facility. Those who had lost arms or legs or had been burned or become paralyzed needed further care and rehabilitation, and sometimes their villages had been bombed and they didn't even have homes to return to. Some were shunned by their families, or their families were dead.

In 1967, AFSC set up the Quaker Rehabilitation Center for injured civilians on the grounds of the hospital. The program began in a warehouse that had once been a tuberculosis center. The original building was altered and expanded several times until it had three main areas in a horseshoe shape. On one side was the physical therapy department and a small surgery room, in the middle was the admissions and administration area, and the third wing housed the prosthetics department. An extra building in back was where patients stayed during their treatment. The buildings were made of cement blocks, with bars in the windows, no glass, and wood shutters. The floor was cement and the uninsulated roof was galvanized iron. The grounds were mostly dirt and sand, with a few trees. One perk for me was that I did not have hay fever, because there was no grass.

Patients stayed with us for weeks or months, receiving medical treatment and physical therapy and learning to use their artificial limbs. Many patients needed "stump revision" surgery to correct how a leg or arm had been crudely amputated after they were first injured, so that they could be fitted with prosthetic legs and arms. Patients also needed braces or wheelchairs or crutches, or all of those.

While I was pregnant we had a patient named Ly who had lost her leg to a landmine. Her husband had abandoned her, believing the common superstition that she would not be able to have more children, so she was there with only her three-year-old daughter. Little Lan was outgoing, talkative, and charming, and I'd often walk through our housing wing to visit with the two of them.

One day they were gone. I quickly learned that Lan was very sick with a rash and a high fever, and she had been moved to the hospital itself, a few dozen yards away. I went right there and found her in a crowded ward, lying on a stained bare mattress in an old baby crib.

Quảng Ngãi Hospital was dirty and crowded, overwhelmed with war injured as well as regular patients. The government paid doctors poorly, so they spent more time in their private clinics than at the hospital. Sometimes two and occasionally three patients shared a bed, sometimes contagious and injured together. They would lie on the bed in opposite directions. Any money the government was willing to spend on health care was going to the military, not to civilian public hospitals like this one.

Ly greeted me in tears and told me they didn't know what was wrong with Lan, and that they weren't doing anything for her. Could I help? I hugged her and cried with her, but there was nothing I could do. The next day that beautiful little girl's fever was higher. She became delirious, and then she died.

A few days after I visited them at the hospital, I was sick with a rash and fever myself. It got worse quickly. Our friends brought me a special dark broth from a northern doctor, a respected local healer. I hesitated when I saw that the liquid contained dead beetles, but I drank it anyway, hoping it would help. It made my heart beat quickly, gave me some energy, and made me feel a little better for several hours. But soon after that, my fetus became completely still, and though I waited and hoped, and cried and cried, it never moved again. I wondered if the northern doctor hated Americans and had poisoned me. But it turned out that German measles had killed beautiful little Lan and also our baby.

It was a medical emergency, and the local American officials helped us by taking Keith and me in the middle of the night to Đà Nẵng in a USAID helicopter. The helicopter flew very low right over the two-lane highway, as if it were a car driving on it. The countryside on both sides of the road most of the way to Đà Nẵng was controlled by the National Liberation Front at night, so only by staying above the highway were we safe. I never understood why the NLF didn't just shoot the helicopter down anyway, but apparently there was tacit agreement that they wouldn't. I don't remember a lot about that helicopter ride except that Keith and I were nervous, and I was shivering, scared, and miserable.

The German hospital in Đà Nẵng said they weren't equipped to help me, so we were taken to a small, private Vietnamese birthing center. The doctors there induced labor, but it wasn't progressing. All during that time the doctors and staff visited with us, cajoled us, joked with us, and tried to keep our spirits up. It was Christmastime, and the U.S. Embassy in Đà Nẵng sent us a large basket of unshelled nuts. The doctors and staff had never seen nuts like these, and our good-humored doctor, Phạm Văn Lương, got a machete and proceeded to smash open exotic Brazil nuts on the cement floor of the room.

After fifty hours of futile labor, I went to the surgery room, a floor below. There was no elevator so they helped me walk shakily down the stairs. They used general anesthesia and removed my dead two-and-a-half-pound baby. The next day they brought him to us in a large glass jar. He had a beautiful face and big bright blue eyes. The staff congratulated us on having had a boy, in an auspicious year for boys, though I was sure they felt that every year was auspicious for having a boy rather than a girl.

They also surprised us by bringing me a newborn they had borrowed from another woman in the birthing clinic. Without hesitation they put the tiny boy in my lap, saying that holding him would give me good luck and would help me get pregnant again very soon. They told me to nurse him, though they had given me pills that made that impossible. This was their form of therapy, and though I appreciated the gesture, I thought the baby's mother might well think it very bad luck that her baby had been held by a woman whose baby had died, and an American woman at that. I also thought it funny that just hours earlier Dr. Phạm Văn Lương had shared his concern that I might not ever be able to get pregnant again.

The doctors asked where we would bury him. But before that could happen, we agreed to have the clinic send him to the German hospital ship moored in Đà Nẵng to confirm the cause of death. The German ship then sent him on to the Seventh Day Adventist hospital in Sài Gòn for more testing. But there, somehow, they lost him. This would have been even more tragic had I been Vietnamese—to have not been able to bury him according to ancient tradition, in a family plot on ancestral ground.

We had fifty-six Vietnamese staff members at our physical rehabilitation center in Quảng Ngãi, quite a few of them former patients we had hired and trained. The highly skilled prosthetists made artificial limbs, metal braces, and wheelchairs, and some of them doubled as carpenters who made crutches. There were also physical therapy aides, social workers, and a receptionist who screened new patients to be sure they weren't armed and weren't soldiers. There were several rehab centers for soldiers in other parts of the country, but none for civilians. We had a sign over the entrance that said no weapons were allowed, and we enforced it. We ourselves, as part of a Quaker organization, also had no weapons at the rehab center or at our house.

In addition to the Vietnamese staff there were eight of us foreign volunteers when I got there, six in Quảng Ngãi and two in Sài Gòn. Everyone was there for a two-year term. We all learned to speak Vietnamese.

Keith's and my job as directors was to oversee the program and the rehab center, import supplies and raw materials, deal with local officials and vendors without bribing them, maintain and pay our staff, and report on what was happening in our center, our town, our province, and in the rest of Việt Nam.

The great majority of our patients had been injured by landmines, and many of those victims were children. Some had been leading or riding a family water buffalo that stepped on a landmine buried on a path or in a rice paddy. Others had picked up pretty, shiny metal objects that then blew up in their hands. U.S. and South Vietnamese troops regularly laid rings of landmines as perimeters around their temporary encampments and didn't retrieve them all when they left. They didn't win any hearts and minds with their devastating carelessness.

In addition to our main work of providing artificial limbs, braces, wheelchairs, and crutches, we treated paraplegics and occasional polio victims, and sometimes people with napalm and white phosphorus burns. Approximately once a week we visited the women's prison ward of the actual hospital, where we met and interviewed political prisoners, most of whom had been brought from the prison to the hospital because of injuries from torture. Sometimes the fluorescent lighting caused those who had been tortured to have seizures.

Our day-to-day focus at the rehab center was to help our patients deal with their injuries and readjust to their lives. Often this involved creativity and customized solutions. Our talented head of prosthetics, Nguyễn Quy, developed an artificial leg that, instead of having a foot, ended like an upside-down golf tee, so the wearer could work in a rice paddy without getting it stuck in the mud. The patient would also have a regular wood and rubber "cosmetic" foot. Nguyễn Quy also created a rubber hand that could be used to grasp a motorcycle handlebar. He and other prosthetists also invented a three-wheeled chair with handlebars and bicycle wheels that could roll on rutted dirt and sand paths. By 1970, the program was producing eight hundred limbs and braces per year, and more each year after that.*

When patients were done with treatment, we usually took them home in our rusty VW bus. One day I went with our social worker to take a single-leg amputee patient home. It took us a long time to get there, and when we were close our little bus couldn't continue on the narrow sand path. We decided to walk, but even the bicycle-tire wheelchair had trouble in the sand. After quite a few difficult minutes navigating the terrain, we reached his small thatched-roof hut between some rice paddies, where we were met at the door by his wife and three small children.

His wife said she had something special for us, and insisted we come inside and sit down. Then, to our dismay, she presented us with a carefully cut pineapple on a plastic plate. We knew that pineapples were an expensive treat. The hungry-looking children were watching us closely. We wondered if we should eat just some of the pineapple, all of the pineapple, or none of the pineapple. Would the children get what we didn't eat? Would it be rude to not eat it, or to not eat all of it? I looked at our Vietnamese social worker for a clue, but his face revealed nothing. It appeared he too had no experience with hospitality toward foreigners. We always tried to be tactful and to handle cultural subtleties correctly, but sometimes we couldn't figure out the best thing to do.

In the end we ate some of it, exclaiming how delicious it was and how generous they were to give it to us. Our patient's wife thanked us graciously for coming, for bringing back their husband and father, and we left, hoping the children got to eat the rest of the pineapple.

---

* Keith Brinton, *The History of AFSC Work in South Vietnam during the War: 1965–1975*. Unpublished study (American Friends Service Committee Archives, 1976).

The small number of U.S. government representatives in Quảng Ngãi did not worry about cultural subtleties and did not try to blend in with the locals. We AFSCers lived in a regular house. We wore Vietnamese clothing and ate Vietnamese food. The CIA and other American government personnel lived in a secure walled compound with razor wire on top of the wall and armed guards in watchtowers. They ate American food, watched American TV, and had air conditioning. We did not want to be associated with them because they were closely aligned with the South Vietnamese government, and AFSC tries to maintain neutrality in war situations.

We avoided flying on their modern Air America planes and instead flew on Air Việt Nam's old DC-3s. You climbed up the stairs into the back of the DC-3, then walked uphill toward the front. Although DC-3s were considered very reliable in World War II, they certainly weren't as reliable in the 1970s. I frequently saw flames coming out of the engines as we took off, but I figured it was just the way those planes were.

Since travel by car or bus was difficult and could be dangerous, these planes were almost like buses for those who could afford them. Passengers often brought on board baskets of fruit or live ducks or chickens carried upside down with their legs tied. Delicious but stinky durian fruits were not permitted on planes because they made people nauseated. Despite that precaution the flight itself frequently caused air sickness, so the planes often smelled bad.

In early November 1973, I flew to Sài Gòn to check on a shipment and to meet with our Sài Gòn team members. The flight was terrifying. It was the beginning of monsoon season and we were thrown around the sky like a yoyo on a string. Lightning seemed to strike the sides of the plane. We were sure we were going to crash. Everyone on board was completely silent, strangers holding hands across the aisle with each other, myself included. Even the babies and animals were oddly silent. We heard only the deafening crashes of thunder and saw blinding lightning flashes that made the plane shudder. Then suddenly the plane hit something and we thought we had crashed, but actually we were on the runway in Sài Gòn, though we still could see nothing but solid gray out of the windows. There was no cheering or clapping. Everyone was still silent, ashen, and sick as we got off. I'd been on a lot of scary flights, but none as awful as this one.

Not long after I returned to Quảng Ngãi, our teammate Rick Thompson flew on Air Việt Nam to Sài Gòn with two young patients he was delivering to the Barsky Unit, an American hospital specializing in plastic and reconstructive surgery for children. Rick planned to spend a few days in Sài Gòn and then come back. His first scheduled return flight was canceled due to bad weather, and he was wait-listed for another flight a few days later, which he couldn't get on. He finally got a ticket for Saturday, November 17. I drove to the airport in torrential rain that afternoon to pick him up. But no flight came. The Quảng Ngãi Airport was very small, no more than a landing strip with a small office, and the weather was fierce, a full-scale monsoon. I assumed the flight had been either canceled or diverted to the much larger Đà Nẵng Airport.

We waited to hear from Rick, to know if he was still in Sài Gòn or had landed in Đà Nẵng. That evening the rest of us—Julie, Tom, Heidi, Keith, and I—were sitting at the kitchen table, listening to the violent storm and to BBC News on the radio. We heard the announcer say, "A civilian aircraft in Việt Nam has gone missing. It was flying from Sài Gòn, going to Quảng . . . ," and he paused. "Quảng" is the first word of many Vietnamese towns, much like "San" or "Santa" for San Francisco, Santa Cruz, or Santa Fe. The announcer then tried to say the second part of the name, having trouble pronouncing it. Listening to him pause made all five of us freeze. The moment felt like an hour. Shivers ran through me. Then the announcer said, "Quảng Ngãi." Our town. Our Rick. We were stunned, unable to speak. Soon friends and neighbors began to arrive, having heard the news. About thirty-five local people had been on that plane, and news traveled fast in Quảng Ngãi.

Keith went to the Air Việt Nam office early the next morning to find out if perhaps Rick hadn't been on that flight. But they confirmed that Rick was on the missing plane. Also on the plane were our medical assistant Bich's aunt and two other relatives, a patient's mother, a friend of our administrator Cảnh, and our prosthetist Nghê's brother-in-law.

Rumors began to circulate that the plane had crashed but there were survivors, that it had landed safely somewhere far away, and even that it had landed on a beach in Liberation territory and that the wounded were being treated by NLF soldiers. There were also rumors that the pilot had been known as a daredevil. I had once chatted with a pilot at the Quảng Ngãi Airport who said to me, "If this is my death day, so be it," and I remember thinking to myself that he was being awfully selfish. I now wondered if he had been the pilot of my terrifying flight to Sài Gòn and perhaps also Rick's flight.

The crash was on a Saturday, but it wasn't until Wednesday that we learned what had happened. The plane had slammed into a mountain near Đà Nẵng, in disputed territory. The South Vietnamese military organized an operation to retrieve the bodies, but said it was in territory controlled by the Liberation Front and they expected armed resistance. The military search party stalled, and some of the soldiers on the rescue team were pressuring families for bribes. So we organized a search party ourselves that included some of Rick's friends and our staff members. But before they set out, Rick's body and those of the other victims were delivered to Quảng Ngãi Airport. No one had survived. Rick's body stood out because he had been thrown free, and at six feet tall he was taller than everyone else. His broken wristwatch told the time of the crash.

We brought his body back, and in a ceremony familiar to our Vietnamese friends he was placed in a white shroud in a beautiful wood coffin that our workers had made using no nails, which was filled with sixty-six pounds of tea leaves. The funeral was a combination of Quaker tradition and Vietnamese "ancestor worship," ensuring that his soul would not wander. We had incense and candles on pedestals, draped red fabric, huge elaborate wreaths, and a black-framed photo of Rick. The hole his death left in our small team was huge. He had a wonderful sense of humor, spoke very good Vietnamese, could fix anything, was a great photographer, was enterprising, dynamic, outgoing, and had many friends. He enthusiastically volunteered for any task. In stressful moments, he reminded the rest of us of the big picture of why we were there. He was unafraid, even of flying, as he had told me about a previous scary flight in a storm. He read his book on that flight and didn't worry, saying if it was going to crash there was nothing he could do about it. I picture him on that last flight calmly reading his book, not looking out the window at the storm, when the plane crashed. I hope that was true for him at the end. Our team was now five in Quảng Ngãi and two in Sài Gòn.*

I was not raised Quaker, but I was attracted to active pacifism as a sensible philosophy. I had participated in American Friends Service Committee programs since high school. I agreed with their philosophy that meeting people from other backgrounds increases understanding and helps to resolve conflicts. In the spring of 1971, after college and graduate school, I applied to be co-director of an AFSC summer workcamp in New Bedford, Massachusetts. New Bedford was a poor community with high unemployment, inadequate housing, and limited academic resources. Local police were regularly accused of discrimination and brutality. In 1970 there had been a violent event during which one person died.

I got the job and drove my $100 old red Corvair van from Santa Cruz, California, to Boston, Massachusetts, arriving on my twenty-third birthday, June 18, 1971. The first person I met was the other director, Keith Brinton. Our main job was to create and run a summer daycamp program for underprivileged local children, but another important aspect of our job was to increase understanding among the fourteen teenage volunteer participants who had been selected from very diverse backgrounds in places like Hollywood, California; Philadelphia, Pennsylvania; and Newark, New Jersey. We lived together all summer in an old warehouse on a weedy lot. Two of our Black participants, both age fifteen, were from Newark, another city that had recently been a center of racial tension and police brutality issues. They thought it very funny that several of the white kids, including a Hollywood movie producer's daughter, wanted brown bread, brown rice, and brown granola, while they wanted white bread, white rice, and white Sugar Frosted Flakes.

Keith and I got married in June 1972. Keith was a Quaker and had

---

* Beth Taylor, *Quaker in Vietnam: Rick Thompson*. Pendle Hill pamphlet 367 (Open Source, 2003); and Beth Taylor, *The Plain Language of Love and Loss* (Columbia: University of Missouri Press, 2009).

attended Haverford College, had volunteered with the Peace Corps in Ivory Coast for two years, and had volunteered as a generalist with AFSC from 1966 to 1970 in a place called Quảng Ngãi, Việt Nam. He was fluent in Vietnamese after being there for three and a half years.

In December 1972, six months after we were married, the U.S. military attacked North Việt Nam's two major cities, Hà Nội and Hải Phòng, with over 20,000 tons of bombs dropped by B-52 bombers. We and many other anti-war Americans watched from afar, furious, helpless, and horrified. In North Việt Nam over 2,600 civilians were killed in the two-week U.S. Christmas Bombing campaign, and the destruction was devastating.

The Paris Peace Agreement was signed a month later in January 1973 by Henry Kissinger and his Vietnamese counterpart, Lê Đức Thọ. *(See "The Paris Peace Agreement" on page 255.)* The two men were awarded a shared Nobel Peace Prize, and Kissinger accepted it, but he did not attend the ceremony out of fear of being assaulted by anti-war protestors. Lê Đức Thọ refused it, stating that the U.S. and South Việt Nam had violated the truce the joint award was based on. With the Paris Peace Agreement signed, the United States declared to the world that the war in Việt Nam was over and the American military was withdrawing with honor.

In the spring of 1973, AFSC asked Keith and me to go to Quảng Ngãi for two years to be the directors of the Việt Nam program. I saw this as an opportunity to actively participate, to personally try to help the people of Việt Nam begin to recover from the killing and destruction my own government had inflicted on them. Another attraction for me was that Quảng Ngãi was very near the beautiful, tropical, warm South China Sea. I imagined coconut palm trees, colorful fish, white-sand beaches. Keith was willing, even enthusiastic, to go back again, and he was interested in seeing the changes now that the Peace Agreement has been signed and the U.S. military had been withdrawn. We accepted the positions.

We got to Việt Nam in early April 1973 and joined team members Julie Forsythe and Rick Thompson, generalists; Heidi Kuglin, physical therapist; and our two Sài Gòn representatives, who went home soon after that and were replaced by Sophie Quinn-Judge and Paul Quinn-Judge. A short time later Tom Hoskins, a physician, joined us.

We AFSC volunteers came to Việt Nam for various reasons. All of us were opposed to war and willing to live in the center of a conflict zone to do humanitarian work. Some of the men were doing alternative service as conscientious objectors to war, or COs, and they could have chosen to work at a safe hospital in the U.S., but instead came to Việt Nam. Others had returned or burned their draft cards or had already done alternative service. Some had been in the military before coming. We women were not concerned about being drafted, but we were fully aware of the American bombing and destruction in Việt Nam and neighboring countries, the use of napalm and Agent Orange, the 1969 so-called secret bombings of Laos and Cambodia, and the Christmas Bombing campaign in 1972. Young people like us were angry and protesting all across America. Many military veterans of the conflict were also protesting and speaking out against the war.

Rick was a Quaker and a commited pacifist and would have qualified as a conscientious objector, but instead he returned his draft card to the U.S. government in protest of the war and the inequities of the draft. Then he came to Việt Nam to help. Keith was also a Quaker and had been a CO for the first two years in Quảng Ngãi, but then stayed on. He later came back with me, so in all he worked with the program for five years and nine months. Sophie and Paul had been working in Paris and had gotten to know Vietnamese students, and had closely followed the progress of the Paris Peace Conference. They wanted to participate in a program helping Vietnamese civilians and reporting on the war. Julie, a Quaker, was well aware of the AFSC program in Việt Nam and wanted to be part of the next step of helping Việt Nam recover and rebuild. She arrived just as the American soldiers were leaving, believing like the rest of us that the signing of the Paris Peace Agreement meant the war was about to be over. Heidi had been working as a physical therapist in North Dakota for two years and was looking for a new challenge. She grew up in Nigeria, and felt well suited for the living and working conditions of a developing and war-ravaged country. Tom was a Quaker, and he came to help the Vietnamese with his professional medical skills. The program hadn't had a full-time doctor for quite a while, so we were very glad Tom joined the team. We were all young, energetic, and committed.

As soon as Keith and I arrived, he went to Quảng Ngãi, while I spent my first two months doing intensive language training in Sài Gòn, sleeping and studying in a tiny house we dubbed "the flophouse," on the same little alley as our small, rented AFSC house. On my first full day there, I went walking around the big city alone, finding landmarks, smiling at people, admiring the beautiful old French buildings and estates, and breathing the polluted air. The city was noisy and dirty, but I didn't care. I bartered for coconuts, mangoes, and rambutans at little street stands, and I quickly learned how to order a variety of delicious hot noodle soups from outdoor stalls, where people sat on low stools and ate with spoons and chopsticks. Hot tea was served with the soup, and the cups, bowls, and utensils were rinsed in a bucket of standing water. The tea and soup were both served boiling, which completed the cleaning between customers. The weather was very hot and very humid, but the hot tea and soup were somehow perfect. Similarly, I found the Vietnamese custom of wearing loose long black pants and a long-sleeved light cotton shirt in that heat surprisingly comfortable.

In Sài Gòn I saw well-dressed women with perfect posture and students on bikes, the girls in traditional white tunics with the long front and back panels attached to their handlebars with clothespins so they wouldn't get caught in the spokes of their wheels, and the boys in white shirts and dark blue pants. I saw families of four or five traveling together on one small motorcycle. If there were only two people and the one in back was a woman, she usually rode side-saddle, as I did when I rode behind Keith. I also noticed the many beggars and bedraggled, barefoot children, but mostly I was aware of the affluence and normality of Sài Gòn.

Keith was still fluent in Vietnamese and had taught me some before we left America, and I tried to use it right away. I wrote new vocabulary words in a little notebook I always carried with me. Vietnamese written language looks somewhat like English, since it uses a modified Roman alphabet with added accents and tone marks. But Vietnamese words have no relationship to English words for clues to meaning, so I constantly needed to learn new vocabulary. Within a few days of arriving in the country, I met my two language tutors, Yến and Dung (pronounced "Ian" and "Yoom"), who would become my close friends. My intensive language work began while I continued to become familiar with Sài Gòn. I met foreign and local journalists, and volunteers and staff working with other programs. I went to demonstrations by anti-Thiệu protestors and visited government ministries to maintain contact regarding our program. The political situation was volatile and anti-government demonstrations were frequent, but as in similar situations anywhere, people went about their daily lives regardless of the political and military conflict.

After two months of study, I flew up-country to join the team. I could see bomb craters on the ground as we approached Quảng Ngãi. My first impressions were of the very small airport, beautiful green rice fields with water and water buffaloes, people wearing conical hats, small thatch houses here and there, and distant mountains. In town there were dusty streets with open-front stores selling soap, metal buckets, brooms, mats, sandals, and other supplies, and people sweeping in front of their shops, even if it was dirt or sand.

There was a crowded open-air fruit and vegetable market, and I was happy to see stands where you could buy pressed sugarcane juice and fruit and vegetable milkshakes, as you could in Sài Gòn. My favorite milkshake was watercress, which unfortunately gave me typhoid fever not once but twice during my time in Quảng Ngãi. Watercress is grown in polluted bogs, but I didn't think of that at the time.

I saw many bicycles and few cars and motorcycles. People were dressed informally, women in black pants with solid-color long-sleeved blouses or pants and shirts in matching cotton fabric, and most men wore short-sleeved white shirts and loose dark trousers. Conical straw hats were commonly worn by most people except soldiers. People in town and on the roads often had a long pole over one shoulder with a large basket at each end, carrying everything from firewood to babies.

I tried to use my new language skills, though I immediately realized the local accent was quite different from what I'd been learning in Sài Gòn. But since almost no Vietnamese I met in Quảng Ngãi spoke English or even French, which I could speak adequately, I had to use my Vietnamese, and it got better and better. I found everything interesting and new, and also dimmer, poorer, sadder than where I'd just come from. It was as if Sài Gòn had been in color and Quảng Ngãi was in black and white.

Contrary to President Nixon's announcement, the war was definitely not over. South Vietnamese bombing continued, still funded by the United States. There weren't American troops in uniform, but there were American advisors. Quảng Ngãi, city and province, had lots of armed South Vietnamese soldiers. Outside of town in the low hills were more South Vietnamese soldiers and, in other positions near them, National Liberation Front soldiers. The South Vietnamese ARVN soldiers often shot their guns out of boredom and frustration. The NLF soldiers were less wasteful of their ammunition. We regularly heard gunfire and artillery, mortars landing, rockets exploding, and distant bombing. It was continuous background noise.

My dreams of a beautiful, tropical beachside town were quickly shattered when I got to Quảng Ngãi. There weren't many trees, nor much greenery in general, and although Quảng Ngãi was quite close to the ocean, the territory in between was disputed. We only went to the beach twice in the entire time I lived there.

The American Friends Service Committee sets up humanitarian programs in conflict zones where people are suffering. Quảng Ngãi had been chosen because it was a very poor town in a very poor province where there was constant fighting for military control, causing high numbers of deaths and injuries. In peacetime most people were farmers who grew rice on plots of land in the countryside. War brought danger to their daily lives and destroyed their homes and fields, forcing many off their land. With the huge influx of refugees, the town was crowded, unstable, and it was either hot and dusty or muddy and flooded, depending on the season.

Most refugees from the countryside had no work and scavenged for daily needs. Street dogs cleaned up bones under tables in the few places to eat out. Begging children waited just outside and darted inside to snatch leftovers when someone finished eating. There were lots of children in the streets, not in school, curious and hungry, and they followed and surrounded us like mosquitos whenever we were outside, chanting "Bà Mỹ" ("American woman") and "Ông Mỹ" ("American man"). They would touch our hair or our arms and shout at us with hands outstretched begging for money. They found blond, curly-haired foreigners especially interesting. We were their entertainment.

Once I was riding our little Honda motorcycle down the dirt main road to the hospital. A toddler was alone in the middle of the road and I braked hard. The road was sandy and I fell over, getting a small cut on my leg. Within seconds I was surrounded by women, half of whom were holding little bottles of Mercurochrome, a red antiseptic ointment, to put on the cut. The women hugged me and bowed to me and thanked me. For what? For not running into the child. They said American soldiers on a tank had done exactly that some time before.

Our house in Quảng Ngãi was burglarized six times in about two weeks in December 1973. One night when Keith was out of town, a robber came into our upstairs bedroom through the window, which had no glass or security bars, and took my purse, my typewriter, and our Sony tape recorder off our desk while I slept a few feet away inside a mosquito net under a noisy ceiling fan. The robbers also got four other typewriters, some of our darkroom equipment, our adding machine, a microscope, a sewing machine, our slide projector, a car tire, some of our medical equipment, an iron, a stapler, binoculars, a fountain pen, and more. One evening after they'd taken our typewriters but not the hard covers, with a bit of morbid humor we set the covers out for them to take too, next time they came.

We always locked our doors, but the robbers pried open our double front door, lifted the metal bar, and came in. They broke into the separately locked kitchen. One night they used a live M16 cartridge to dig around the frame of the dining room window, and left the cartridge. They knew we were not armed, and they kept finding new ways to get in. We felt helpless. On the other hand, even if we had been armed, we would have been no competition for their skills and weaponry, so in that way it was safer to not be armed. Soldiers and police ruled the streets but couldn't be trusted.

The series of burglaries ended only when our workers and friends who lived in our compound suggested we take turns standing on the roof all night to confront the robbers if they came. Three friends took the first shift. Several armed men arrived in the street below at 1:30 in the morning and yelled up at our friends on the roof, asking them why they were protecting the Americans. They told our friends to leave so they could burglarize the house. Our friends refused, and one of the soldiers fired at them with an M16 rifle. The bullet went right between two of our friends who were standing close together. Although it missed them, one was slightly injured by flying concrete when the bullet hit the barrier on the edge of the roof. The men fled, no doubt thinking they might have killed someone, and all of us gathered in the kitchen in the middle of the night to calm down and to take care of our injured friend. The break-ins ended that night. The police arrested and briefly detained two adults and five or six children, ages thirteen to nineteen. Prior to these burglaries, the program over the years had experienced only a few similar incidents that we knew of, and none as damaging as these.

Some days later our friend Lê Anh, the city photographer for weddings, births, and other special events, came to tell us that a soldier and a policeman had tried to sell him a microscope that had "Hoskins," Tom's last name, engraved on it. The soldier and policeman thought it was a photography tool and had offered it to Lê Anh to try out before buying. Lê Anh took the risk of giving the microscope back to us before the soldier returned to complete the transaction.

The province chief of police was a first cousin of our physical therapy assistant Nguyệt, and she told us he had recovered some of our belongings. At the police station he showed us our typewriter and a Grateful Dead tape that had been in our tape player, but said he had to keep them as evidence. We never got them back. We were pretty sure that more of our belongings had been found by the police, but nothing except the microscope was ever returned to us.

Soon after the burglaries in 1973 came the biggest flood in Quảng Ngãi since 1964. There were places downtown where the water was very high and swirling dangerously fast. At the hospital it was up to my thighs. Tom, Julie, Heidi, Keith, and I spent an afternoon hauling people and belongings from the single-story pediatric ward to the second story of a nearby ward. We carried smelly, dirty, sick children in our arms and on our backs. The electricity was out. When I was walking back home through the water, I stopped to help a man whose foot was bleeding badly after he had stepped on a piece of glass. We were near the home of an American missionary who was also a nurse, and she took him in and attempted to stitch his foot with a sewing needle, without anesthesia, while I tried to hold him still. But it was too painful, so he limped back into the dirty floodwater.

Many of our workers spent two days and nights sitting in the rafters while water raced through their houses. Luckily, none of them or their families were injured. At our own house we moved what belongings we could to higher places, though it turned out that the house was on a high spot of ground. Still, the water rose to within an inch of floor level. During the days of the flood Tom gave us all typhoid shots, since we had been in the polluted water.

Soon we had company, people whose homes had been damaged or destroyed. Our worker Anh Ry's family of twelve briefly moved in with us, as did our worker Anh Tiên's family of five, plus a few other individuals who hadn't been able to get home. After several more days the water receded and the cleanup began. During this flood time, soldiers were more and more out of control, shooting their guns randomly on the streets. One soldier I walked by hit me lightly with his hand, which was extremely unusual. Another soldier trained a rifle on Julie as she walked past, then followed her with it, making sure she noticed.

One time a bullet came through the tin roof of our rehab center and missed Keith by a foot. It had probably been randomly fired into the air by an ARVN soldier somewhere. Another time a staff member and I were taking some patients home to their village when our Honda mini pickup truck was shot at with an M79 grenade that exploded about fifteen feet in front of us. They certainly could have hit us if they had wanted to, so they were just having fun scaring us. Back in 1968, when Keith was first in Quảng Ngãi, on the first night of the Tết Offensive a hand-sized piece of shrapnel ripped through his mosquito net just above the mattress but missed him. He had gotten out of bed a moment earlier. Many aspects of war are random, just good or bad luck.*

We often hosted visitors in Quảng Ngãi, including American govern-

---

* The Tết Offensive was a coordinated campaign of simultaneous attacks planned by the Vietnamese Communist leadership in North Việt Nam and carried out by troops of the North Vietnamese People's Army of Việt Nam and the South Vietnamese National Liberation Front at the end January 1968, the beginning of the Vietnamese Tết (New Year) celebration. It struck thirty-four of forty-four South Vietnamese province capitals and sixty-four district towns, which resulted in the insurgents holding parts of most of the towns or cities for periods ranging from a few hours to twenty-four days in the case of the ancient capital of Huế. Although it failed to achieve its ultimate aim of forcing the United States to agree to a neutralist government, and resulted in very

ment officials. In February 1975, the U.S. Congress was considering another military aid package to the South Vietnamese government, and President Gerald Ford asked that a bipartisan congressional delegation go to Việt Nam on a fact-finding mission before the decision would be made. The delegation included Bella Abzug, Donald M. Fraser, and Representative Pete McCloskey, Republican from California, all opponents of continuing military support. Others in the delegation were in support of continuing to send American financial support, including Senator Dewey Bartlett, Republican from Oklahoma.

McCloskey and Bartlett came to Quảng Ngãi. Before they arrived at our rehab center, they had already visited with and been briefed by the province chief and the local USAID/CIA officials. They came to us in a jeep motorcade, complete with sirens and guards, kicking up dust. They stayed for thirty-five short minutes, during which time Senator Bartlett was completely uninterested in our patients and everything else about our program. *(See "My Congressional Delegation Trip to Việt Nam," by Pete McCloskey, on page 231.)*

Representative McCloskey, on the other hand, asked quite a few questions and listened to our answers. He had run for the Republican nomination for president in 1972 on an anti-war platform and was defeated by incumbent Richard Nixon. (He switched to the Democratic Party in 2007.)

As we were taking them on a ridiculously short tour of our facility, Keith said, "Almost all our patients here are amputees or paraplegics." Senator Bartlett replied, "Anti-Ts? Oh, I see. You accept patients only on the condition that they're anti-Thiệu." He had obviously been briefed that our AFSC program was anti-war. But was he deaf? We thought he might have been. The delegation had probably already met with President Thiệu in Sài Gòn. The senator seemed to have nicknamed him "T." When he referred to "T," his aide had trouble keeping a straight face. Keith corrected the senator,

---

heavy losses to PAVN, it also created serious doubt among U.S. news media figures and some administration officials about the possibility of a U.S. military victory in Việt Nam. It thus accelerated the development of popular anti-war sentiment in the United States.

loudly, saying, "No, they're amputees. AMPUTEES, not anti-Ts." Later in the half-hour visit Bartlett, apparently already considering himself an expert on Việt Nam, told Keith that the Communists were kidnapping people and forcing them to marry them, to "assure their permanence."

We were furious that Senator Bartlett seemed to be using his short visit with us only in order to claim he had learned about all sides and all opinions during his fact-finding trip. When the delegation returned to Washington, Bartlett strongly supported continuing military aid to the South Vietnamese government to avoid, he said, "a Communist bloodbath." The term "bloodbath" was used more and more by American government officials leading up to April 1975. It was the prime scare tactic in a last-ditch effort to keep the U.S. from abandoning the war effort in Việt Nam.

Representative McCloskey opposed sending additional aid. The members of the delegation were unable to agree on a unified position, and this was part of the reason further military aid was not sent.

In addition to hosting visiting diplomats and dignitaries, we were regularly visited by Vietnamese or expatriate friends from other programs, team members from Sài Gòn, and most frequently, journalists. They were from the *New York Times*, AP, Reuters, UPI, BBC, and other news organizations. They wanted to tour our center, and they wanted to visit the nearby site of the 1968 Mỹ Lai massacre, just one of the American war atrocities. The village of Mỹ Lai was very poor, and whenever we were there sad survivors, mostly old women with betel nut–stained teeth or no teeth, approached us in tears, gently touched our arms to get our attention, and told us about family members who had been killed by the Americans. As they described the nightmare they would point at the ditch where the victims had been thrown into a mass grave. Though I was American, they did not see me as the enemy, probably because I was a woman and also not a soldier. They begged us to tell the world what had happened there, and we translated these requests for our visitors. *(See "War Crimes against Vietnamese Civilians" on page 243.)*

Nearly every time I was on the road to Mỹ Lai, rifle shots were fired toward us, but they always missed and seemed to be only warnings. We assumed the shots were coming from National Liberation Front guerrillas, since they controlled the area around Mỹ Lai. We felt they were making sure we knew who was in charge, and that while they were allowing us to go there, we had to be careful. This certainly impressed the journalists, all of whom were based in Sài Gòn. We had gone there quite a few times and had never had any problems, except once.

Not long after I arrived in Quảng Ngãi, Sophie, Paul, and Diane Jones, our former AFSC Sài Gòn representative who was back in a short-term position, were on a small dirt road near Mỹ Lai on their way to visit a refugee camp. All three were riding on our little blue 110cc Honda motorcycle. The road deteriorated, and Diane got off and walked ahead to ask a local ARVN soldier if it was safe to continue. He said the road was temporarily secure, so she got back on the bike and they went on. A kilometer down the road Paul got off because the road was bumpy and three people on the bike were too many. Sophie and Diane drove on toward the camp. Then Diane got off, and Sophie went back to pick up Paul.

Suddenly three armed National Liberation Front guerrilla soldiers, two women and one man, dressed in floppy hats and loose khaki clothing, stood up from where they'd been hiding in bushes about twenty yards from Diane, who was alone on the narrow road. They shouted at her and gestured for her to come to them. She'd never seen NLF soldiers, but it was obvious that was what they were. This was very close to the refugee camp and also close to two South Vietnamese Army outposts. She realized how physically close the soldiers of both sides were to each other.

The three soldiers had their rifles pointed in her direction, and she saw no option but to obey. She approached them, hoping there were no buried landmines where she was walking. They made her put her hands over her head and move out of sight of the road. A few minutes later, when Sophie and Paul returned on the motorcycle, the soldiers shot warning shots to alert them and motioned to them to come too.

The guerrillas brought Diane, Sophie, and Paul to meet their higher officers, who seemed displeased that they had captured our teammates. They immediately began to try to figure out how and where to release them, since they knew that holding foreigners was a very sensitive issue. Diane, Sophie, and Paul were told they would need to walk for three days to a more secure area, where higher-level authorities would decide how to release them. They walked through many villages, where local peasants were generally friendly and curious about them. Some villagers, remarkably well informed, asked them about the Paris Peace Agreement and why, since it had been officially signed, the war was still going on.

Diane, Sophie, and Paul were kept captive for twelve days, during which time they walked a lot, often very close to ARVN outposts. They even crossed the main highway, at night. They were given plenty of rice, some sweet potatoes, and some green vegetables. One night they heard an explosion very near where they were resting. In the morning they learned it had been caused by a wild boar that had tripped a Claymore mine. Their captors cooked the boar and shared it with everyone, including them.

One day they were in a very poor village where several people told them how dangerous and difficult it was living in a buffer zone between the two sides. At night, the National Liberation Front was in control, and in daytime, South Vietnamese Army soldiers were in charge, checking ID cards and often stealing chickens. They were back near Quảng Ngãi at this point, and on the last day a nine-year-old boy guided them out of the village they had slept in and on toward town. He stopped partway there and showed them a path to follow. After about half a kilometer more of walking, they were on a familiar road heading into Quảng Ngãi.

They were near the airport when they passed a large number of ARVN tanks heading toward them. The tanks were followed by more military vehicles and weaponry, and soon after that a large ARVN military operation was carried out in the same area where they had just been. Diane, Sophie, and Paul thought of the people they'd met who were now being attacked and bombarded.*

While the three were being held by the Liberation Front, some of our staff members with contacts assured us they were fine and wouldn't be harmed. We asked these staff members to use their connections to try to get them released, and perhaps that helped. I flew to Sài Gòn to assure both Vietnamese and American officials that their capture had been entirely unintentional. Neither our team members nor their captors had wanted it to happen.

---

* Diane Jones, *Tet with the Provisional Revolutionary Government* (American Friends Service Committee Archives, 1974).

There had been journalists who were intentional guests of the NLF, and we wanted to be clear that in this case our team members were actually captives. We were concerned that if the governments, both American and South Vietnamese, thought the incident had been planned, they might have rescinded AFSC's right to be in the country, and the three might even have been arrested when they returned.

On that twelfth day, early in the morning, our teammates walked through the doorway and into our house. We jumped up and cheered, hugged them, and welcomed them home. They seemed tired but fine, and we were all very relieved. A few days after they returned, the three were interviewed by local South Vietnamese special police, who were interested in military information about the areas they had been through. They refused to participate since they felt it was inappropriate for them as foreign volunteers in a neutral humanitarian program to give information to any government. They willingly spoke of their experiences, but not military details they might have been aware of. Their non-cooperation gained them the enmity and resentment of those police officers and the province chief.

In the ensuing days we tried to get back our motorcycle. It had been found in a nearby Liberation Front–controlled village during a South Vietnamese Army operation. The ARVN soldiers had confiscated it but wouldn't return it to us. How did we know they had it? The situation was always close, intimate, just as the Liberation Front and ARVN outposts were often very near each other. Rumors traveled quickly. People in town told us when they spotted our motorcycle, and we ourselves saw it around town a few times. But we never got it back.

The National Liberation Front soldiers and the South Vietnamese soldiers were essentially in the same places and indistinguishable, except by their clothing. If they wanted to blend in, even their clothing was the same. One could never be sure which side one was interacting with. It was a confusing war.

After decades of fighting, in early 1975 major changes began to happen on a national scale. The North Vietnamese and National Liberation Front soldiers moved in forcefully and took control of the mountain city of Ban Mê Thuột. The South Vietnamese Army offered no real resistance. They simply fled. It was quick and unexpected that the South Vietnamese military was so easily defeated. The same thing soon happened in Pleiku and Kontum, mountain towns even closer to us in Quảng Ngãi. Momentum was building, and people were beginning to think about the possibility of the war actually ending, but with which side winning?

On March 9 a group of more than a dozen National Liberation Front soldiers, dressed as South Vietnamese ARVN soldiers, walked into the southern end of Quảng Ngãi, ate at a cafe, and then shot a small rocket into a nearby police station, killing a policeman. One of their group died also. On March 14, other Liberation Front soldiers also dressed as South Vietnamese Army soldiers threw hand grenades into a small police station just two hundred yards from our house. Some Self-Defense Force members came out of a nearby house where they were visiting and found themselves directly in front of the Liberation Front soldiers.* The Liberation soldiers opened fire, killing three and wounding others. News came to us quickly that among the dead was our own prosthetist and former patient and amputee, Nguyễn Liệu, who was with the Self-Defense Force members. He left a wife and two young children. Sadly, we participated in another funeral.

Now soldiers were posted every one hundred yards in town, and there was a 10 p.m. curfew. Some of our rehab center workers warned us of danger, that a shift of power would soon be happening in our town. We heard that the Liberation Front had warned people in the city to "dig deep bunkers," so it was clear they planned action and expected retaliation from the ARVN. We sandbagged the front of our house for added security. At the bank the line was unusually long, and I waited more than two hours to withdraw some cash. The next day I realized I should have gotten more,

---

* The South Vietnamese Self-Defense Force was a part-time militia created after the Tết Offensive in 1968. Their duties were to support the police and the military and to ensure "pacification and security." The people we knew in both Quảng Ngãi and Sài Gòn expressed fear of the Self-Defense Force members, who they felt used their positions and weapons to intimidate people, especially powerless or displaced people.

but by then the bank was closed. Tensions were rising all around us, verging on panic.

Heidi's two-year term was over, and she had already left and hadn't been replaced. Julie was out of the country on vacation and would return soon to Sài Gòn. Tom was on his way there to meet her. Sophie and Paul, our Sài Gòn teammates, were with me and Keith in Quảng Ngãi for a few days. The four of us began to discuss whether to stay or to leave. Our friends Earl Martin and Pat Hostetter, who lived near us, were volunteers with the Mennonite Central Committee, leading a program focused on investigating and removing unexploded ordnance like landmines.* They told us that Earl was planning to stay but Pat and their children were leaving. The local American station chief and the CIA and USAID people were also preparing to leave right away and were pressuring us to go with them. They said the situation was getting more dangerous by the hour, and we needed to evacuate immediately. They said their sources had told them the city of Quảng Ngãi would be attacked not just by the Liberation Front soldiers but by regular North Vietnamese Army soldiers, and we would be captured and taken prisoner or killed.

We considered our situation. We didn't have a bomb shelter and didn't want to impose our American selves on any Vietnamese family's bomb shelter. Some of our Vietnamese friends thought we should stay and would probably be safe. They said the local Liberation Front leaders knew about us and wouldn't harm us, though they weren't sure about the North Vietnamese. Others felt we should leave temporarily. They were worried about what might happen to us and also to them if we were with them. We didn't want our presence to put them in an uncomfortable or dangerous situation, and we were getting more and more nervous for ourselves.

---

* The Mennonite Central Committee is the relief and peace agency of North American Mennonite churches. In Quảng Ngãi Province the program focused on the survey and removal of unexploded ordnance. In other parts of the country they focused on various civilian relief and medical needs. MCC had programs in Việt Nam since 1954. For a complete account of MCC work in Việt Nam see Luke S. Martin, *A Vietnam Presence: Mennonites in Vietnam during the American War* (Morgantown, PA: Masthof Press, 2016).

On March 18 an American consular official visited us again, warning that they expected bombing. He said he could give us only half an hour to get to their headquarters to make it onto their flight to Sài Gòn. We huddled together, tried to stay calm, considered the offer, and decided a half hour wouldn't work. So we declined.

The next day the situation was even more intense. Many of our Vietnamese staff were leaving, some taking their families to Ly Sơn Island, where they felt they would be safer. The ARVN forces had now fled from the two closest provinces to ours, leaving them open to the Liberation Front soldiers to take control right away.

Early on the morning of March 20 the American official was at our door again, now quite panicked. He said he could get us out on a flight at 11:15 that same morning, and he pleaded with us to leave, more urgently than he had two days before. With the tension increasing by the minute and no way to predict the future, we four huddled together again. There was no time and no way to contact our main office in Philadelphia about this decision, since telegraph services were no longer functioning. We had to decide for ourselves. We decided that the responsible thing to do would be to leave, for now.

We quickly went to the rehab center to tell the workers who were still there our plans and to draw up papers giving official responsibility to a committee of department heads. We left them the bulk of the money I had gotten from the bank, though it was only enough to keep the center running for a short time. We hugged, said goodbye, and said we'd be back soon, but we felt ashamed. We were going to be safe from bombing, but would they?

Back home, each of us packed a small bag of clothes. We were leaving behind our center, our possessions, our library, our friends, and even our commitment to avoid flying on Air America. But we vowed we would return to Quảng Ngãi as soon as possible. I looked back with tears streaming down my face as we drove to the U.S. compound in a USAID car. The driver seemed to think he was James Bond as we raced down the street, leaving a cloud of dust behind. We were whisked into the compound toward a tall building inside the barbed wire–topped perimeter wall, and a guard slammed the metal gate behind us. It turned out that our friend

Pat and her kids hadn't left yesterday and were on the flight with us. There were also some fifty to sixty Vietnamese people the embassy was evacuating. Pat's husband, Earl, was there to get Pat and the kids onto the plane, and then, against the request of the American consul, he went back to Quảng Ngãi.

We passengers were told to quickly get on the C-47 military transport aircraft and prepare for a fast takeoff. We followed orders and arrived at an airbase in Đà Nẵng at 1 p.m. As we entered the spacious, modern military terminal, it suddenly was as if we were back in America. It was comfortable, well furnished, air-conditioned, and clean, and we even ate American BLT sandwiches for lunch. After a few hours we left for Sài Gòn in a sleek Air America jet, arriving at 8:45 p.m. We took a public bus to the Quaker house and got there at 9:30, just before the 10 p.m. curfew, which we knew was enforced. We surprised Julie and Tom, who were at the house and hadn't known we were coming. We unpacked our few belongings and settled in with no idea how long we would be there.

On March 24, 1975, only four days after we left Quảng Ngãi, the town and the province were taken over by the Provisional Revolutionary Government, the governing arm of the National Liberation Front, and not by the North Vietnamese Army. There had been some shelling of the city, but overall it had been a peaceful handover of power. And it really was more of a handover than a takeover, since the ARVN forces had fled before the Liberation soldiers even arrived. Earl had stayed and later wrote a book about his experience there.*

But we were in Sài Gòn and hadn't gotten the news of the change of government in Quảng Ngãi. At the top of our minds was the fact that we had left our rehab center workers without salaries. So we withdrew a lot of money from a bank in Sài Gòn, and Paul and Julie flew to Đà Nẵng to try to deliver it to Quảng Ngãi. When they arrived in Đà Nẵng they realized that there was no way to get to Quảng Ngãi. The situation in Đà Nẵng was quickly becoming out of control as people panicked, trying to flee but not knowing where to go or how to get there. Julie and Paul decided to come

---

* Earl S. Martin, *Reaching the Other Side* (New York: Crown Publishers, 1978).

back to Sài Gòn immediately. The only exit route they found was by forcing their way onto a large barge in the harbor that was dangerously overcrowded with fleeing refugees. In the chaos, most of the money was stolen from them. But they made it safely to Cam Ranh, and from there they got a flight back to Sài Gòn.

Meanwhile, Tom was trying to follow Julie and Paul north to Đà Nẵng, but like the rest of us in Sài Gòn, he didn't know how bad the situation already was there. He got onto a flight from Sài Gòn to Đà Nẵng, but when he arrived he quickly realized he wouldn't be able to find them in the increasing chaos. So he headed for a Buddhist temple where he felt he might be able to stay and where his medical skills would be useful.

The day after Tom left, and before Julie and Paul returned, Keith and I bought ourselves plane tickets to Đà Nẵng, with the goal of delivering more money for salaries to our staff in Quảng Ngãi. We did not know Paul and Julie had been unable to deliver the money they had carried. We were completely unaware of what was happening in both Quảng Ngãi and Đà Nẵng. There was no information and no communication—no phone calls, no telegrams, no cables, no news at all.

At the airport we learned that the flight before ours was the last one to Đà Nẵng. Ours had been canceled. We returned home, and Paul and Julie came back soon after that. We learned later that Tom had found work at the German hospital in Đà Nẵng, and he ended up staying and working there, away from the rest of us, for many months.

We now accepted the fact that we weren't going back to Quảng Ngãi, so Julie, Sophie, Paul, Keith, and I started working on how to organize ourselves and where to sleep. Usually only two people, Sophie and Paul, lived in the house in Sài Gòn, and now there were five of us.

The city of Sài Gòn was a very different world from Quảng Ngãi. It was a cultural and material glutton, with big hotels and nice restaurants, night clubs, cars, theaters, and lots of well-dressed citizens and foreigners having a good time. There was plenty of food, delicious and to us exotic fruit, lots of stores full of merchandise, big banks, traffic congestion and pollution, and a thriving black market where you could buy almost anything. It had elegant old buildings, large, graceful houses and embassies, lovely parks with lakes, and wide boulevards. It was cosmopolitan and prosperous, not at all like Quảng Ngãi.

Most of the time it was easy to forget the war if you were living in Sài Gòn. We did not hear artillery or any other shooting. We did not feel the ground shiver from bombing. We didn't see lots of soldiers and tanks. Life seemed normal and we enjoyed it, but we also thought about Quảng Ngãi. We listened to BBC on the radio and visited news offices in Sài Gòn, and followed the progression as more and more cities and provinces in South Việt Nam changed from South Vietnamese to National Liberation Front and North Vietnamese control. As each city "fell" to the Communists or, more often, was abandoned by the South Vietnamese military and local government, it seemed more and more possible and likely that the action might soon reach Sài Gòn. We began to ponder the same decision we had had to make in Quảng Ngãi, whether to stay or to leave. We wanted to stay, as we had wanted to stay in Quảng Ngãi, but would we actually do it this time?

An important part of our job as directors was to regularly write detailed letters to the main office of AFSC in Philadelphia to keep them informed. Now communication with America was becoming more haphazard and unreliable. The telegraph office was often closed, and when open it frequently couldn't or wouldn't send telegrams to the United States. Letters weren't going out. Time seemed accelerated, as the South Vietnamese government lost control of provinces and cities almost daily. The speed with which panic traveled and created chaos was as powerful as the military offensive, and the PRG and North Vietnamese were hard put to keep up with the fleeing ARVN soldiers and South Vietnamese government officials.

We knew we were in a historic time, that something momentous was happening. I began to keep a daily journal, aware that after this long war, so costly to Americans and Vietnamese alike, I might be a witness to how it ended. By April 30, 1975, we were among only about a dozen Americans we knew of left in Sài Gòn to witness the end of the American War, as Vietnamese call it.

What follows comes entirely from my journals, my letters, and other firsthand sources, covering the months between March and July 1975 in Sài Gòn, Việt Nam.

# 1

# INCREASING TENSIONS

**TUESDAY, APRIL 8, 1975**

We are in Sài Gòn now. The palace was bombed at 8:30 a.m. Apparently a single South Vietnamese ARVN pilot got disgusted, bombed the palace and a nearby storage area, and flew on to Đà Nẵng.* Paul was taking a shower in the roofless tiled area next to the kitchen, Sophie and I were getting dressed in the middle room, and Keith and Julie were in the living room. As the loud zoom of the swooping plane came on, Paul, covered with soap, ran from the shower to the middle room. Sophie and I thought the shower had burst or something in the kitchen had exploded, so we ran toward the living room. At the same time, Julie and Keith ran from the living room toward the middle room, thinking the explosion had been on

---

\* On April 8 an A-37 South Vietnamese Air Force jet dived on the Presidential Palace, releasing a bomb load originally intended for the Communists. The plane's pilot was Lieutenant Nguyễn Thành Trung of the South Vietnamese Air Force. He escaped, as did President Thiệu. It was later revealed that the pilot had been a member of the Communist Party since he was a student. He had gotten his pilot's license in the United States and had joined the South Vietnamese Air Force while actually working for the North Vietnamese.

the street. We all ran into each other and started laughing uncontrollably, because the situation was hilarious and terrifying at the same time. Our little Sài Gòn house doesn't leave much space for maneuvering around each other. The roof over the living room and middle room doesn't offer any real protection, but it feels safer than the kitchen and roofless shower area.

## THURSDAY, APRIL 17

What is happening is completely different from anything we've experienced until now. The war seems to be coming to an end, town by town, and people have been talking about this, hoping for this, waiting for this for decades. It is happening so quickly that in many towns the South Vietnamese local government officials and soldiers fled as many as twenty-four hours before the North Vietnamese could even get there to take over.

It may not be the ending they want, but it's going to be some sort of an ending. This is something happening in the whole country. There are many unknowns. Will it reach Sài Gòn? Will it be violent? Will the U.S. military retaliate with bombs? Will the South Vietnamese government? Everyone is worried and scared, and no one knows what's going to happen. We've been waiting for our replacement directors to arrive since January, when we would have begun a two-month overlap. We would have left and gone to Nepal for a vacation before heading home. But our replacements have been stuck all this time in Hong Kong, unable to get visas for Việt Nam. We don't plan to leave the country with the American evacuations. We're planning to stay, no matter what.

Paul and Keith got "Liberation haircuts"—short—so they don't look like hippie contractors. Today the rumors fly again, that Saturday the 19th will be Liberation day, or at least a PRG attack on Sài Gòn. I don't think so yet. One tidbit we learned today is the secret code that the U.S. Embassy will broadcast over the radio when they decide to evacuate. They'll say, "The temperature in Sài Gòn is 105 degrees and rising." Then they'll play "I'm Dreaming of a White Christmas." It's April, of course, and of course there's never snow. I guess that's the point.

The main AFSC house here in Sài Gòn is small, with no room for guests except on the living room floor. For a while AFSC rented the little house next door to the main house, our "flophouse," where I did my language study when I first arrived. But that's not available now. Since we expect to be here for weeks or maybe months, Keith and I are sleeping in a new flophouse we've found, which is actually just a single bedroom in a sort of compound of similar single rooms. The Vietnamese owner has all exits locked up tight, and we're locked inside at night. The owner has been ridiculous about keys, not letting us or even his employees have any, so we've spent a lot of time hollering and banging to get out or in the gate. There's an old caretaker and he said of the owner, "Rich Vietnamese are very cruel." Butch, the faithful guard dog (yes, "Butch"), is still here, and he might just bite a nasty intruder for us—maybe. If anyone came to rob us here, they'd be so disappointed they'd probably shoot us. We have almost nothing. And I'm always hungry. There's a bánh mì (bread) boy who comes around sometimes. He walks along the streets calling "Bánh mì đây," a slightly abbreviated version of "Bread here!" I reach through the bars on our door to give him money for his dry bread laced with weevils. We don't have a refrigerator or storage area. Just a small bare room.

There are still quite a lot of Americans and other foreigners around town. They haven't all left yet, though many have. We and the Mennonite Central Committee folks, some adoption agency people, Dick Hughes of the Shoeshine Boys Project, the U.S. government, and some journalists are still here. We're waiting to see what happens, to decide where to stay. If there's "rape and pillage," as predicted by the U.S., not that we expect that, we'd like to be with the Buddhist nuns and their fifty orphans. Our friend Hùynh Liên,* the head nun of the Buddhist monastery, is quite important and also quite funny. *(See "At a Demonstration Led by Buddhist Nuns" on page 235.)* She invited us to join them to cho vui (have fun together). But the nuns' temple and orphanage are pretty close to the airport, so if there's fighting and rockets and mortars, we'd rather be with the others in our little AFSC house, even though we don't have a bunker or bomb shelter. I don't

---

* Hùynh Liên was the chief nun of the Vietnamese Mendicant or "begging" order, followers of the Theravada tradition. She was born in Phú Mỹ village, Tiền Giang Province. She was ordained in 1947 and was one of the first female disciples. Both monks and nuns of this tradition wear yellow robes and carry alms bowls. She was a leader in Sài Gòn of many demonstrations for peace and equal rights, and she was an active participant in the Third Force movement.

know anyone here who does. We've prepared ourselves with extra rice, a charcoal stove and charcoal, plywood to cover the windows, thermoses with water, little medical kits, and each of us has a bag of personal possessions to grab and run with.

Sài Gòn is a great place for rumors. It seems as if people all over the city catch on to the same rumor in very few days. The main rumor going around changes every week or so. Today our friend Chị Hiền told stories of South Vietnamese soldiers raping refugees in Vũng Tàu. She also told a tale of a U.S. Navy refugee rescue boat from Đà Nẵng where the crew was afraid they'd be killed by the refugees, so they locked them in holds under the deck and didn't give them food or water. Supposedly when they docked in Vũng Tàu, they discovered that over a hundred people had died from lack of air and from thirst. She claimed they threw the bodies into the ocean instead of burying them. Her final comment was "Now we should be careful eating seafood."

We've heard there are two or three hundred Provisional Revolutionary Government delegates at the airport who arrived there recently for official negotiations with the GRVN, but they're stuck there now and negotiations have broken down. We were told they are resigned to being killed. They have no way to leave the airport or return to the north with the current conflict situation. They figure that if the South Vietnamese ARVN doesn't get them first, they'll be killed when the North Vietnamese attack the airport, presumably a prime military objective. Or maybe the Americans will bomb the airport. How terrible. Surely there's a way this can be avoided.*

Each day there is less and less South Vietnamese government territory actually controlled by the South Vietnamese government in South Việt Nam. We expect the North Vietnamese will be coming soon to Sài Gòn. Luke Martin of MCC said today that the Hong Kong Shanghai Bank won't take dollar checks anymore, only cables. Nothing that takes time to process.

---

* There were nearly two hundred delegates of the Provisional Revolutionary Government and of the Democratic Republic of Việt Nam in a U.S. Army compound at Tân Sơn Nhứt Airport, participating in the Joint Military Commission established by the Paris Peace Agreement. See Gareth Porter, *A Peace Denied: The United States, Vietnam, and the Paris Agreement* (Bloomington: Indiana University Press, 1975).

When we were back in Quảng Ngãi we listened to the news on the radio every evening, marking every province as it fell. We continue this evening ritual in Sài Gòn, where we have a map on the wall and we can track the provinces.

## FRIDAY, APRIL 18

Several things now will take a week. In a week we may get some of our money back from our bank that closed down in Quảng Ngãi. In a week the Logistics office may agree to ship our large shipment of prosthetic and therapy supplies to Hong Kong for sending on to liberated Đà Nẵng and then to our rehab center in Quảng Ngãi. And in a week we may have two children, ages four and six.

At Logistics we were surprised when we got an enthusiastic response. We told the man in charge that our shipment was goods and equipment specifically useful only in a physical rehabilitation center, and therefore we wanted to send it to our rehab center in Quảng Ngãi via Đà Nẵng, although of course both cities are liberated now, not under South Vietnamese control. The man seemed to like the idea, amazingly enough. We were sure he'd say that nothing could be sent to "liberated" or, more likely, "Communist" places. We urged him to remember we were only asking for help freeing up the shipment, not shipping it all the way to Đà Nẵng and on to Quảng Ngãi. We would take care of that. He said he would try to help.

As for our new children, my close friend and former language tutor, Yến, asked us two weeks ago if we could take her two older boys to Laos for her, and from there send or take them on to Hà Nội to their grandfather. I asked at the U.S. Embassy two weeks ago, speaking to Vice Consul Mary Lee Garrison, telling her that I wanted to adopt them, which of course wasn't true. She said there was no way to do that.

Then yesterday Yến asked us again, so we went to the embassy again. I managed to avoid the long line and got right into the consulate office. I saw Ms. Garrison again, and this time I decided to tell the truth. I said, "I don't want to take these children to America. I want to take them to their grandfather in the north, via Laos."

"Well, that's nice to hear," she said. "I'm completely fed up with this wholesale export of children." She then offered a legal way of getting guardianship of them, which will take a week. They're two of the nicest children we know, and we'd love to accompany them to Laos and Hà Nội.

I had felt funny the first time I talked with Ms. Garrison, pretending I was adopting the children to get them out of the country, since I'm firmly opposed to that. Telling the truth was much nicer, and I was amazed that she agreed with me. She had some other comments on the general situation. She said no feasible evacuation plan exists, the U.S. Embassy is dreaming, and she's about ready to just pack up and leave. While we were chatting, she asked if Keith and I were really legally married, since we each kept our last name. She kept her own last name too, as did her husband. Obviously I should be a bit more open-minded about U.S. government officials.

## SATURDAY, APRIL 19

It's raining for the first time since we've been here—one month already. Today we received some publications of our own writings, from the head AFSC office in Philadelphia. We wrote back and caught them up on things here in Sài Gòn.

Today's prediction, or rumor: The PRG would like a negotiated settlement. That requires that President Nguyễn Văn Thiệu resign. He doesn't seem to be planning to resign, therefore . . . an attack on Sài Gòn, destroying the airport first and foremost, then Biên Hòa and Cần Thơ. Careful aim at specific targets. Sappers getting Thiệu's palace.

We were told that PRG people in our area know us, know who the "good people" (non-military, non-government Americans) are, and we shouldn't worry. Keith points out that many Sài Gòn soldiers have never had to fight. They've bought positions in safe Sài Gòn, or at the safe airport, and hopefully these inexperienced soldiers will just give up without a fight. We all keep hoping for a negotiated peace, but Thiệu won't resign.

We wish the U.S. Embassy would pull out quickly, but they're not going yet. They know that their leaving signals the end of the Thiệu government, so they stay on. We, and the PRG, would like them out of the way. They make everyone nervous.

Today it was rumored that Sài Gòn will be liberated before the end of the month. If it's an artillery barrage it will be noisy and scary. How I wish it would hurry, whatever it's going to be.

Scare stories are going around and the newspapers are picking them up, perhaps because there's a lack of other news here. The government is telling people "don't believe all you hear on BBC" as more and more people turn to BBC for good reporting. The GRVN also says to not believe *Newsweek* or *Time* magazines. One day last week they even censored their own anti-Communist Sài Gòn English language daily, the *Saigon Post*.

Yesterday I visited our American friends and their new daughter, Tuyến. She's four, beautiful, half (Black) American, half Vietnamese, and she is sad. Her birth mother is said to be rich, owns a house, car, a clothing store, is twenty-four or twenty-five years old, and is giving up Tuyến because she is scared, thinks bi-racial children of Vietnamese women will be harmed or killed, and also she says she wants to get married and assumes that having a mixed-race child will make that more difficult. The little girl has gone to nursery school, been well treated, and has always lived with her mother.

Four days ago, her mother gave her to the Holt Adoption Agency, which accepted her. Yesterday she went to our friends, her new family. We know Holt, unlike ISS (International Social Services), is not urging people to keep their mixed-race children. They think the children will suffer terribly under the PRG. Our friends, her new parents, want to help her, and certainly will be good and loving parents, but at least if her birth parents were poor, or dead, it would be easier. But this is her situation, and our friends are going to do all they can for her.

## MONDAY, APRIL 21

Thiệu resigns! Whoopie! Now the president is Trần Văn Hương.* Keith and Paul went to watch Thiệu's speech on TV with some BBC journalists,

---

* Nguyễn Văn Thiệu was president of South Việt Nam from 1967 until he resigned under pressure on April 21, 1975. Trần Văn Hương, a South Vietnamese politician born in 1903, became president immediately after Thiệu resigned. Hương was president for one week, until April 28, 1975, when he resigned and handed power over to General Dương Văn Minh, who presided over the surrender of the government on April 30.

and to translate the speech for them. Curfew seemed to be 8 p.m., or maybe still 9 p.m., unclear. They plan to sleep downtown somewhere.

As Thiệu spoke, jets flew overhead, perhaps not daring to stay on the ground. Sophie, Julie, and I and an assortment of friends went next door to watch Thiệu on TV. It was worth seeing. He didn't actually resign until over fifty minutes into his speech. Bitter, angry, saying that if only the Americans were still here with their B-52 bombers, they would have won the war. By saying that, presumably he admits he's lost it. He said the U.S. abandoned him, especially with the Paris Peace Agreement. He said the U.S. needs to send aid or they won't be able to negotiate. He said the U.S. will cheer his resignation, because they know he is against the peace agreement they made with the Communists, the Paris Peace Agreement.

Now we six women are sitting, reading, and feeling just a bit edgy about noises outside. One of our guests is sleeping here because she's been told her house will be raided tonight. I wonder where Keith and Paul will sleep. Maybe in the Hotel Caravelle. They can tell us how people reacted downtown. It's very good that Thiệu resigned. A relief. I didn't really think he would.

## TUESDAY, APRIL 22

This morning we went to watch a peace demonstration of all religions at the downtown cathedral. It certainly didn't incite a riot; in fact it was quite a staid presentation, including some Cao Đài, members of a religious sect in the Mekong Delta region, who humorously mimicked and quoted Thiệu in his resignation speech, saying, "Now maybe America will give aid." The police were out in full force and much of downtown was blocked off. When Sophie and I tried to get there by car we found it impossible and had to bring the car home, go downtown again by motorcycle taxi, and then walk to the demonstration.

Keith and Paul had been inside the air-conditioned Hotel Caravelle, so they and all the journalists didn't hear all the jets in the air as Thiệu resigned. Reaction to his resignation seems to be very subdued. Faces on the street don't express anything. Our motorcycle taxi driver didn't say anything. Julie said her driver repeated what Thiệu had said, that he hopes now there will be U.S. aid. We don't hope that. We don't want the Americans to get involved again. For the many Saigonese who know that the PRG and North Vietnamese said Thiệu's resignation was not enough, was too late, and that the whole government has to go, there was no joy.

As yet we don't know the form of the new government. Apparently the U.S. ambassador went to call on new president Trần Văn Hương as we went by the U.S. Embassy this morning.

Paul is British, and the British consulate is increasing pressure on Paul and Sophie to get exit visas and to leave. Unlike the U.S. Embassy, the British consular office is relatively empty. Many staff people have left, and it looks like they all may be leaving soon.

We got our Laos visas just in time. They're closing their embassy tomorrow. I think Thailand is also closing up today.

Yến never sent us her letter giving up the kids, so I guess the fake adoption won't go through. Just as well, since we don't want to go to Laos unless we have assurance of being able to return to Sài Gòn or Quảng Ngãi. We wonder if she didn't send the papers because she decided against it, or because of the military situation out at Biên Hòa, where they live. We heard there was fighting between where we are and there. It's very close!

The jets are in the air. American? South Vietnamese? The ARVN still has firepower, but not much will to fight. More U.S. supplies are coming into Sài Gòn, we think. The military aid only postpones the possibility of peace. We say no to more U.S. support. Let the Vietnamese work it out themselves.

Yesterday there was a broadcast of a very good idea that wasn't true. It said that the PRG announced the offer of a twenty-four-hour ceasefire during which the U.S. could evacuate all its personnel, a total pardon for all Vietnamese who worked for Americans, and an invitation to non-government foreigners to stay on and continue working. But unfortunately, it was apparently a misinterpretation, or another rumor. It would have been nice.

# 2

# FEAR AND PANIC

**WEDNESDAY, APRIL 23**

Things are really moving again. Now the big day is to be two days away, Friday, April 25. The PRG has apparently stated a deadline for either a new government here, a surrender, or a PRG attack on the city. Deputy Hồ Ngọc Nhuận, General Dương Văn "Big" Minh,* and other good people in the South Vietnamese government want a new government in order to avoid a breakdown in the ARVN, which they fear would cause many deaths

---

\* Deputy Hồ Ngọc Nhuận was a prominent writer, an editor, and an opposition deputy in the Assembly of the Republic of South Việt Nam. He was one of the leading organizers of the Third Force during and after the signing of the Paris Agreement. After April 30, 1975, he was elected a member of the Fatherland Front, a consultative body with little actual power.

Dương Văn Minh, also known as "Big" Minh, was a South Vietnamese politician and general in the Army of the Republic of Việt Nam. In 1972 he advocated for a compromise solution to the war, and after the signing of the Paris Agreement he openly identified as a member of the Third Force. After President Thiệu resigned on April 21, 1975, the legislature asked "Big" Minh to be president and to handle the surrender. He was president from April 28 to April 30, 1975.

and much destruction. As for us, we feel pretty safe in our corner of Sài Gòn—neither too rich nor too poor, and with a good strong gate at the end of the alley.

One thing we didn't think about when we considered going to stay at the Buddhist Mendicant nuns' temple and orphanage is if there is chaos and the ARVN soldiers lose control, then what about the people who have been coming to *our* house for safety when it gets scary? How can we go away and leave the house empty, thus scaring all our friends and neighbors by our absence? We can't.

I feel the panic began today in earnest, kicked off, as predicted, by the stepped-up U.S. evacuation. Planes, big ones, are leaving constantly, continuously in the air, taking anyone and everyone somewhere, it seems. We hear these people reach Guam or the Philippines and must stay in refugee camps in tents, crowded and uncomfortable. Just today we've had half a dozen requests for us to take people out of the country, or sell them dollars. We are getting tired of hearing all the propaganda people are repeating to us, which they get from Thiệu's banners and billboards and the TV, about the Communists being cruel and wicked. People believe women with makeup or long fingernails will be arrested or raped, children will be murdered, men will be arrested, and so on.

We heard the South Vietnamese ARVN dropped a bomb called a CBU-55 that takes all the oxygen out of the air, and we heard that hundreds of PRG and NVA troops, and presumably civilians, were found dead near Xuân Lộc, with no visible injuries but with hands clutched to their throats. The Agence France Presse News report is that the South Vietnamese ARVN withdrew from Xuân Lộc and dropped the illegal bomb as they left.*

Today we all had a picnic on the roof of the flophouse, and the landlord asked us to help him get to America and to get him dollars. For our picnic we had some good bread and some good La Rue beer, and we enjoyed

---

* The Battle of Xuân Lộc was the last major battle of the war, from April 9 to April 21, 1975. The South Vietnamese used cluster and "Daisy Cutter" bombs and a CBU-55B fuel-air bomb, the first ever used in combat. See Tiziano Terzani, *Giai Phong! The Fall and Liberation of Saigon* (New York: St. Martin's Press, 1976) and "Battle of Xuan Loc: April 1, 1975" Vietnam War Commemoration, www.vietnamwar50th.com/1975_the_fall_of_saigon/Battle-of-Xuan-Loc/.

ourselves while chatting and watching the helicopters and big transport planes in the sky. We waved at a few of them before we realized they might think we were trying to get their attention and wanted to be rescued. So we stopped waving, finished eating and drinking, and went back downstairs. The brief escape from reality was refreshing.

At noon we had lots of visitors. Yến's lovely two nieces, with her younger boy, came and brought a message from Yến confirming cancellation of the plan for adopting her kids to take to Laos and on to Hà Nội. She says things are happening too fast, and the various embassies are closing up too quickly. The Biên Hòa airbase is being rocketed regularly, and the road to Vũng Tàu, Highway 15, is cut. Maybe Biên Hòa will be liberated tomorrow. By noon tomorrow there may be a coup, too. If so, there may be a peaceful settlement.

But in a way, now I don't want a negotiated solution. I want a victory and a surrender. I'm afraid an "agreement" can be too easily abused, as in Laos, as happened with the Paris Peace Agreement. I want to see a clear victory. Americans should leave. It might be nice to be the only Americans left in Sài Gòn. We probably won't be, though. There probably isn't even time for everyone to leave, if the attack will really be on Friday.

We know the propaganda teams are working hard, because the rumors are flying and plentiful. I hope the revolution comes quickly, so people don't go completely crazy.

Chị Hiền has been sleeping here every night, and we aren't comfortable with it. She comes quite early, at 6:45 p.m. tonight, and showers (in our cold-water, roofless shower) and makes herself comfortable, letting the whole world, and especially our cook Bà Hai, know she's sleeping here, which is illegal and a bit risky. Besides, we don't really think she's in danger, and if she were, she'd never sleep at the same house every night.

Today we took some red, black, and white fabric to our favorite sewing shop to have an AFSC flag made. They're very busy, and we won't get it for at least a week. They said lots of people are having clothes made to wear when they leave the country.

Tonight we learned that GRVN deputy Hồ Ngọc Nhuận was offered a secure place to stay by the other side. ("The other side" is the neutral and more friendly way to refer to the National Liberation Front.) They told him that after the change of government he may be welcome to become some sort of official in the new government. But he didn't accept, because he wants to continue to work for a coup here, followed by a political, peaceful, multilateral solution.

The U.S. should spend its evacuation aid money on airplane engine silencers. They sure are giving away their "secret" evacuation by all the airplanes and helicopters. Some of the planes may be spotter planes, but most are probably evacuating frightened rich people. We don't know.

I find it difficult to hide my enthusiasm when talking to people about the coming events. They say to me with downcast faces, "Oh, the Communists are so close; they're right near Sài Gòn." "Yes," I reply. They're not only near it but surrounding it, and by tomorrow they can hit it with their largest guns. It's coming, so we might as well relax and experience it. Many people in Sài Gòn have been largely shielded from the war all these years and have been pretty oblivious.

If many more people tell me how wicked the Communists are, I think I might agree. In one conversation today I asked a man, "If the VC are so cruel, why don't they just bomb Sài Gòn to complete destruction?" He thought about it and offered that the Communists like to look good at first and then they change.

## FRIDAY, APRIL 25

Surely it still will be soon, but now it looks like it won't be until the beginning of next week. For part of the day I was depressed and irritable, thinking about the miscarriage. Late in the day we were cheered by the news that the U.S. Embassy personnel should all be gone by Monday or Tuesday. We were interviewed by Peter Arnett of the Associated Press. We gave him a long interview, complete with photos of us, and later Paul came home and told us he was the same reporter who had misquoted Paul when he was telling about getting out of Đà Nẵng. But maybe he'll do a better job on us.

Our alley gate is now apparently our responsibility. The two nicest and most responsible families have left the country, so we're stuck with their refugee relatives and friends from Huế and Đà Nẵng. Not the nicest neighbors to be "liberated" with, but they could be worse.

Max Ediger, of MCC, came for a few minutes and looked worn out from all their visitors asking for help to leave the country. We've gotten much less of this than they have, but we've gotten our share, and it's frustrating and discouraging. It's hysteria, even from people with no American or South Vietnamese government connections. The American officials themselves are causing it with their bloodbath stories and their urging people, us included, to leave. They pressure us a lot, every day, and we thank them for their concern and politely decline. Sometimes we think it's not just concern on their part, but rather a desire to leave no American eyewitnesses to what is going to happen. What if it's not a bloodbath? We are determined to stay, to see what happens. *(See "Why So Many South Vietnamese Feared a Bloodbath" on page 240.)*

Some reporters are planning to stay. The French and Indian Embassies are staying. The French Embassy is telling its citizens to stay put because it's dangerous to try to leave now. Sometimes we pretend we're French, on the streets. I don't encounter anti-Americanism really, though. Generally, the streets still feel normal and safe to us, though we now try to avoid crowded places, just in case they get blown up. People in cars and on motorcycles and bicycles and on foot still smile at us, and we at them. We don't stand out here in Sài Gòn the way we always do in Quảng Ngãi.

Today Sophie received a gift of mangoes from Huỳnh Tấn Mẫm's mother. He is a former medical student and an active student leader, in fact the former president of the Sài Gòn–Gia Định Student Union for four years. He has been imprisoned eleven times since 1972, and has some paralysis from having been tortured. She says all the prisoners except him were brought from the Bình Thủy airbase, and she's convinced he's been killed. She's having difficulty coping, as we can easily understand. We hope she's wrong.[*]

[*] Huỳnh Tấn Mẫm is a politician and medical doctor who was a prominent leader of the student movement in South Việt Nam, protesting against the Thiệu government and the American involvement. The student movement was very strong and helped lead to the eventual end of the war. Huỳnh Tấn Mẫm was arrested on January 5, 1972, and was imprisoned until early 1973, when he was released in a prisoner exchange under the Paris Peace Agreement. However, he refused to be released to the PRG, as he insisted that he was a non-party resident of Sài Gòn. After that, he remained at the prisoner

Airplanes are still going overhead, but it seems like fewer than yesterday. We heard there was some rioting at the airport and at the U.S. Embassy, by people trying to get on flights to leave the country. It's so sad to think of some of the people who have left. We've been told that the Barsky Hospital doctors and staff got onto a "secret" flight. And we've learned that Committee of Responsibility director Bill Cooper sent his local director, Chính, to America while he himself stayed here. Unnecessary and dangerous. One friend told us that a third of her teachers at Sài Gòn Medical College are gone. She believes they left because they fear they won't be able to make as much money under the new government as they do now.

## SUNDAY, APRIL 27

Yesterday morning Sophie, Julie, and I went around downtown, vaguely trying to track down new president Trần Văn Hương's speech location where we had been told he would announce his resignation, but we didn't find it and he didn't resign.

In the afternoon we joined Australian journalist John Pilger and *Newsweek* correspondent Loren Jenkins at the British Embassy for a swim, believe it or not. The embassy staff have all left, and they had given the keys to the journalists, who invited us today. It's a grassy, pleasant location on Hiền Vương Street, and the first swimming pool I've been in in Việt Nam. They were interested in the story we'd heard of a surgeon leaving with the American evacuation in the middle of doing an operation, and also about the Barsky program pull-out.

Last night, or actually this morning around 4 a.m., Sài Gòn was rocketed four times, but we all somehow slept right through it. Six killed, twenty injured, many houses burned.

This morning we had a set of visitors. First came an absurd woman we'd

---

release center at Lộc Ninh until April 28, 1975, when President Dương Văn "Big" Minh ordered his release. Mẫm was a founder and first editor-in-chief of *Thanh Niên* newspaper, the paper of the Communist youth movement in the south. Following reunification, he was a member of the Sixth National Assembly, and after completing his medical studies he became head of the Red Cross in Hồ Chí Minh City.

never met before, who said she's the daughter of the old woman next door who moved out and went to New Zealand to be with her other daughter. She said she has eleven children and used to work for Air Việt Nam. She is sure the Communists will kill her, and therefore she wants to go to France. Air Việt Nam, the Vietnamese airline, not Air America. Later in the day, she emptied the house of absolutely everything, and when I offered to keep an eye on the house for her, she had the bright idea of offering to rent it to us. We declined.

Another visitor was a young man who worked for the Barclay (New Zealand) Quakers relief program, who says that he likes the PRG, but his fiancée is scared and wants to leave the country. He said the Barclay Quakers told their workers there was nothing to worry about, and then, he said, they took off forever. As with the Barsky Hospital staff, I question whether the local foreign Barclay volunteers actually wanted to leave, or were obliged to by their home office. He asked us for a letter of introduction explaining who he worked for, who Quakers are, that their program is from New Zealand, not the U.S., and that they're not part of any government. We obliged.

I remember on our last day in Quảng Ngãi, people were reading horoscopes and wondering about the future. No one could predict what was going to happen, and everyone was tense, and reading horoscopes was one way of calming fears.

Tonight Keith and I went to dinner at Chez Albert Restaurant. We ate extravagantly—steak, clams, brains, flan. The cost was 3,800 đồng, or $2 U.S. on the black market, or $5 U.S. for us, since we change money in banks. We generally ate very little in Quảng Ngãi, just like everyone else, and got very skinny, so we aren't used to this kind of rich food. It was delicious. Tonight we splurged, thinking why not, who knows the future?

And apparently we weren't the only ones with that thought. To our astonishment, every table was occupied, the place fuller than we've ever seen it on previous trips to Sài Gòn. There were mostly families with children, one old man alone, two younger men, a woman with four children, all very happy and talkative. The waiters were working very hard and seemed as amazed as we were. The fun atmosphere dampened only for a moment when a loud fighter jet seemed to come unusually low overhead. It felt like an evening in Paris or New York, definitely not Sài Gòn right now. What is it? What are they celebrating? Do they feel peace is coming? Do they feel their money will lose its value so they might as well spend it? These people certainly don't seem to be leaving the country and don't seem concerned.

The constant noise of the airplanes and helicopters of the evacuation, however, is enough to cause panic all by itself. They never used to be allowed to fly over the city or the Presidential Palace. Now they do because there's so little space outside the city that's safe for them to fly low over. It reminds me of once when we had such a steep and fast landing at Phnom Penh Airport that I thought we were crashing, but actually it was to avoid being shot at, because the area around the airport was not under government control.

## MONDAY, APRIL 28

President (for one week) Trần Văn Hương has now resigned, and the much more popular General Dương Văn Minh was installed as president. He gave the order to free all political prisoners and told the U.S. government to leave the country. Yes, the president of the South Vietnamese government gave the U.S. government an ultimatum. Not the PRG, not the North Vietnamese, but the South Vietnamese government kicked out the U.S. government. We're told "Big" Minh is prepared to surrender to the PRG.

A scenario we didn't imagine is what just happened. We were told there was an attempted coup d'etat by Air Force commander Nguyễn Cao Kỳ, who I guess decided Minh's peace declaration sounded too much like surrender.*

At 6:10 p.m. Sophie and I and my language tutor Yến's niece Thanh Bình were sitting on the front steps. The electricity was out and we'd been listening to a lightning rainstorm. It was dinnertime and our cook, Bà Hai, came to tell us dinner was ready. She also passed on the rumor that the ARVN bombed Highway 1 to Biên Hòa this afternoon. Biên Hòa is only about twenty-two miles from Sài Gòn. Right then, there was a loud boom

---

* There was actually no coup attempt on April 28. South Vietnamese air marshal Nguyễn Cao Kỳ and others did plan one to take place around April 10 with the object of removing Thiệu and not allowing surrender to the Communists, but the plan did not materialize. A major political and military figure, Kỳ left the country on April 28, 1975.

and Julie thought it was bombing, but we laughed at her and said it was thunder. Then came another, and the scream of an airplane. Then more explosions, and sharp cracks of rifle fire, machine gun fire, and anti-aircraft fire. Thanh Bình went home quickly, and Bà Hai did too, and we went inside and locked up the house. We were very worried about Paul, who had been out since 7:30 this morning with a BBC TV crew going to Biên Hòa, which has been heavily hit and is apparently in PRG hands now.

It turned out that Paul couldn't get very far. The BBC car was stopped by the South Vietnamese ARVN soldiers less than two miles outside the city, at a large bridge. He spent the morning watching twenty or so PRG guerrillas holding out against many more ARVN soldiers with heavier firepower. He spent most of the time flat on his stomach by the bridge, with bullets whizzing at all angles around him. He saw an old man, standing, not taking cover at all, on his same end of the bridge, actually smiling and saying, over and over, in the general direction of the ARVN soldiers, "Thua rồi," meaning "You've lost already." The ARVN soldiers weren't trying very hard. They had other things on their minds. Later in the day Paul saw the big military PX (post exchange) warehouse being looted by ARVN soldiers, while the local military police were trying to stop them.

Since Paul and Sophie live in Sài Gòn, they have contacts with many people. At around 5 p.m. Paul went to President Minh's compound. Minh had just been inaugurated minutes before. Paul chatted with Deputy Hồ Ngọc Nhuận and other officials and acquaintances.

Then they heard a big explosion, like us assuming it was thunder. They saw an airplane that seemed to be heading straight for them. Their first thought was to hide in the building, but then they ran out instead. Paul bumped into President Minh himself, the only time he'd seen him up close. He got out of the way and let Minh and his wife run out first. Minh went quickly to a small French car, his wife to an American car, and both cars took off fast. Paul ran all the way home from Minh's compound, including past police and soldiers. We all applauded with relief when we heard him arrive.

At our house we checked that the alley gate was locked, barred the door, put our plywood in the back window, closed the new shutters in the front window, pulled the kitchen table into the center room instead of under the open sky in the kitchen/shower area, and sat down to a candlelit dinner. We had a silent moment holding hands amidst what now sounded like lots of bombs and machine guns and anti-aircraft fire. It was pretty deafening. No one could really eat, but we all drank water.

Finally the noise let up, and by aim or coincidence the electricity came back on, and we cleaned the dishes, showered, and moved to the living room. We were now scared. I reminded myself that we're here because we want to be here. I thought of the book I'm reading about climbing Annapurna. The climbers chose to be in danger for the experience of living it and to tell about it. So did we. I have no regrets. I know I'd be more scared for friends in Sài Gòn if I weren't here with them. I'm sorry our friends and families in America must be frightened. I'm sure it's terrible for them. We need to tell them our Sài Gòn house is well located, halfway between the airport and the palace, not near the port or any military installations. We're as safe as we can be, all things considered.

The evacuation is clearly still going on, and I wonder what those people are doing and how they're feeling. The thought of going anywhere tonight, especially on an aircraft, is hugely frightening. It's dark, loud, and we hear lots of explosions. Being here where we are is much safer. There's a song by Holly Near with the refrain, "If you can die for freedom I can too." I remember once thinking those words were unrealistic. As for me, I definitely don't want to die, but I want to see Việt Nam be at peace, and we here must suffer some fear in order to see it. We all must remember we could die in many ways, and we must accept risk sometimes, despite our fear.

I've been studying some new words like đầu hàng (surrender) and đảo chính (coup d'etat). My political vocabulary is growing as the daily need arises. There's a twenty-four-hour curfew on now, so more time to read and study.

## TUESDAY, APRIL 29

Doing the dishes tonight was an ordeal! The electricity was off, it was 7:15 p.m., dark and stormy. Lightning and airplanes in the sky, first a string of ten of the big Huey helicopters they're using for the evacuation, then some small helicopters, and then the fighter jets. I counted eight I could see go by through the patch of sky in the open kitchen/shower area. Very loud and scary. Anti-aircraft fire and rockets and guns going off, flashing in the sky. I was kneeling in the sink area doing the dishes, as if crouching low and kneeling would help, and with every bang or close helicopter, I'd jump up and go into the room with a roof.

The jets seem to be heading south. I wonder if they are going to Cần Thơ. I hope the PRG makes sure to close down the Cần Thơ Airport as well as the Tân Sơn Nhứt Sài Gòn Airport before they bring in tanks. Otherwise, I'm really afraid some of the ARVN pilots who are left will come bomb the tanks and us, right in Sài Gòn.

All of us are tired from the tension, but controlled. Paul went downtown early this morning but the atmosphere was tense and unpleasant, and also he heard there was still a twenty-four-hour curfew (that few were observing), so he came back and we all spent the rest of the day together at home.

We had several visitors who brought news. Looting has become fairly widespread at the airport, the airport PX, Newport PX, USAID 1 and 2 cleaned out, and at houses of people who have left. Our neighbors and a visitor said the looters are teenagers for the most part, and unarmed.

Some soldiers are wearing soldier uniform pants but have changed to civilian shirts. Lots of soldiers are running away, some even to our alley, and others are still at their posts but have their civilian clothes on top of their uniforms, or under them. The streets are strewn with discarded military clothing and gear.

This morning looters were selling their loot, like Marlboro cigarettes, on the street for high prices, but by afternoon they lowered their prices to sell them faster, as tanks are reportedly arriving in Gia Định tonight and could easily be in Sài Gòn in a few hours.

The helicopters overhead and the anti-aircraft fire are very wearying, exhausting. We think, and BBC also reported, that the anti-aircraft fire is the ARVN, the South Vietnamese, not the PRG, firing at the U.S. evacuation planes. They're angry. They feel abandoned. I definitely would not want to be in a helicopter or on an evacuation plane right now.

The PRG apparently quit attacking the airport this morning and allowed the U.S. evacuation to go on there. Small helicopters are ferrying people from special locations to the big helicopters at the airport. They must be taking out many Vietnamese as well as Americans, because they only needed about twenty flights to get out nine hundred Americans, but there have probably been over a hundred. Several families whose homes are near the airport (one to two miles away) have fled here to our little six-house alley. They say the fighting and looting there is widespread. The airport this morning was still on fire in several places. The PRG may wait until midnight for their next big hit, since they know newly installed president "Big" Minh ordered all the U.S. officials out by that time.

BBC radio had a report we applauded merrily tonight. They said the Americans had all left, except for a few journalists and a few "hard-core expatriates." That's us! We wonder how many of us there are tonight in Sài Gòn. They didn't mention the probably thousands of French people who are here.

The sound of rockets makes my heart jump. My hands are still shaking from a close boom, maybe a rocket fired from a helicopter almost directly overhead. A boom and a slam, launching and exploding. Heart pounding. Four of us are sitting in the living room listening to all the war sounds. This intensity is an unusual experience for pampered Saigonese, and for us foreigners as well, even though we lived in Quảng Ngãi. This is bigger and very close. It certainly isn't the political settlement we were hoping for. We are, each of us, involved in our own thoughts, waiting only to survive the difficult next few days. We're looking forward to the relief we will feel when this ends, if all goes well.

Thanh Bình, Yến's niece, was here with us as the liberation of Biên Hòa was announced on the radio. We cheered and hugged. Then she became serious and said quietly, "My father was Aunt Yến's older brother. If only he could have lived to see this day. He and so many others gave their lives for the revolution. American troops cut open his belly and tortured him to death."

Now all the secrets can come out. It's hard to believe that time is really here. *Điện Tín* and other banned newspapers reappeared again yesterday. Today I guess they couldn't publish. The South Vietnamese government radio station is broadcasting the Paris Peace Agreement and announced the release of political prisoners including Nguyễn Hữu Thái, president of the Student Association Revolutionary Committee of Sài Gòn, and student leader Hùynh Tấn Mẫm, who, happily, is alive and okay, contrary to what his mother had heard. He gave a talk on the radio, telling the Americans to get out and calling the Provisional Revolutionary Government by its name, not "the Communists" or "the VC."

Today many people ignored the curfew and either ran from Gia Định, the airport, and Chợ Lớn, closer into town, or went out to loot. People on our Yên Đỗ Street stood in small groups talking. I saw several cars with people and suitcases going somewhere, with French flags on the sides of the cars.

Weeks ago the PRG published its new rules for taking over a large city. One point was to quickly secure the electricity, water, and telegraph facilities, so no one could sabotage them. The electricity factory is on the road to Biên Hòa and is already held by the PRG, and those polite folks seem to be doing their best to keep it on a lot of the time. We don't care about the lights, but the ceiling fan means a lot in this weather.

Our AFSC flag wasn't ready when we went to pick it up. They were completely surprised when we walked in, since they didn't really expect to ever see us again. We have a Buddhist flag, a PRG flag, a white pillowcase flag, but unfortunately no French or British flag. We'll probably use the Buddhist and white flags if we have to go anywhere, like if our house is hit by a rocket or mortar and we, hopefully, survive.

A British Broadcasting crew stayed, while most all other newspeople seem to have left in today's evacuation. Thus we can still get some local news from BBC. We heard that some French men taking pictures were beaten up today at the airport, and two other French reporters are missing.

Voice of America radio* seems to be saying that all those deafening jets are American. Miserably scaring us and all of Sài Gòn just to create a dramatic American evacuation? President Ford said the evacuation would take place without violence, and in another sentence said a U.S. Air Tactical Command marine aircraft was fired on and returned fire. We think we might have actually heard it. The Voice of America station said the Huey

---

* Voice of America radio is a U.S.-funded international broadcaster established in 1942 and headquartered in Washington, D.C.

helicopters are being escorted by fighter jets. And the airport is closed to fixed-wing aircraft. They have to fly to aircraft carriers at sea.

I can just see those U.S. pilots, who don't know the geography of the city, returning fire coming from angry ARVN soldiers in town, and blowing up downtown Sài Gòn. It's all very close now, and the planes and rockets are the scariest so far. We worry they may be off their targets by just a little bit in places, which would mean they could hit us or anywhere else in the city, but what could the targets even be at this point? What's there to bomb? It won't change anything.

It's a relief but also infuriating to hear that all those terrifying noises all day long were the U.S. busy "saving" people again. They could have left weeks ago without all this drama. It is historic, and ironic, that in the end they were ordered out by the government they supported, and now they are hurrying to meet the deadline.

Thanh Bình told us that PRG tanks are already in Gia Định, maybe a quarter mile from us. How wonderful it would be if they take over by morning. Then by the next day, May Day, it might be all over. It is reassuring for the moment, as I write this, to hope all the jets are only American, and that there won't be any more jets in the sky once they're gone.

# 3

# LIBERATION, OR THE "FALL" OF VIỆT NAM

**WEDNESDAY, APRIL 30**

This is it, a new government, LIBERATION OF VIỆT NAM, 10:30 a.m.

**THURSDAY, MAY 1**

There was no time yesterday, April 30, to write at all, so I'm doing it now.

Yesterday was a memorable day. At 4 a.m. we woke on our thin pads on the living room floor of the main house to the sound of rockets and heavy artillery. It had been quiet since about midnight, when the American evacuation finally must have ended. We heard that a few U.S. Marines were stuck at the U.S. Embassy, but in the end I think they got out. Paul learned that helicopters were bumping into each other on the aircraft carriers, some being pushed over the side to make space for others, some crash-landing on the deck.

Some very close bangs, less than a quarter mile away, got Sophie and Paul and Julie into the living room to join us, all of us listening intently and trying to guess what was happening. We cooked very ancient oats for breakfast that tasted like rusty metal. At about 9:10 a.m. our friend Mạnh

Tường was at the door. He had come in a jeep he got somewhere, and he could climb in and out pretty well even with his braces and crutches, which he uses because he had polio.

He told us the airport has been taken. We discussed the situation and talked about what to do if our block of houses catches fire from a rocket. With this rather sobering precaution in mind, we all started re-packing our bags for running on foot, as opposed to by car. We took extraneous stuff out, made sure we had medicine and bandages, took extra rice. These preparations were while we were listening to the ever closer war noises. There had been a few rockets into the city in the last three days, and even yesterday the fighting was general, seemed to be widespread, and if the ARVN had not accepted defeat, the fighting would have continued right to the center of town and the Presidential Palace itself.

Out on the street yesterday morning there were hundreds of people moving, going, coming, running from the airport, from everywhere to everywhere. There were ARVN soldiers walking slowly, some looting, some shooting, throwing away their uniforms, dressed only in their underwear. There were ordinary people all over the streets, going anywhere. I went out for food, but everything was locked up against looters so I came right back.

The tanks of the PRG were already on Trương Minh Giảng Street and in Gia Định on the bridge by Phan Thanh Giản. The bangs and repercussions were close, and electricity was off. Thinking of the possibilities didn't make us feel good. Also, the nearest Buddhist temple to go to was much too far away to consider as a destination.

Happily, Mạnh Tường came back about an hour later to announce that President Minh had SURRENDERED. We cheered, shouted the news to our alley neighbors, who peeked out their doors and stared at us, stunned, stone-faced, amazed at our enthusiasm. Not that they want the war to continue, but they of course are fearful based on the widespread propaganda. We, by this point, have experienced a lot of American propaganda and just don't believe the northerners will pull out fingernails, rape women, slit throats, cut men's long hair, and round everyone up and shoot them. We trust our friends who sympathize with the Liberation movement, who said those things won't happen. Maybe the neighbors don't know anyone who isn't afraid. Fear is contagious.

There's a saying that if you want to live rich, go into government administration. If you want to beat people, join the police. If you want to threaten people, become an informant, and if you want to lie, go into propaganda. The propaganda has been very effective.

Mạnh Tường went away and said we should be careful and not go out on the streets until the afternoon, since there were scared and still-armed ARVN soldiers and police on the streets, and he worried they might shoot us foreigners. So we walked around the tiny house grinning somewhat nervously at each other, and then sat down to lunch, leftover fried rice. But we hadn't gotten a single mouthful in our mouths when Mạnh Tường was again at the door, shouting, "Come out, all of you! You don't need anything but your flags." We left the Buddhist flag on the porch, left the white one too, and took only the PRG one.

We all ran out, got in the Subaru, flew the flag out the window, and were accompanied and driven by Mạnh Tường's friend Anh Tùng, who had a rifle and a pistol. We headed to Vạn Hạnh Buddhist University, a major Sài Gòn university where the students were organizing. Four of us crowded into the back seat.

Along the way we saw a Sài Gòn tank and a well-dressed civilian man lying right next to it in the street, dead. His was one of three bodies we've seen. Another body was in front of the university, apparently a student who went out with a PRG flag a little too early and got shot in the head by a diehard GRVN policeman.

We arrived at jam-packed Vạn Hạnh University, where we heard a lot of shooting. But the shooting was only to empty cartridges of rifles they were collecting there, and also to keep order on the street in front of the gates. I saw two angry-looking ARVN soldiers driving a big truck on the street in front of the school and not wanting to stop and disarm. The Vạn Hạnh students stood in front of the truck and shot in the air a few times until the truck went in the gate. It came out again a short time later.

All this was happening before the non-local PRG or the North Vietnamese actually arrived. Local people, primarily students, were already in charge here, remarkably well organized, polite, firm, and excited. They were going out in jeeps, collecting discarded soldier gear and clothing from all over the streets, bringing it back, dividing it into piles, and taking all the weapons to a locked room.

For two days ARVN soldiers have been discarding rifles, helmets, clothes, and their identity papers and have been going around in shorts or just their underwear, until and unless they could get home to put on civilian clothes. The clever ones have been wearing street clothes under their uniforms for a while now. The streets are full of papers and furniture and junk. When the surrender came, soldiers stopped their tanks, trucks, jeeps where they were, got off, undressed, and dropped their uniforms, papers, and weapons by their vehicles. Then they ran. The students are out trying to collect all that and are trying to disarm and organize any non-cooperative soldiers. The streets are heavily littered with papers, including lots of identity cards of spies, police, and Self-Defense Forces. We were told there are trucks with loudspeakers telling fleeing soldiers to come to Vạn Hạnh University to turn in weapons and be issued papers confirming that they've done so.

At the university it took a half hour for the first official papers of the new government to be made. They prepared a stencil, but the first stencil had a fake name the chairman used, so they cut another one with his real name. We are numbers 1–5, the very first to get our papers. The papers are important. They allow us to travel and take pictures freely, except in places that aren't yet safe, like the airport itself.

The first tanks on the street came at about 4 p.m. In other places they came in earlier. The street was mobbed with people, and the tanks could only proceed slowly. The first six or so tanks were followed by slow-moving buses and trucks carrying hundreds of curious PRG and NVA uniformed soldiers who were looking at the buildings and waving at the crowds of people all around them. People near us on the sidewalk giggled and waved at them, as did we, and someone tossed them a pack of cigarettes. Then came more busloads of soldiers, grinning out the windows at us. We waved at them and they waved back. Everyone was out on the street watching, happy, children playing all over, vehicles packed, jammed, more buses and trucks of PRG and NVA soldiers arriving, and then there was an intermittent line on each sidewalk of PRG soldiers on foot. These fellows did not smile. They probably felt very vulnerable among these crowds. The foot soldiers were carrying rifles and rocket and grenade launchers. They kept their eyes straight ahead and walked quickly. They looked hot and tired, and they used their black-and-white checkered scarves to wipe their faces.

Most of the soldiers walking in were wearing rubber sandals like mine, made from tires. These sandals, and the checkered scarves, are commonly worn by people in the countryside and in smaller cities like Quảng Ngãi, and I've had rubber sandals and a scarf since I first got there. But today some people on the street stared at my sandals and asked me how I got a pair of Communist sandals so quickly.*

I want to mention the Westerner I saw on the second or third tank on our street. He was tall, dark-haired, had a thick beard and mustache, and seemed to be giving orders. About twenty-six to thirty-two years old, probably an American.†

Someone on a tank asked Paul—yes, Paul—if this was really Sài Gòn! Our friend Mạnh Tường was asked that too.

Also on the streets were many looters who were only paying attention to getting their loot home. They took anything and everything. We saw a computer, lots of pillows, couches, chairs, refrigerators, vases, windows, chandeliers. They were taking them on bikes, motorbikes, and on foot. The looting was at houses of people who had left, and at abandoned offices and stores.

The looters we saw were not armed teenage boys as I'd imagined they would be. And I think the ARVN soldiers who had changed out of their uniforms were by then too scared to loot. But women, men, kids, unarmed, were all over the streets pushing their treasures along. One boy, about twelve years old, pushed three soft rolling armchairs on top of each other.

---

\* The sandals were called dép Bình-Trị-Thiên, named for the three central Việt Nam provinces where they probably originated: Quảng-Bình, Quảng-Trị, and Thừa-Thiên.

† I wrote those words in my journal, but later thought, but didn't write down, that he could have been French or British or another European nationality, or American, or half Vietnamese. Many years after I was in Việt Nam I obtained my thick and heavily redacted Defense Intelligence Agency Freedom of Information file and read that I was credited with having said I had seen an American POW on a tank on April 30, 1975, "giving orders in fluent Vietnamese." The location where this "evidence" was gathered was Fort Chaffee, Arkansas, where Keith and I had stopped on a speaking tour in the late summer of 1975. The informant's name was redacted. This became a statistic of the U.S. government of the existence of an American POW. I attempted to refute this, since whoever he was he wasn't a prisoner, and I didn't know his nationality, and I hadn't heard him speak, but I was not able to alter it.

A very poor-looking woman and her small son carried a heavy desk, filling its drawers with things other people had dropped, like pillows and fabric. In general, we're told that looting didn't get as far out of control here as in Đà Nẵng, probably because here the new government arrived faster than it did there and established control more quickly.

Embassies were looted, though the students tried hard to keep that from happening. By today they had the Malaysian and Taiwan Embassies locked up again. We haven't gone by the U.S. Embassy yet, but at noon today someone borrowed our car to go help stop out-of-control looting there. They announced very early on that looters would be punished, but so far we've seen no punishment except people being told to not do it.

News filtered down quickly about the leaders who had climbed onto evacuation planes and left. Some twenty or more ARVN jet pilots were said to have flown themselves and their families off to Thailand. The Thai government only lets them stay a limited amount of time though, we're told.

We heard fantastic BBC reporting of the evacuation fiasco, as it had to have been. BBC confirmed what we'd heard about too many helicopters trying to land on aircraft carriers, and ARVN helicopters following the American ones and trying to land too, but there was no more space, so some helicopters had to be thrown over the side.

We went in our car, with Anh Tùng accompanying us, to pick up some journalists to invite them to see the activities. We stopped at a gas station and Anh Tùng shot into the air to stop some looters. We had a Liberation flag flying on the jeep, and people waved at us and asked in astonishment what our nationality was. We surely couldn't be American. Must be Russian. Now instead of street kids shouting "American woman! American woman!" at me, I've heard "Russian woman! Russian woman!"

We went to the Presidential Palace, which had dozens of tanks facing it right up to the gate. The first tank had smashed through the barrier, and an officer with a pistol had gotten off to receive the surrender from President Minh. I wandered around talking to PRG soldiers, along with several hundred other curious bystanders.

Keith and Paul at one point went home to get something. They left the car with the PRG flag at the end of the alley, near two cadres standing there. When they came out of the house again, our well-meaning neighbors told them to go back inside, saying, "They're here! Don't go out! They'll shoot you!" The neighbors had been hiding in their houses the whole time and saw the jeep and the cadres through their window, but hadn't seen Keith and Paul when they arrived in the jeep. Keith and Paul told them it was okay and went out to the jeep again, and when they reached it, they waved back at the neighbors. The neighbors were, to say the least, surprised.

There was a curfew beginning at 6 p.m., but the streets didn't empty until 8 or 9, and no one seemed to care. Our whole area was controlled by students, not uniformed soldiers. The soldiers all seemed to be downtown, or were still arriving. We stayed up talking with people at the university until 11 p.m., so we decided to sleep there. We climbed five flights of stairs to the roofed, wall-less temple meditation area. We slept in our clothes on the marble floor with three refugee monks from Đà Nẵng, Quảng Ngãi, and Pleiku. They said they were glad for peace, and they wondered what the future would bring.

We heard and saw flares shot into the air, probably just for fun. Some tracer bullets too. At one point we heard a single machine gun, perhaps at the airport, probably some last dissident ARVN soldier. As I lay there I couldn't believe how safe I felt. I realized I'd never really felt safe in Việt Nam before. I definitely never would have slept outside before, and especially not on a tall building. It was calm and peaceful.

# 4

# SUNRISE

**THURSDAY, MAY 1**

Now I'm writing about today, May 1. This morning we saw the sun rise over a peaceful Sài Gòn. First Sài Gòn sunrise, and Liberation and end of war. We were up at 6:30 or so, and Keith and I walked home from Vạn Hạnh. Some people we met on the streets thought we had come in with the troops from the north, just because of our sandals.

We showered and changed clothes, ate some breakfast, and walked back to the university. On the way I bought medicines for the infirmary there. The streets were packed worse than yesterday, with all the curious people who hadn't dared come out before now. It was very hard to move, even on foot.

Later, we were sitting outside the post office on stools at a rice stand, waiting for some food. A young NLF soldier in a floppy hat and green uniform was sitting at another table, shyly and hesitantly ordering rice. The rice stand woman, also embarrassed, was grinning and asking him some questions, and now is getting his food. It's so strange to watch enemies personally meeting each other for the first time.

One of our neighbors in the alley is a doctor from Đà Nẵng. On April 29, he and his wife were petrified and panic-stricken and came to us at 11 p.m.

asking for our help in attempting to SOS the American helicopters in the sky to come down and take them away before the "devilish, cruel Communists" came and surely killed them.

Today I saw the doctor and invited him to go to Vạn Hạnh University to help out. He said he wanted very much to go, to "prove his new attitude," and we took him in our car. When we reached the infirmary, people there stood and clapped for him, grateful for a doctor. The doctor was surprised, relaxed a bit and smiled, and got to work.

There are flags everywhere. People have quickly painted over their old flags and now have PRG ones on their outer walls and fences. Cars and motorbikes have flags. We have flags. Lots of flags.

At the university we were taken in a press jeep for a tour of the city. Today no one is allowed to shoot guns anymore. Traffic police students have rifles, but are supposed to not fire them. Every direction we drove we got stuck in incredible traffic. It was actually a lot of fun, since everyone was laughing and good-humored, but a waste of gas. There was a fire on one street, so we and thousands of others, mostly on motorcycles, had to turn around and go back. Two big buses full of PRG soldiers turned around too, all of us waving and laughing.

We made our way to the airport. We tried to go into the chiefs of staff building, but as a military installation it was still off limits. There were groups, lines, of newly arrived PRG soldiers and some air force (a blue insignia on their collars) walking into town, waving, hot, friendly. I saw nothing to distinguish officers from non-officers. I saw no women troops except for three uniformed women cadres. We went to the airport gate and asked permission to enter. A smiling man in a jeep asked us to wait because it wasn't yet entirely safe in there. Later we heard some big booms, perhaps an artillery dump blowing up. Still later at the airport, we saw vehicles destroyed, almost all military, and one Honda car. We saw one PRG or North Vietnamese tank that got hit too, perhaps the only one in the whole attack on Sài Gòn.

There's a perimeter around central Sài Gòn the ARVN tanks were either retreating to or arriving at when the surrender order came. The tanks are still sitting in the middle of the roads, making terrible traffic jams of their own. There is one on our corner and one on Công Lý and Yên Đỗ too. We finally made it to downtown, which had very few cars, actually little traffic at all.

Yesterday hundreds of uniformed North Vietnamese troops stayed right downtown, camping in the big park in front of the palace. They were chatting, cooking, doing their laundry, and hanging it on clotheslines strung between trees. A few hundred Sài Gòn civilians went to talk to the soldiers in the park yesterday, and by noon today some thousands were sitting on the grass with them, talking and smoking. Then later in the afternoon, they'd gone out of the downtown area. The park has had the grass badly trampled, but it's not littered on at all.

The soldiers covered the barrels of the tank guns and anti-aircraft guns, and now they don't look so scary. By today, they've moved most of the tanks to various locations outside the center of town, including a little alley around the corner from us. They've also taken down most of the barbed wire and barriers from around the Presidential Palace.

The troops just coming in are so cool, so calm, so confident, their assurance spreads over the city. At this point I'd almost leave our house unlocked just because of the relaxed, secure feeling in the city. The gentleness of the "conquering invaders" is also very much in contrast to some of the local students. Some students, at a festivity today, clapped loudly when they were called the liberators of the south, but didn't clap when the announcer said the hard work was still ahead, that it wouldn't be over in only three months or five years, but a whole lifetime. Also, like students everywhere, they groaned when, after one speaker had quickly read aloud the PRG Ten Points, which promised peaceful reunification, freedom of thought and worship, and gender equality, another speaker said she would read them to the students again. I do expect they'll be hearing them again and again.*

---

* The PRG Ten Points included that the Americans had to unconditionally withdraw, and destroy their bases in Việt Nam. The Vietnamese would choose their political system without foreign interference. A provisional government including members of all political groups would be formed. The north and south would re-establish normal relations and negotiate reunification peacefully without foreign intervention. The Americans would bear all responsibilities for damage incurred in Việt Nam during the war. *A Ten-Point Policy of the PRG of the RSV toward Soldiers and Personnel in the Government of South Vietnam* (Wilson Center Digital Archive Citation: January 25, 1972).

The Liberation anthem, "Liberate the South," was led by a cultural group whose members had only just learned the words. The whole audience at the festival stood up spontaneously, but no one seemed to know the song yet. But I did! Yến, my language tutor, had taught it to me the day she told me about her husband. During my first two months in country, when I was doing language study in Sài Gòn, she came every day to tutor me. But then she was gone for a week, and we didn't know why. When she came back she said she had had to go visit some family members.

Once we were alone, she broke down in tears and told me about her husband. She said he was a Liberation fighter with the National Liberation Front in the mountains, but he didn't carry a gun. He was a poet, and his job was to keep up everyone's spirits. A poet, in the army. She told me she had learned he had been shot, and that's why she was gone for that week, trying to see him. But he had died before she could reach him. Also, she had just learned she is two months pregnant with their third child. She said they've been married for eight years, but have only lived together for a total of two years. He was in prison some of those years, and then wasn't really safe in the city, so he had gone to live in a writers' community in the countryside, in an area held by the NLF. He had huddled in caves while B-52 bombs crashed overhead. He had bled from the ears and mouth from the bomb concussions, but other than that, he had never been injured. She had visited him in the countryside about once a year, for just a few days.

She and I cried together. It was very intimate, raw, painful, so very sad. She was on a chair and I was on the floor at her feet, and we were both wiping our eyes on the front panel of her aó dài tunic. Instead of doing any language study that day, she taught me the words to "Liberate the South," and we sang it over and over. One line is about killing Americans, but she stressed that it didn't mean me. She shared with me that she was actually a National Liberation Front cadre herself. Before she left the room that day and every day after that, she put on her public face and didn't let any emotion show. Like so many other cadres, she was invisible in plain sight.

The students are still in control of security at local areas, while the uniformed PRG and NVA soldiers have the palace, airport, and other important places. To be honest, it feels safer with the soldiers in charge of security rather than the students. The students are good, but not as mature or experienced, of course, as the soldiers.

The students took over a government building and turned it into a student center, and are having meetings there all day. They divided into action groups to organize locally, since at the moment there's no apparent local administrative structure. They also are organizing teams to clean up the city. By this afternoon looting seems to have ended, and things are much calmer. Tonight we've heard two large explosions—no idea what they were, but in general we feel safe.

These PRG soldiers are tough. One man from the north today told Julie he hasn't been home in four years and wants more than anything to go back. They're tired and happy and want to go home to tell their families they're still alive. Many others whose homes are in Sài Gòn have just come back for the first time in years and decades. I see lots of embracing as people meet and re-meet each other.

Bửu Chỉ, political prisoner and artist, has just come out of hiding, and Nguyễn Hữu Thái, of the Student Association Revolutionary Committee, was just released after some three years in prison. We also had a long talk with Lê Công Giàu, who was imprisoned from 1971 to 1973 for his politics, and who has now also come out of hiding.

Lê Công Giàu talked of how well they have faked ID cards over the years, so well that only an X-ray machine can tell them from the real Sài Gòn ID cards. He told of how the PRG brought weapons into the city on pushcarts under piles of smelly, salty fish, and how ARVN soldiers wouldn't inspect the carts because of the fish. He talked of how carefully and quickly the PRG got control of the electricity and radio stations so that they couldn't be sabotaged.

Another man sitting with us said, "Yesterday I saw people I recognized as secret police. They had changed clothes and shook my hand as if they were my good friends. I just shook their hands."

Lê Công Giàu said they're still concerned about armed former ARVN soldiers who haven't yet come to the locations set up to care for them and where they're supposed to turn in their weapons. He fears they'll keep their weapons and use them to steal, since they have no military income anymore.

He said a system is being set up to help locate and inform families of their relatives who have died. They're working on traffic organizing too. He pointed out that under the PRG, medical care is free. So are many films and movies, both documentaries and just entertaining ones.

When Lê Công Giàu was first imprisoned in 1971 he was tortured so badly he almost died. His friends didn't dare go visit him in the hospital in Sài Gòn. For two months he had what Mạnh Tường called "administrative torture," meaning he was tortured eight hours a day. He is thirty years old. He says now that there is peace he dares to think about having a family.

We were talking near the open door of Lê Công Giàu's small room, sitting on some mattresses on the floor and drinking hot water from thermoses. A PRG uniformed photographer with a German camera was walking by, and Lê Công Giàu invited him in. He joined us and we discussed cameras and the events of the last two days. Has it really only been two days? Then we went outside to take pictures of all of us posing together. The photographer wanted a souvenir picture of himself with Americans.

Then we met up with Huỳnh Tấn Mẫm. He told of his three years in prison and all the times he was moved in the last few weeks. He was released two days ago when the last GRVN president, General "Big" Minh, freed him and all other political prisoners.

On one of his recent moves, Huỳnh Tấn Mẫm was the only prisoner in a huge truck with lots of guards. In the last prison at Long Hải, he had only seawater to bathe in, and he still has sores on his legs, which he showed us. In prison he was never allowed books or paper or medicine, and the little food there was, was terrible. He spent eleven months and twenty days in solitary confinement in a small windowless cell. He said he urinated and defecated in there too, and only rarely was allowed out, only at night. He tried to exercise to keep fit and not go insane.

In the last place he was held he had fifteen trustees just for him, but they fled one by one until only one was left. The one who was left was the supervisor. He opened Mẫm's jail cell and said, "Premier Vũ Văn Mẫu frees you," and then he formally begged Mẫm's pardon and apologized for what the Thiệu regime had done to him.* We're told that in the Delta there are

---

* Vũ Văn Mẫu, a politician who served as foreign minister under Ngô Đình Diệm, was prime minister of South Việt Nam for two days, from April 28 to April 30, 1975. He declared April 30 to be "pardon day," when all political prisoners were to be released. He was succeeded by Huỳnh Tấn Phát, prime minister of the Provisional Revolutionary Government of South Việt Nam.

some ARVN military divisions left, but they are surrounded and no resistance is expected from them. This morning we heard on Sài Gòn radio an announcement that the station is now called "Liberated Sài Gòn Radio."

Today everyone is looser and friendlier than yesterday. The possibilities of a country at peace, of freedom to travel everywhere, of men not having to be soldiers and instead finding jobs they want, near home, are beginning to really sink in. It's a wonderful feeling. As we traveled on a jeep this afternoon I sat backwards, legs hanging over the back. People on bikes and motorcycles behind us smiled and waved and asked our nationality. One young woman yelled, "Vui không Chị?" ("Are you happy, sister?"). I answered, "Vui lắm" ("Very happy"). She was thrilled, maybe because I answered in Vietnamese, and then she asked, "Cách mạng vui không?" ("Happy with the revolution?"). "Vui lắm," I said again. She followed us for several blocks, smiling.

Tonight the landlady came over to ask us, in a roundabout way, to help her go to the U.S., where her husband has apparently already gone. She said the separation of families is the fault of the Communists. She talked to us as we climbed out of the official PRG jeep with PRG flag that we'd just come home in, and we have official red armbands and ID papers. She still thought we could somehow help her.

When Sophie saw the landlady, without thinking she began to take off her red armband in fear of what the woman would think. We laughed and reminded her that she needn't be secretive. Similarly, this afternoon I was asked by a well-dressed and obviously rich man, who introduced himself as a lawyer, if he could take our picture. I felt oddly paranoid and thought he shouldn't see my armband or my black-and-white checkered Liberation scarf. I refused the photo opportunity, and by the time I realized it didn't matter, he was gone.

# 5

## THE FIRST FEW DAYS

**FRIDAY, MAY 2**

This morning traffic is still clogged in places but better than yesterday. Great improvement in garbage, people gathering it in huge piles on the streets, and big trucks picking it up. Buses are running today, and were yesterday also. There are lots of vehicles of all sorts. Uniformed PRG soldiers are more spread out. They're living in empty buildings. They walk around the streets unarmed and alone today, smiling or just busy or eating or chatting or resting.

We haven't met many people who are still scared of the North Vietnamese, now that they've met them. Some who are still scared nonetheless have told me the uniformed soldiers are polite and dễ thương lắm! (very cute!). They're more afraid of local PRG guerrillas and sympathizers, either because they fear those people know a lot, perhaps about them, or because they fear locals may do bad things, much as the "cowboys" (draft dodgers, Self-Defense Forces) did under Thiệu.

BBC radio reported that the PRG announced confiscation of all public *and private* property. We know this isn't true. It has to have been an incorrectly translated broadcast from Liberation Radio. It's true that all public and U.S. property is confiscated, claimed by the government. But private property, if the owners are still here, is not confiscated. And foreign embassies are being protected as best they can be.

One former U.S. building that was still being looted this morning had a sign on the gate by the afternoon saying looters would be "threatened," and that those who stopped looters would be "praised."

We understand that there are three Associated Press journalists, two United Press International journalists, one Indian, three British, at least one Italian, and several French journalists still here. But what they do all day, I don't know. We hardly see them.

Looted houses are all locked up today. No more looting at all as far as we can tell. One can't see now if houses were looted or not, unless the windows are broken. Local brigades are organizing to clean up after the looters. A student group went to Long Khánh by car and came back, collecting the dead bodies on the way. One friend said he saw quite a few there still. Sound trucks are going around asking people to not dump garbage in the streets, and also to not burn it, for fear of unexploded munitions going off.

We went to Thiên Thanh sewing shop and the woman's mouth fell open in surprise when she saw us. She couldn't believe we hadn't left. She hadn't made our AFSC flag yet, and no doubt wasn't going to since she thought we were gone, but she gave us a new little PRG flag as a souvenir.

We walked through the Presidential Palace park, slowly, with hundreds of others, stopping to chat with several soldiers. Most of the ones there are North Vietnamese, because the battalion guarding the palace is North Vietnamese. The bộ đội foot soldiers are nice and fun to talk to. They seem as calm as Buddha, with a long concept of time. They refer to several years as a short period of time.

Some we met were students just a few months ago who were asked to volunteer for the final push. They're not particularly curious about us, and they seem to listen to what we're saying instead of commenting on how good our Vietnamese is. In conversations today they proudly told of their victories against the B-52 bombers, and could quote how many were shot down and how many U.S. troops had been involved.

One described an American pilot who was shot down, who had come from a base in Thailand. The soldier motioned behind him to a rocket launcher, apparently the very type that they use to shoot down B-52s. Keith mentioned that the Vietnamese used a lot of restraint in not killing the captured pilots, imprisoning them instead. The man said that killing them wouldn't be the right thing to do. And I'm sure it was useful for negotiations or propaganda too. *(See "I Was a Prisoner of War" on page 233.)*

In the Presidential Palace park, we sat on the sidewalk and on the low wall, along with many curious soldiers and civilians. One soldier had "adopted" a street boy of about seven and was playing with him, and picked him up off a bicycle he'd knocked over. Another soldier was sitting next to a civilian whose arm was draped around a fellow soldier, and another leaned against his knee, and one leaned against Keith. In Việt Nam, men in public hold hands with and touch other men, women with women, but not women with men.

We walked around some more, got to the Student Union, and looked at a photo display there called "The Life of Hồ Chí Minh."* There I met a broadly smiling cadre with an AK-47 rifle, apparently an officer of some sort. She's twenty-four, from Cần Thơ, has beautiful, thick black hair in a braid down her back, is relatively big and definitely strong, and has been a cadre since the age of fourteen. She was easy to talk with. I noticed she was wearing blue flip-flops instead of rubber sandals, and when I pointed that out, a male cadre near her said, "She's in the city now and has to look pretty." I wasn't sure how to react to that, but she smiled at him, so I did

---

* Hồ Chí Minh, born Nguyễn Sinh Cung in 1890, was also known as Nguyễn Tất Thành, Nguyễn Ái Quốc, Bác Hồ, or simply Bác ("Uncle"). He was a charismatic and revered Vietnamese revolutionary and political leader and the first president of the Democratic Republic of Việt Nam. He was the founder of the Vietnamese Communist Party in 1930. A longtime anti-colonial activist, he led the effort to defeat the French, ending with success at the battle of Điện Biên Phủ in 1954. Fearing the spread of Communist power in Asia, the United States declined to sign the Geneva Agreements in 1954 and instead helped to install anti-Communist Ngô Đình Diệm as head of state of the southern half of the country. Diệm also refused to follow the final Geneva Accords that ended the "Indochina War," and the "American War" began. Hồ Chí Minh served as prime minister of North Việt Nam from 1945 to 1955 and president of Việt Nam from 1945 until his death in 1969. Sophie Quinn-Judge, *Ho Chi Minh: The Missing Years* (Oakland: University of California Press, 2003).

too. I told her I didn't know how to shoot a gun. She smiled again and said, "It's easy. Want to learn?"

In the evening we got a surprise. Earl Martin and Yoshihiro "Hiro" Ichikawa, our Mennonite Central Committee close friends and neighbors in Quảng Ngãi, arrived at our door. They left Quảng Ngãi on April 9, sixteen days after Liberation there. They described the transition in Quảng Ngãi and their trip from there to Sài Gòn.

A few days after we, and Earl's wife and kids, left Quảng Ngãi, Chị Mai, our friend and the receptionist at the rehabilitation center, arranged a visit for Earl at his request to meet some local Liberation Front cadres on March 23. Around town people were packing and trying to leave, but the main roads were closed. Earl was curious and wanted to find out how the cadres felt about him and Hiro not leaving. He took a circuitious route through town and past the airport into disputed territory, and shortly before reaching a rendezvous point was stopped by armed South Vietnamese soldiers. They warned this American that if he went farther, he would encounter dangerous Việt Cộng. But they let him continue. Eventually, following a guide at a distance, he reached a thatched-roof pavilion completely hidden in tall grass and leafy bamboo trees. There he met several apparently high-ranking uniformed PRG soldiers. They seemed to already know about him, and gave him the impression that he would be safe and welcome to stay in Quảng Ngãi. They asked if other foreigners were still in town, and he said he knew of one, Hiro.

The cadres suggested that Earl make sure to have a good camera so he could take pictures in the upcoming days. They told him to be at the Quaker house, our house, when shooting began, and to make a small sign, with the numbers 3, 5, 7 in white on a dark-blue background, and to hang it on the door at the first sound of gunfire in town.

Earl left to return to Quảng Ngãi in the late afternoon, but was stopped by a squad of ARVN soldiers. They took him to their outpost and questioned him. They accused him of having gone to see the Communists, but he said he had just gone for a walk, and was also looking for a possible village to stay in if Quảng Ngãi was bombed. They asked him other questions, including, specifically, why the U.S. Congress had voted against the military supplemental aid appropriation.

He was still there well after dark when suddenly there was machine-gun fire nearby. The soldiers ran to their positions and Earl started to run away from the outpost, but they yelled at him that there were landmines ahead, so he turned back. A lieutenant offered to take him to spend the night with a family in a nearby village. To his surprise, the family let him stay, even though, they said, guerrillas often visited at night. Very early the next morning one did, and he told Earl that he was the same man Earl had met yesterday "in the liberated zone." Earl was relieved that it was a cadre who knew him, but later the same man said he had been kidding and had actually met Earl in the ARVN outpost, and he was actually an ARVN sergeant. The sergeant took him back to the outpost for questioning, but soon let him leave, providing a driver on a motorcycle. Earl thought he was free, but the driver took him to the infamous Provincial Interrogation Center. He was questioned for a few more hours, then released. The soldiers holding him seemed to have more important things on their minds. Tension in town had increased dramatically in one day. He returned to the Quaker house, where Chị Mai greeted him and asked how his adventure had been.

Soon it became apparent that the ARVN military were fleeing, leaving Quảng Ngãi. Citizens raided the military warehouse and took supplies home. It was midnight, March 24, and there didn't seem to be any government in charge in Quảng Ngãi at all. A few hours later, at 2:15 a.m., the guerrillas appeared outside their door. Apparently they had just walked into town and had taken over the government, with no encounters and no fighting.*

A month later Earl and Hiro were invited to leave, for their own safety, they were told. They have been stuck on the road from Quảng Ngãi to Sài Gòn for three weeks, treated extremely politely but slightly suspiciously. Their news depressed us and dimmed our hopes for going back by car. Now they've come to Sài Gòn to join two other MCC workers, Max Ediger and Jim Klassen, who, like us, stayed to witness the takeover in Sài Gòn. That night Earl and Hiro and Keith and I slept in a row on the floor of the flophouse.

---

* Earl S. Martin, *Reaching the Other Side* (New York: Crown Publishers, 1978), 42–47.

## SATURDAY, MAY 3

Another very full day. First thing in the morning, Sophie and Julie and I made our way to the Khất Sĩ temple and orphanage to see our friend, the anti-war Buddhist head nun Hùynh Liên, and the children in the orphanage. This was where we had been invited to stay before Liberation. These nuns had always been very active in the anti-war Third Force movement during the old government. *(See "The Third Force" on page 248.)* We visited and saw their banners that read "Chào mừng quân đội cách mạng." ("Welcome to the Liberation army.")

Then I walked over to Dung's house and by luck found her home. A relative of hers was there whose husband was a secret policeman and is still scared. I just now learned from Dung that she and her husband, Ba Minh, had been political prisoners under the Thiệu government. She told me they were arrested for having poems in their house calling for peace. He was imprisoned for four years, she for six months. They had been active in the anti-Thiệu student movement, but only after imprisonment did Ba Minh join the Liberation Front, she said, and she participated to a much lesser extent from home in Sài Gòn. Like many others, they were politicized in prison. So they were guerrillas, cadres, as were Yến and her husband. Ba Minh was a writer and Yến's husband was a poet, and these were their actual jobs as guerrilla soldiers with the Liberation Front. They used pens instead of rifles.

Dung told me what she did as the surrender was announced. She and her sixteen-year-old sister, Thu, went out to the street, pulled down a flag on the local government outpost, and put up a PRG flag. They stood there, unarmed, and shortly dozens of panicking, half-dressed soldiers were putting their guns at their feet. Dung and Thu picked up rifles, which they didn't know how to shoot, to show others that they had authority and to encourage more ARVN soldiers to give them their guns, which they were all too happy to do.

I left Dung's house and went home, where I found Mạnh Tường and lots of friends, including my other language tutor, Yến. Our cook, Bà Hai, who had always been ardently anti-Communist, was there too. Today Yến told Bà Hai, jokingly confessing, that for all these years that they've known each other, Yến was actually part of the other side, part of the National Liberation Front, one of those revolutionaries Bà Hai has always been terrified of. There was only one moment of complete shock on Bà Hai's face before they were both laughing and hugging each other. The rest of us were in on the hugging too. Then things got more serious as Yến started to cry because, she said, her husband couldn't live to see this day. That makes my heart ache.

Our friend Chị Hiền saw us on the street at about 2 p.m. and asked us to attend a meeting where local religious leaders would be presented to PRG leaders. We went to Vạn Hạnh University at 3:30 p.m. to meet up again with Mạnh Tường and his friend Anh Tùng, to go to the meeting together by jeep. It was a crowded jeep, with us plus three journalists, one a PRG guerrilla, one a monk, one a student, who interviewed us and took pictures as we drove. The guerrilla was from somewhere north of Quảng Trị, about twenty years old. He's been a Liberation fighter since he was ten.

At that afternoon meeting, we stood in a large crowd in the blocked-off street, an air of festival everywhere. People crowded around each of us to ask who we were, and they found it hard to believe we were Americans. The women asked me all sorts of questions about the new government, as if we were part of it. Will we have to work from 4 a.m. until 6 p.m. every day? Can we still wear colored dresses? Can we have long fingernails? Will they change money to other money? Can we still get in contact with friends in America? Can Vietnamese students in America get back here? If our families were originally from the north, do we have to go back there? What will they do to people who ran from the north in 1954? What about people who ran more recently? Well, in fact, we do know more answers than most of them do, so I answered what I could and told them to work through their local committees, which are quickly being organized.

The speech and the meeting were set up right on the street, but a small house was open for the use of "special" participants, including us. We were invited inside to sit down and drink tea while we were interviewed and asked questions ourselves. An older man, who was the owner of the house, asked me and Sophie if we would adopt their adopted son, a strikingly handsome five-year-old boy, half Caucasian-American and half Vietnamese, who had been left on their doorstep when he was a baby. I was surprised to hear this, after Liberation, and from a man involved in the new organizing.

The man said he refused to give the boy up to the U.S. evacuation, but we were "sympathetic" Americans, so he hoped we would take him. We talked more with him and his wife and I don't think they were ever really serious, just worried. He also said he was afraid that, being a merchant, he would no longer be able to get imported goods to sell, so their family would suffer.

# 6

# YẾN IS IN CHARGE

**SATURDAY, MAY 3, CONTINUED**

We left the afternoon meeting at a quarter to 6 Sài Gòn time, and were just in time at Bình's and Thúy's house for dinner. They are sisters of our friend Phương-Hằng Phan, who works with MCC and has visited us and the MCCers in Quảng Ngãi. *(For Phương-Hằng's story, see "How I Came to Live in America" on page 228.)* Thúy has a little girl named Cún, half white American, half Vietnamese, and they have been very worried about what will happen to her. I right away invited them to the women's meeting that night. Yến had suggested they and I come, as a way of relieving their fears.

There seems to be no curfew at all, and people are on the streets until quite late. Bình and Thúy's mother came in by bus last night from Tuy Hòa, and the trip took from 6 a.m. to 9 p.m., five hours longer than usual, because many bridges were destroyed. The checkpoints were few, she said, and the guards always courteously said to her, "Mother, please go right on by." She said it reminded her of the old days, before Việt Nam was split in half in 1954.

Bình and Thúy can remember a little about life back then, though they were very young. They remember a birthday song to Uncle Hồ, and other songs about washing and keeping clean and behaving correctly. Bình recounted when all the five-year-olds in school were told to kill flies, and the more they killed the more they were praised. The same with rats. She said they were each expected to kill three rats a day. They would kill the flies and pick them up with their hands, but were not taught to wash their hands afterwards. They would save the rat tails to take to school and carry them in their pockets or lunch pails. We all laughed and agreed that the fly and rat killing wasn't bad, but further hygiene education was needed.

At 7:15 p.m. we three went off on their Honda 50, all sitting straddling, across the Phan Thanh Giản bridge toward Biên Hòa. We turned into a crowded refugee camp, noticing that the Biên Hòa highway still has lots of tanks and trucks parked along the way. We came to the local revolutionary committee building and asked inside where the women's meeting was being held. A very friendly young man smiled and asked if we were Thu Thủy, Thúy, and Bình. We said yes, and identified ourselves. He didn't show any reaction to the fact that one Vietnamese name, Thu Thủy, belonged to me, a foreigner. He said Yến had asked him to take us over to the meeting. We walked for two minutes and came to an empty area to the left of the road, fenced in with barbed wire and set up with many low plastic stools close together. Yến was there and greeted us warmly.

Pretty soon there were about two hundred people crowded together, calmly chatting in the dark under one light bulb strung on a wire. A woman named Chị Cuốc talked with me before the meeting began. She asked if I thought communication with the U.S. would still be possible, because she has friends at CARITAS (an Episcopal social charity) and Catholic Relief Services, and she wants to write to them in America. She wanted to talk to me in English, but I didn't want to be noticed as a foreigner any more than I had to be, so I asked her to speak Vietnamese with me.

Chị Cuốc is the head of the local women's committee, and she stood up with a hand megaphone to welcome everyone. She introduced me to the audience, I imagine because she knew people were curious about the only non-Vietnamese person there, and then introduced the guest speaker, Chị Sáu, otherwise called . . . Chị Yến, my dear friend and language tutor.

Chị Yến! Chị Sáu! (which means "sixth older sister," a common nickname). Same person! To our astonishment, she is in charge of one of the seven arrondissements (sections or boroughs) of Sài Gòn. She's important. She was her wonderful strong self, all four feet ten inches or so of her. Her voice is low, slow, and soothing. She welcomed all the relatives of "our Uncle Hồ," and throughout her talk referred to all Vietnamese that way, as Uncle Hồ's children. The audience was eager to listen, and they chased away nuisance children who came to play in the dirt and who made a lot of noise.

She began by saying, "Many of you sisters have heard propaganda and gotten scared. You are wives or mothers of soldiers, policemen, GRVN officials, and you've heard you'll be arrested. We're now a country at peace, and there's been enough killing. We don't want to arrest anyone. Now we want to work together to build and reconstruct. Some of you have American husbands, or half-American children. The revolution is not angry at children, or people. The enemy was the domineering American government. Children and families of Americans are Vietnamese and the revolution will care for them with as much love as for all of Uncle's relatives."

Yến continued, "You women will want to know about the revolution's health care and education programs. The revolution has always provided free health care. No private hospitals; you don't have to borrow money to survive illness or injury. The hospitals are public, but *good*, not corrupt. The nurses and doctors care about the people. Right now there are few doctors because many GRVN doctors only wanted money, and have joined the Americans in going off in the retreat, abandoning their patients. But very soon there will be doctors from PRG areas in every hospital, so take your sick family members to the hospitals, and don't be afraid." (Hùynh Liên has in fact sent most of the other Buddhist nuns at her monastery off to be nurses at hospitals.) "I have worked for ten years with the revolution, and I've never once had to pay a doctor or pay for medicine. All medicine here will be free.

"As for education, there will be daycare centers and good schools for our children. Many mothers who must work lock their children in the house and leave them and go off to work. This is very dangerous, especially because of fires. The new government will provide healthy, fun centers with teachers and caretakers for the children, for the convenience of the mothers. If the mothers must go to work at 8 a.m., the center will open at 7:30 a.m. There will be cookies and drinks and toys, and the children will learn songs and games. Higher-level schools will also benefit the children. They won't be overcrowded, and they won't cost money. Schools now are expensive, and only the rich can get higher education. From now on the best students will be able to achieve as high as they are able, based on ability, not money."

An audience member asked about older people who never went to school, and if they would be able to attend. Yến said, "Those older people who never got to go to school can go now. In the revolution, you don't need to be ashamed of being eighteen or fifteen or thirty and never having gone to school. In areas long held by the PRG, many people forty or fifty years old also learned to read and write for the first time.

"Some people say the revolution will force people to wear different clothes, cut their nails short, work all day. People working to improve their society have often found that long nails made it hard to do some work, and that nice clothes are harmed by some work done in them, like nurse work, so we save our nice clothes for holidays, when we all dress up and celebrate and make our country beautiful with our bright pretty clothes.

"In the new society, women can go out on the streets after dark with no fear at all." (This statement drew the greatest response from the audience.) "Women have had to be afraid of the Self-Defense Forces, but no more." (This drew a standing ovation from the audience of women.)

"Those of you boys listening here who were Self-Defense Force members, don't think that we hate you. The revolution understands why some of you were not doing your best to help your people. In the future you will all come to learn how to use a gun only for self-protection, not to attack, and how to correctly and uprightly defend all of our brothers and sisters and parents." (Audience clapped and laughed in agreement.)

"As for money, let me explain that if the Sài Gòn money is changed to new money, it will be at an exact correct exchange rate and you will still be able to buy just as much with it. While the Sài Gòn đồng in the last week rose as high as 4,000 to $1 U.S., the Hà Nội đồng is still 2 đồng to a dollar. A bag of rice costs 5 đồng in liberated areas and 25,000 đồng here. The money each of you has is your own private money. The revolution won't take it away from you. If some of you have more rice, you'll eat more. Those who have less will eat less." (Laughter.) "The propaganda you've heard says that if you have a chicken you'll have to eat it in the dark of night because you're not allowed to eat well anymore." (Huge laughter.) "You who have chickens get to eat chickens and you who don't just don't, that's all. The new government won't take away anyone's food or money.

"Industries will be nationalized, in a manner mutually acceptable to the government and the private owner. Everyone will continue in their work, and the government will find new jobs for soldiers."

A student asked how they can take the test for the high school baccalaureate—twelfth grade. Yến said that in Huế after Liberation it took only about three weeks to get schools running normally again, and their baccalaureate test was given. She assumes the same will happen here. At the moment most students are helping reorganize, taking care of refugees, but soon will probably resume their studies.

A woman asked if the new government would fulfill the promise made by the old government, but never carried out, to pay the family of a dead soldier a large sum of money. Yến started to answer, "Everyone will receive enough to live on, but beyond that . . ." and then she paused, looked down, then continued more firmly. "Thousands of Liberation soldiers have fought and been sacrificed for decades for the revolution, with never a thought about compensation on their or their families' behalf. Since they have sacrificed, the GRVN families must also learn to sacrifice. Families will not be paid large sums of money just because a family member has died. Every family in Việt Nam is in this same situation, and more Liberation families than GRVN families."

The women hearing this answer, certainly for the first time, seemed to be having new realizations, and nodded in agreement or at least understanding. After all the propaganda about the filthy Communists, now they see and are listening to this small, friendly woman talking about sacrifice. The emotions behind Yến's words were evident to all. She had known suffering too.

At the end of her speech, a man of about fifty was introduced as the chairman of the local revolutionary committee. He gave a short speech, and then he lectured the little boys, who had been misbehaving and interrupting throughout the meeting, on their bad manners. Considering we were in a crowded refugee camp where these boys lived with little discipline and probably no schooling, I thought they actually weren't as disruptive as they might have been. Maybe I'm used to Quảng Ngãi street kids.

Each family at the meeting who lived in the refugee camp was asked to send one volunteer with a broom at 8 a.m. the next morning to clean up the littered streets. Volunteers from a high school were coming, and the chairman said it would be disrespectful to let students come and clean their streets without helping themselves. As the meeting ended, people were enthusiastically talking about what had been presented.

Back at our house, sitting in the kitchen eating watermelon and drinking water, we discussed it all. We talked about how education might change and how nationalization of businesses might take place. If stores are supposed to remain private, then will pharmacies also remain privately owned? If so, will the government buy the medicine and then distribute it for free to patients, if medicine will be free? It will be interesting to see how all this will be organized.

Bình told a story of a woman who works in her office, the Revolutionary Press Agency, who has always worn gorgeous clothes, lots of makeup, and not only had red fingernail and toenail polish, but also had a flower painted on each nail. Since Liberation she's been wearing an old purple áo dài and has short plain nails. No one in the office has said a word to her about it, and Bình thinks it's very funny. She says that even though the woman is free to dress up as before, she would be embarrassed to now, simply because it's not "fashionable" as it was during the strong American mini-skirt influence.

## SUNDAY, MAY 4

Sài Gòn has been liberated for only four days and yet the changes already are remarkable. Cyclo and motorbike and taxi drivers we've asked tell us they're thrilled by the changes. They are talkative and pedaling hard to make lots of money during these festive and expensive days. Traffic continues to be jammed, so gas must be available, and families are moving here and there, perhaps to better houses that relatives abandoned when they left the country.

The highway is now open all the way to Hà Nội. Buses are expensive now, but will be cheaper when the regular (not black market) gas flow is operating, probably very soon. That's a little too bad. I was hoping for a gas shortage so the air in Sài Gòn would clear up. Have to hope they will have muffler laws, at least.

Friends predict a train all the way north very soon, perhaps as soon as in a month. I can hardly believe that, but even Yến predicts one month. It's the most economical way to link the country, not just to get people from place to place, but more importantly to supply all parts of Việt Nam with necessary goods and merchandise. Maybe we can send up our medical shipment by train to Quảng Ngãi.

People on the streets are eager to talk, especially to the uniformed PRG and NVA soldiers, who now go everywhere, sightseeing, shopping, visiting, unarmed and often alone. The North Vietnamese Army soldiers are "extremely correct" about paying for what they buy, but no one knows the exchange rate, so some end up paying too much, some too little, and hopefully it all averages out in the end.

The PRG soldiers wander around, often with civilians talking casually with them, sometimes with arms around each other, or two soldiers hand in hand. People seem completely unafraid of them, and those who are afraid say they're afraid of the "fake" Communists, people from before who still have guns. The PRG soldiers are so calm and strong, and good-looking, probably because they look happy. They're young and old. One man of fifty or so, in a jeep, asked with a broad smile who we were. We told him we were Americans, and he reached out his hand to shake ours.

People are discussing the changes. Should they really believe that these things the cadres are saying are true? Or will people be arrested later on? But as each day goes by, more people seem to believe in the change, believe the Americans really aren't coming back, believe that each individual may have a say in the new government, as they've been told.

I feel like I'm on vacation in any Asian city not at war. We walk on the streets at night, go into a refugee camp without secret police following and asking questions, and I am treated in general pretty much like a Vietnamese. We feel we can talk freely, and even those who used to only whisper no longer add, "If I say this on the street I'll be arrested." The new soldiers are remarkably calm, not hostile or antagonistic. Brothers and sisters and cousins, same language, same blood.

A PRG journalist saw Mạnh Tường and ran up and hugged him. He had known Mạnh Tường when they were students together in Sài Gòn. He said he had been arrested by the GRVN military police for trying to avoid the draft, and was conscripted. But he later deserted and became a

PRG journalist. He said the PRG did not make him join their army, but appreciated him being a journalist working with them. So now we have Yến's husband, a poet; Dung's husband, a writer; and this guy, a journalist, all with the National Liberation Front.

Ex-president Thiệu is as if dead a hundred years already. So quickly forgotten. He was never revered, and I wonder how respected he actually was. No one seems to regret, at least out loud, that Thiệu and the others left the country. Those who have mentioned them to me talk about how they must be suffering by being so far away from their homeland.

But everyone over the age of twenty knows of Uncle Hồ Chí Minh, and even anti-Communists recognize him as the father of Việt Nam. His birthday this May 19 is sure to be a wonderful celebration. I wonder how many people know that his 1945 Declaration of Independence is in part based on the United States' 1776 one.

Many workers in Sài Gòn were back on the job two days after Liberation. Most people are at their normal work now. Civil servants, like post office workers, are back at work, some grumbling since they're not being paid.

A huge steam shovel was putting garbage into a truck three days after Liberation. Local elementary schools are administrative centers for the new government. All people are urged to participate and make themselves part of the new organization.

Our cook Bà Hai said a lot of people are spending their last money on very overpriced Western goods and pretty things, thinking that from now on there won't be any more pretty things to buy, or any more money. Looted items from American houses are being sold widely.

People with sewing machines are making blue, red, and yellow flags as fast as they can. They sell for 500 đồng for a big one, and they're flying all over the city. Even the Khất Sĩ Buddhist nuns said yesterday they're making flags and they've already sold five hundred of them. Some rich anti-Communists have covered their houses with flags, not because they believe in the revolution or because they were told to do so, but simply because they think they're safer that way.

I've now distinguished four revolutionary groups. One is the uniformed PRG and high-ups, who must be organizing on high levels like ministries and cabinets and foreign affairs. Then there are the students, the visible security control in local areas, who have rifles, and they guard police stations and control traffic. Then there are guerrillas, local men and women in floppy hats who have been working for the revolution outside of and in the cities in the south. Last are the mostly middle-aged and old people who have quietly worked for the revolution for twenty-five years, right in Sài Gòn, organizing, communicating, mailing, and providing materials. I find this last group most touching, being true to their cause for so long while living in the heart of the "enemy." This is like my dear Yến, though I don't think she's quite middle-aged.

We keep being late or early, because half the city is on Sài Gòn time, half on Indochina (Hà Nội) time. Sài Gòn time is an hour later than the rest of Indochina, but many people who have just arrived don't seem to know it.

At 2 p.m. Sài Gòn time, Anh Tùng came and took us to Vạn Hạnh Buddhist University and later to the student center downtown. We interviewed a man who drove with us, named Anh Hằng. He was born in 1933 and had been in prison from 1954 or '55 until 1963, and again in 1965, and again for two months until Liberation. He's a civil engineer, and he was old when he graduated in 1968, because of all the time he had spent in prison. He's never supported the GRVN. Since he got out five days ago, he's decided his first revolutionary interest is to help clean the city. He knows where all the big machinery is, and he plans to call on the radio for all operators to come back to work and to clean up the trash in the city. "In the revolution if you have initiative, you can do what you want and get a lot done. You're not ordered to do it," he said. "It's done by committee."

I asked if all prisoners were released and he said no, just political prisoners. "But the government gave political prisoners papers like criminals, so how did the PRG know who to let out?" I asked.

"One, we all know each other in prison and know who is who, but also, despite the false common criminal papers, they still kept all the political prisoners locked separately from the criminals, because they didn't want them to influence them," he said.

We walked around downtown and saw quite a few PRG soldiers having their pictures taken in front of the General Assembly building, the old Opera House. The soldiers seem extremely polite and also meek. Journalists, who mostly stay downtown, say the soldiers are naive and are buying overpriced watches and radios and souvenirs.

We attended a rather silly meeting of some journalists at the Hotel Continental. The more experienced journalists we knew weren't there. One speaker, Canadian I think, referred to the new government as the VC, and another man referred to them as "the Communists." I found an opportunity to privately tell the man who used the term VC that he might want to refer to the government as "the government," because then he would be more successful interviewing people. And I suggested they refer to the current government in power by its name, the Provisional Revolutionary Government. He seemed receptive to my suggestions.

Back at our alley, the store at the intersection of our alley and the street had a TV set up so people walking by could watch it. We stood and watched a movie of Hà Nội, Christmas 1972—the downing of thirty-four B-52 bombers, five F-111s, the destruction, the missiles, the captured U.S. pilots at a press conference, the hospitals, the injured babies. It said the bombing went on for thirteen days and nights. After having just experienced one day and night of rockets and mortars, and not right on top of me, I can't imagine how people mentally lived through the horror of that length of time. Not to mention the actual physical destruction done by B-52 bombing raids.

I'm disappointed to see how many journalists still don't seem to know much or anything about what's going on. They think only the soldiers are in control, and don't seem aware of the organizing by local groups, by students, and what's happening in the suburbs. One well-meaning British cameraman asked several soldiers, "Hà Nội?" That's all he could say, and he had no interpreter. The response was "Yes," but of course an astute questioner would realize that it might mean a soldier is from Hà Nội, or he likes Hà Nội, or he didn't understand but wants to be polite. From such silly one-word questions, whole articles get written in the foreign press.

Julie had a funny incident today with a very old cyclo driver. He found out she was American, and he was very disturbed. He asked if that meant the Americans would come back. She assured him that wasn't so. Then he asked if there were any American men here too. She said there are only a very few, and he relaxed.

# 7

# GETTING ORGANIZED

**MONDAY, MAY 5**

This morning we three women drove our own car to Logistics, where we requested permission to go in from the officials at the gate. Every worker is back on the job, though as yet trucks aren't on the road. Now they're doing an inventory. They said they'll try to get our shipment that's still here at the dock up to Quảng Ngãi soon. We agreed that our medical center and the shipment are now the property of the Vietnamese government, but we do hope the essential prosthetic supplies can reach Quảng Ngãi soon.

On our way home we went through the Chinese neighborhood of Chợ Lớn and passed a striking sight—an almost intact tiny spotter plane on the side of the street, tangled in electric wires, covered with children playing on it.

It happened at 2 p.m. on April 30, and the pilot either parachuted out or stepped out and got into a jeep and ran away, they told me. No one was injured or killed. We talked to some little boys about it, and they sent us to another street to see the hulk of a helicopter that crashed trying to take off, overloaded. Again, they said, no injuries. An eyewitness told us they all got out before it burned. They told us of a less lucky plane crash, also in Chợ

Lớn, where twenty-some people were killed, but we didn't go to see it. This being Sài Gòn's Chinatown, Chinese flags (mainland China) were being sold on the streets alongside PRG ones. Until now I've only seen Taiwanese flags and of course GRVN flags here.

We visited our friend, Catholic father Chân Tín, an anti-war activist and Third Force leader for many years, just like Buddhist nun Huỳnh Liên. We took photos together. He was excited and happy, asked if I'd seen Yến, his niece, and noted how she is always being followed by others and what a fine leader she is. In Vietnamese saying someone is your niece or younger sister (Em) or older brother (Anh) and so on can mean that's true in family lineage, or it's just a way of referring to your relationship. I don't know if she is actually his niece, or he is just close to and older than she is. But I also didn't even know he knew her, so it was a surprise to learn he does.

He said that on April 29 he was part of a "reconciliation delegation" visiting the PRG military delegation that was stuck at the airport. I'd had no idea about that, either. The bombing started and he had to stay there, and he was still there until the airport was liberated on the 30th. When the PRG soldiers arrived, they all shared a "feast" of a chicken and coffee liquor in the bomb shelter. The above-ground buildings were destroyed, but all the delegation people were fine. The new soldiers had all heard of Father Chân Tín but had never seen his face. He said he was definitely very flattered.

Television is becoming fascinating to watch. They're showing war documentaries of the PRG and NVA shooting down B-52s, defending and repairing the Hồ Chí Minh Trail, and the lives of guerrilla soldiers living in jungle areas. Now we see how bombing looked from the ground. GRVN television used to be very boring. "Newsreels," for example, before movies, were of Thiệu reviewing a military academy or welcoming some visitors, not even mentioning the war except for jingles against the "nasty, fierce Communists."

Saigonese are already impressed with how hiền (polite, calm) the PRG soldiers are, and it's so true. They stroll arm in arm, have their pictures taken, take pictures, buy radios and toothbrushes. Twice I've seen them meekly and politely beg the drivers of otherwise empty small cars for a short lift, but sadly, in the two instances I watched, the drivers refused. Others of us have observed times when they did give them rides, and Paul saw some soldiers insist on buying their driver a cold drink as they got out of the car. It made me feel sad when they refused, because the soldiers are so extremely courteous and friendly, and I was embarrassed at how unfriendly Saigonese can be.

This afternoon I went to the military administration office in the former premier's palace. I was trying to get permission papers to take pictures at the Liberation Celebration event on Wednesday, May 7. That celebration is being combined with Điện Biên Phủ Day, which commemorates the famous 1954 battle when the Vietnamese fought back against the French, paving the way for the Geneva Accords that ended the French war in Việt Nam a few months later. Very polite officials at the administration office shook my hand and explained I should go to the Ministry of Foreign Affairs.

Then I headed to Vạn Hạnh Buddhist University's infirmary, which is treating eighty to a hundred patients a day, mostly injuries from explosives. Though propaganda teams are telling people not to burn trash, many still burn it and bullets and grenades explode and people are injured. A student health worker told me that their first concern there is health, but second, also very important, is that in the city as a whole there are former secret police and soldiers who still have weapons and may be pretending to support the revolution, but are secretly working against it and are dangerous.

The PRG soldiers are almost all completely unarmed, all over the city. We heard that two were murdered by former policemen out past the airport, two or three days after Liberation.

## TUESDAY, MAY 6

I spent the morning writing letters to Quảng Ngãi, with the hope of sending them with a friend by bus tomorrow. In the afternoon we had a short visit with a military commissar and relative of North Vietnamese prime minister Phạm Văn Đồng, whose name, he told us, we can't properly use in any article until and unless we have press credentials. Late in the afternoon Em Yên, Yến's niece, came to make sure we remember Yến's invitation for us to come celebrate the second anniversary of Yến's husband's death tomorrow, May 7.

## WEDNESDAY, MAY 7

We got up at 6:15 a.m. I put on my áo dài tunic for the first big celebration of the revolution. At 7 a.m. we picked up Mạnh Tường and newly released political prisoner and artist Bửu Chỉ at the Oxfam office, where he was being interviewed by our friend, Indian journalist Nayan Chanda.

Then we went to the Presidential Palace. What a beautiful palace! It is now decorated with an enormous picture of Hồ Chí Minh, probably fifteen by thirty feet, and huge red and blue banners and streamers, and up on a balcony we could see the whole military committee governing Sài Gòn and Gia Định. My guess is there were half a million people, lots of students, lots of flags and banners in the crowd. Later I was told the official count was a million people.

Some young people were giggling as they cheered. They're still getting used to this dramatic change from what Sài Gòn was like only a few days ago. Many people were emotional. There were framed cloth pictures of Hồ Chí Minh, held tightly by old people who had probably had them hidden in closets in their homes for decades. It was illegal to display them before. In the huge crowd there were no armed guards that I could see. Way up on the roof of the palace we could see two soldiers with binoculars.

The crowds went right to the steps of the palace, as never before. Always in the past people had to stay well away, behind barriers, barbed wire, and armed guards. It's amazing that there's so little security only a week after Liberation, while many guns must still be in the hands of people who have not turned them in. I guess this new government really believes that the people, even those who have been fighting them all these years, are with them. I mentioned this surprising freedom to a military official I met later in the morning, and he answered that the new government isn't afraid of the people; it *is* the people.

It was exciting to stand and listen to the excellent sound system playing the National Liberation Front anthem, "Liberate the South." Everyone stood still while it played, and then when it was over, moved in closer to the palace. The chairman of the governing military committee for Sài Gòn and Gia Định spoke for only a short time, and the whole ceremony lasted less than an hour.

At the end it was still cool, and we walked with the crowds up the almost car-less boulevard toward the zoo. I forgot to mention that we found a place, earlier in the morning, to buy gas, and bought eleven liters at a whopping 1,100 đồng per liter, a cheap price, believe it or not. That's about $12 U.S. per gallon, as I calculate. Could it be? Surprisingly though, a lot is being sold and being bought. We heard the price of a bicycle is 100,000 to 200,000 đồng. And a motorcycle is only 5,000 đồng, or four liters of gas, cheaper than a bicycle. Bicycles are precious and motorcycles almost valueless right now. But people have told me that soon there will be a lot of legal gas. We'll see.

# 8

# WE ARE DETAINED, AND OTHER EVENTS

**WEDNESDAY, MAY 7, CONTINUED**

Keith and I couldn't find Em Yên and everyone else after the ceremony, so we headed home, intending to go right away to Biên Hòa to see Chị Yến for her husband's death day celebration. When we got home, we found we didn't have the gate key, so we had to climb over the fence in front of our house. I went in, washed up, and then found myself, half-dressed, looking out the front window at five fully armed PRG soldiers at our gate. Keith quickly went out and, embarrassed, had to explain that we didn't have the key, and invited them to climb over the fence. They found that suspicious and wouldn't climb the low fence. Keith heard one say to another, "How did they get in? Go get the hacksaw out of the jeep." Keith said that really wasn't necessary, and to demonstrate that we truly didn't have the key, he climbed over it to be on the outside where they were.

The neighbors came out to enjoy the scene, and I, now dressed, got water and drinking glasses, thinking at first they were doing a routine house-to-house check. They wouldn't drink anything, and I didn't have time to drink anything either before a very polite official explained that they were inquiring into the activities of foreign personnel, and would we mind coming to the police station.

They left two guards at our house, outside the gate, and checked carefully to see if there was a back entrance. That required climbing over the fence, so now they did. The higher officer told the lower ones who were to stay there that they were responsible for all the possessions in the house, and so even if someone else came in and took anything, they would have to take responsibility. So for their sake, I barred the kitchen door so they'd feel more secure. We told them they were welcome to stay inside the house under the fan, drink water, sit down, but they refused, the officer explaining that the neighbors might misunderstand and not realize that we had invited them in.

So off we went in their jeep to the Gia Định military security office. Keith and I sat on the porch separately, waiting for our interviews. We were invited into a cool room, served tea (which I was now too nervous to drink), and we shook hands with two polite middle-aged men who called me Chị (older sister—a polite, friendly term), even though I was definitely younger.

They took me, alone, into a room, and asked me very carefully worded questions to find out who we are. I explained about Quaker work and principles, told them the exact day I had come to Việt Nam, told our term of service, what our work is in Quảng Ngãi, and so on. He seemed to already know about our work and wanted to learn more about me and my opinions. He asked me to write my name and all the names of my friends and references, American and Vietnamese. For Americans, I wrote Keith, Sophie, Paul, Julie, Tom, and our four Mennonite friends' names.

The officer had already mentioned Bill Cooper in our conversation. Bill, an American, had been on our AFSC team before I got here, and after his term with AFSC ended had come back with the Committee of Responsibility (COR) and was running their program for injured children in Quảng Ngãi. We had considered him a close friend until recently, when we had a major falling out.

Cảnh, a former patient missing the lower part of one leg, had been working at the rehab center as office manager. He and Bill were close friends, and together they had come to us saying that our medical assistant Anh Bích and other staff were stealing from us. We really did not believe it and did not pay much attention.

Soon after that, our physical therapy assistant Tuyệt asked for a meeting with me and Keith and asked us, "Do bars of soap have wings to fly out of the supply closet with? Do towels fly on top of them, and never come back?" That was so odd it definitely got our attention. She was telling us, very carefully, that fellow physical therapy assistant Nguyệt and her husband Cảnh, who with Bill had accused Anh Bích of stealing, were themselves stealing from the rehab center's supply closet. She was speaking cautiously, especially since Nguyệt's cousin was the province police chief, but she managed to convey to us foreigners, in an appropriately subtle and face-saving way, that we were not seeing theft that was happening right in front of us on a regular basis.

We thought back. Bill's program shared our safe that was inside our house in Quảng Ngãi, and often Keith would ask Bill or Cảnh about a money discrepancy. Sometimes the discrepancy would disappear after he asked Cảnh about it.

Cảnh and Nguyệt had recently had a lovely wedding in our covered cement patio area. It was soon after the wedding that we learned about the thefts. We had a group meeting with the entire staff, careful to be diplomatic, and in the end we fired Cảnh. We didn't fire Nguyệt, since it was Cảnh who had the keys, but we suspended her for two months. Only after we fired Cảnh and suspended Nguyệt did we learn from a number of other employees that he had been skimming money from their paychecks, claiming he could get them fired if they did not contribute to him. We were appalled not only at what he had been doing, but that we hadn't realized it. They were brave to come forward, and we were ashamed we hadn't been aware.

Bill and Cảnh had been very close friends for a long time, and Bill was quite upset when we fired Cảnh. He immediately hired him to work for COR. We took COR's money out of our safe, gave it to Bill, and changed the combination. We were still on speaking terms with Cảnh and Nguyệt and Bill, especially since they all lived across the street.

A few days after we fired him, Cảnh asked Keith for a loan of 15,000 đồng to buy a motorbike. Keith refused. The next day, Bill came to Keith and asked for a short-term loan of 15,000 đồng for his program. Keith gave it to him. A few days later Cảnh had a new motorbike. That was right before bigger things started to happen and right before we came to Sài Gòn.

Needless to say, I left Bill's name off my list of American references, though one of the men interviewing me noticed and specifically asked if I knew him.

He asked very briefly about the Mennonites, then concentrated solely on Bill, his Committee of Responsibility program, and its relationship to AFSC. Did he come to our house often? No. Did we know him well? We thought we did. Did we know Anh An? At first I couldn't hear if he meant Anh An or Anh Anh or Anh Ân, since they sound almost the same and I didn't want to misunderstand or make any mistakes. I was realizing this was a serious interview, so I concentrated hard and had them repeat a number of questions to make sure I correctly understood them. Then one of the men pulled out three photos, one of a young man I don't know, apparently the Anh An he was asking about, one of Peggy Perry (former AFSC Sài Gòn representative), and one of Bill and Cô Lệ, our cook Bà Hai's daughter. I identified the people I knew.

I was completely honest in all my answers, especially about Bill, since I was beginning to think this whole interview might be about him. The fact is he's not someone we trust, or even like at this point, though I didn't say that. The man asked me if I knew for sure that Bill didn't do anything besides care for the children. I didn't know what he was thinking of and he didn't tell me. I said I didn't know of anything else. I tried to be tactful. I said he was someone I could live with, but he was very hard to work with.

The two men were very nice and we talked about Việt Nam and the American peace movement, and about what we did in Việt Nam politically, such as that we gave dignitaries and journalists tours of our rehab center and nearby Mỹ Lai, mailed out notes from political prisoners, and wrote articles for American magazines. I stated that we feel the American people are not the enemy and that they support the Vietnamese people. When asked why I stayed, I said I had regretted leaving Quảng Ngãi and wanted to stay in Sài Gòn to be a witness to what was happening. I also said I wanted to stay because I was telling my Vietnamese friends to stay, so I felt I should do so myself. I told them I wanted to see the revolution and then return to America to tell the truth about it.

I said we were sad only that our voices are so small and Henry Kissinger's voice is so big. I mentioned that we'd really like to go back to Quảng Ngãi, and the man smiled and said not to worry, that when things are settled he is sure we can go back.

He asked what our plans for the future are, and I answered that before Liberation we were planning to leave very soon. But now with Liberation we want to stay and see what we can do to help. We'd like to spend more time in Sài Gòn, then go back to Quảng Ngāi, and if we're not needed, go home in a few months. If there is work we can do, we'll stay as long as we can be useful and are welcome. He thanked me again and I was led out, and Keith went in for his own private interview.

I was writing in my notebook outside when a man invited me inside to write at a table. A few minutes later an older man came in and said he needed to ask me one more question. His question was "What does Bill look like?" What does he look like? They knew what he looks like. They have photos of him. I misunderstood at first, so he simplified it and said, "What is he like? His nose, body, arms, hair, etc.?" Ah, I got the point. The discrepancy between the photo they had of him and him today. They've probably seen him wearing a wig.

I said he was bald but sometimes wore a wig. The man asked why, and I said, "To look better." Then we looked at each other and we both burst out laughing. He, the cadre, was balding. I said wigs were not uncommon in America. My interviewer seemed flabbergasted. We could barely stop laughing. I guess he does look suspicious to them.

We wonder if these interviews are being done with all foreigners. We don't think so. We think these interviews today have more to do with Bill than anything else. We know he had some GRVN police friends, so maybe they're suspicious about that. Then there's the connection to Cảnh and Nguyệt and her police chief cousin. At any rate, it's sort of lucky for us, because we hoped to get investigated as soon as possible, so we can get credentials to, hopefully, travel. And now they have our information.

This all-day visit lasted until after 5 p.m. We had late lunch with the highest officer we'd met, who was very fun, in his office. All was very friendly by then, and he asked us to wait just a little longer so they could meet and decide if they had to ask us more questions or not. We waited outside, and Em Yên joined us. Turns out she too had been there, since 12:30 p.m. or so. She said Paul and Sophie and Julie were at another office, and after we left they were brought to our office for their turns. A real marathon. We were all unhappy about not getting to Yến's husband's death anniversary celebration.

While we were gone, Bà Hai had arrived at our house. The two soldiers still "guarding" our house accepted her hospitality, and she served them coffee and dressed the finger of one who was recently injured by a bomb fragment. She told us she talked with them and heard what it's like to be "under the bombs." She said her "consciousness" opened. I'm not the only one learning new vocabulary.

Meanwhile, Bà Hai's daughter Sương either just recently found out or just recently told her mother that her fiancé's family is mostly PRG. And now Bà Hai claims that her own younger brother has been PRG for many years. Really? Who knows what to believe! It's very hard to know.

Probably they're just acting, playing it safe, but we frequently hear Saigonese say they were duped, were puppets of the Americans, and that they now realize that people just like them in look and language, including their own relatives from the north, were "the enemy" they were afraid of. I imagine part of that is true, the part about their surprise that the North Vietnamese are so similar to them in language, culture, and appearance. People come to see very quickly that they were fed a lot of propaganda over twenty-five years, and now they're looking at the reality and the truth. Living it, in fact.

Some PRG soldiers have warned us that as "people's consciousness" grows, they will be better at distinguishing between the American government and the American people, but that until then we should just lie and not say we're American, for our own safety. But we haven't encountered any problems with being American.

We got home at 5:30 p.m. and right away two visitors arrived, Anh Hằng, the engineer we'd met a few days ago who said he had spent ten years in prison, and a friend of his named Hoàng Lộc. Hoàng Lộc showed us several news clippings of himself. He said he was in prison for twenty years, and every day in prison, he told Bà Hai, is like a month on the outside. They invited Keith and me to a special meeting at 8 a.m. tomorrow, to be held inside the Presidential Palace. They said about 180 people will be present. After they left, two more visitors came, a Scot and a Japanese, who said they're from the YMCA. Is there really a YMCA in Sài Gòn? I found myself suspicious of the Scot. He said he came from America to Việt Nam just four days before Liberation. That could not have happened, not from the U.S. How could he have come? He dropped a lot of names, but his story just didn't make sense.

Then, even more visitors. We had a fine visit with some of Yến's relatives—Hồng Vân, Hồng Quân, Sơn, Tú, Vân—and finally to bed. We were really sad to miss Yến's husband's death day anniversary celebration. She had prepared a fabulous feast for us. I really wanted to be there. But it certainly wasn't intentional on our part. Luckily her niece Em Yến got home and told her what had happened at the military security office that day and why none of us had made it out there. I was very disappointed, especially knowing how busy she is and how she must have put a lot of time and preparation into making it a wonderful celebration.

## THURSDAY, MAY 8

I've had a cold and my energy is a bit low, so I've been less aware of the rest of the world these last few days. This morning I dressed in my new yellow áo dài, and Keith and I went to a side entrance of the Presidential Palace to meet the delegation Hoàng Lộc invited us to join, which we were to accompany right into the palace. It was to be a meeting of North Vietnamese soldiers with representatives of various local groups, including students, teachers, workers, and business owners.

We paraded with banners into the palace but then found confusion about the time, which would make us either wait an hour or do the ceremony outside. A military official apologized and requested that we go ahead with it outside, because his soldiers are suffering from the change in climate and need to be inside. As we paraded around the palace, a large number of foreign press people were attending a press conference nearby. Some really stood out in their faded blue jeans and straggly hair. After the press conference was over, a few came to see what our event was about, but they didn't have an interpreter so they only talked with us English speakers. One correspondent thought our event was just students meeting soldiers, so we explained who the participants were.

The actual main point seemed to be just for people to meet people, including people who favored, or supposedly favored, the revolution, meeting and visiting with actual revolutionaries. For example, there was a bank president who gave me his business card and said he has spent several years in prison. Another man, a teacher, said he was severely beaten by the former government and is permanently handicapped in one leg. A political prisoner was there who had opposed the old government. It was all a bit confusing, as it often is these days.

The ceremony included speeches welcoming the liberation of Việt Nam, a local group singing songs, and the soldiers singing back their own much more lively songs. The civilians put garlands around the necks of the soldiers and gave them gifts. Keith and I were asked to present gifts, which we did with embarrassment. When it was over we went to Hoàng Lộc's house for a few minutes. Then he drove us both home on a one-seat Lambretta.

## FRIDAY, MAY 9

This morning Keith and I took a cyclo to the downtown bank area, where we met Em Yên and her cousin Hoa, who is Yến's brother-in-law's daughter. We walked together to the house of her father, Lạc, where we visited through lunch. He brought up a problem he's having. A company contracted to the U.S. Navy owes him over $1,000 U.S. He worked as an airport groundsman, and as things got hectic he didn't receive his last paycheck, separation pay, or bonus pay. He asked if we could help, but I don't think there's any way to. But if we get to Bangkok, the company headquarters, we'll try to see if there's anything we can do.

Some "cowboys," alias hoodlums who were often ex-Rangers or ex-ARVN Self-Defense Forces,* ripped off Paul's camera. He was visiting Madame Ngô Bá Thành, a major leader of the Third Force in Sài Gòn.†

---

\* ARVN Rangers were the light infantry of the Army of the Republic of Việt Nam (South).

† "Madame" is an honorific showing respect when speaking of important women leaders. It replaces the Vietnamese quý bà (precious woman), a phrase no longer in common usage. The French word Madame no doubt came from the days of French Indochina and is also used in English.

Paul was coming out of her house on a fairly empty street, about to take a picture. They hit him in the kidneys, took the camera, and ran. Luckily they didn't also take his bag, which had another camera in it. The cowboys are having a wild time stealing cameras from journalists all over town. It's increasing.

Tonight we had a dinner party. Hoàng Lộc and a man named Anh Tấn invited themselves, and were joined by Tú and Dung and Em Hương and her friend Lý. I barely know them, except for my dear tutor Dung. Hoàng Lộc says he's a Communist Party member, and probably so is Anh Hằng. Both Hoàng Lộc and Anh Hằng seem a bit immature for their ages. They're not young.

At dinner someone, I don't remember who, mentioned that in the north and PRG areas of the south the salaries of women are slightly higher than men's because they need to have sanitary napkins. True or false, I don't know.

Many discussions these days center on how to control the cowboy hoodlums. Even an armed bộ đội cadre had his camera stolen, and two cadres saw the thieves hit Paul and take his camera, but they couldn't catch them. Often it's crowded, and they can't shoot into a crowd, and many soldiers aren't armed anyway. We were told that two were severely knifed while guarding a rice warehouse a few days ago.

Former secret police are a real problem. They're often posing as cadres. A secret cop who used to follow Yến around in the old days now has a job driving a jeep she travels in, to her annoyance. And Paul saw a former secret cop, who once hit him in the stomach at a demonstration where he was taking pictures, enter the Senate building with a red armband on his sleeve.

Hoàng Lộc told us that special secret police will be coming in from the north to help in the south. The bộ đội soldiers seem quite innocent and naive when they encounter crimes and corruption here. For example, they're not used to locking their bicycles. So their bikes are being stolen, and the PRG is warning soldiers to not leave them unattended, and to get bike locks.

---

Madame Ngô Bá Thành was an internationally recognized scholar, lawyer, professor, and leader of the Third Force movement in South Việt Nam. As an activist and prominent Third Force leader, she spent time in prison for her views.

We learned that the military government will continue to govern Sài Gòn and Gia Định for three months, not just one month. We also learned that since the revolution there hasn't actually ever been an official curfew, and there isn't one now. That is a surprise.

## SATURDAY, MAY 10

Lazy day today. Before Liberation, lots of friends depended on us as a source of information. Now there are so many direct sources, they don't need us in the same way as before. This is very good, since our former role was an abnormal one—foreigners helping Vietnamese learn about events in and relating to Việt Nam. We had access to national and international news they just couldn't get.

I never before saw people so glued to their TV sets. In every house that has a set you can see families watching. The TV programs seem better made and produced, and the subjects are fascinating to Saigonese. This evening I went next door to watch a puppet show, the news, and then a movie, *Đường Về Làng Mẹ* (*The Road to Mother's Village*). It was a sad love story.

This morning we again attempted to get papers at the Ministry of Foreign Affairs. But before we left, Paul and Sophie's friend who had been part of the airport delegation dropped by and suggested we wait a few days and let all the crazy (my own adjective) foreign press people get theirs first. The lack of awareness of many foreign journalists is notable. One BBC reporter said, "The government just isn't organized yet," based on the fact that the government hadn't let foreign press coverage be wired out of the country yet. The government may be restricting the foreign press, but they're definitely getting organized.

We also heard that the very first report out of Sài Gòn since Liberation was by a Reuters reporter who stayed in his hotel room for two days before and four days after the change of government. Half of his report was about the British Council swimming pool, how the press could still go there, and the food and wine they consumed. Apparently even other press people found this outrageous and aren't speaking to him.

One journalist told me there isn't anything to report on. I asked him if he'd been out to the suburbs to see the organizing going on there. I was asking in all seriousness, thinking he might say that grassroots organizing isn't really "news," so he wasn't covering it. Instead, he was defensive. He seemed almost intimidated. Many of the journalists think we AFSCers know a lot since we speak the language, live outside the downtown area, and we've had people in the country for a long time. I guess we do.

We sent off a report—a cable—sort of a news report. We had to cut out all greetings to family as well as information about our own program, or they wouldn't send it. Presumably our families know we're fine by now though, through an earlier French report that was sent out.

There's a fourth-hand report that Bill Cooper hasn't yet (two days and two nights) come back from his own interview with the local officials. We're not really worried, but definitely curious. Maybe he deserves the questioning and suspicion he's getting. I honestly don't know what he's about, what he's been doing to create this interest from the government.

I really marvel at the dedication and stamina of the Liberation forces. If I were one of those soldiers I think I'd resent the spoiled Sài Gòn hippies, the overdressed young women, the cowboys. I think I'd show off, brag about what I'd done. But when these soldiers brag, they speak of all of them as one, as a group: their achievements against U.S. bombs, against incredible firepower and military might, and against U.S. poisons, including Agent Orange, napalm, white phosphorus, and CBU-55 bombs. *(See "Agent Orange and Birth Defects" on page 246.)*

Julie and Sophie said they wished they'd had a flash camera to take an indoor picture of all the soldiers in the post office today sending letters home. There's a special letter box for letters to the north, and lots of divided families, not just NVA soldiers, are now sending off letters, something they of course haven't been able to do in decades.

# 9

# CHANGES, CHANGES

**SUNDAY, MAY 11**

Today's newspaper, *Nhân Dân* ("The People"), from the north, has an article describing what Saigonese thought the PRG soldiers would do, all the rumors started by the U.S. Embassy and the old government. It said people thought they would use pliers to pull out fingernails painted red and would throw anyone who dared to speak English into a dungeon.

Last night on the radio we heard that the Sài Gòn military government said people are required to hang PRG and North Vietnamese flags and pictures of Hồ Chí Minh for the three-day national celebration beginning on May 15. We didn't believe it really said "required" until we read it ourselves in this morning's Sài Gòn newspaper, on the front page.

This morning we strolled around the park by the palace. It's closed off temporarily while soldiers build scaffolding for the victory celebration. We watched dozens of sharks trying to sell watches and radios to innocent-looking young soldiers. I walked up to four women soldiers in uniform, with long braids and ponytails. A man was trying to sell one of them a cheap, secondhand woman's-style watch. I asked the price and he said 15,000 đồng, over $20 U.S. I told him the cadres were friends and he shouldn't cheat them like that. The embarrassed women took off, and the seller looked embarrassed and, maybe, ashamed. The women cadres generally seem to melt away.

A while later we heard a voice from a sound truck slowly and calmly saying through a loudspeaker, "Anh Em Bộ Đội, đừng mua đồng hồ giả." ("Older and younger Friend Soldiers, don't buy fake watches.") The speaker was being kind and didn't say the watch-sellers are behaving badly and cheating, but rather told the soldiers to only buy in stores and to get receipts. He told them to not believe the stories the sellers tell, such as "I'm poor. I need to sell my watch to have money to go home to my village. I'm the only one who has owned it. It's a very good watch." The PRG soldiers don't seem to know about bartering, since it seems there are set prices in the north and in PRG areas, and also they want to be kind and they're definitely naive, so they believe the tales they hear from sharks. It really is sad to see the soldiers mistreated by Sài Gòn crooks.

As for that newspaper statement requiring posting flags and pictures of Hồ Chí Minh, my explanation for it is that they want the city to look good for future foreign press coverage, or maybe they figure that the foreign press will say it was required even if it wasn't, so why not require it. Paul had a better idea, that the new government feels the PRG deserves a show of support and affection. Saigonese people may or may not like the PRG, but essentially everyone loves Hồ Chí Minh, the "father of the country," and many people have hidden embroidered or printed pictures of him in their homes for many years that they're happy to now be able to bring out and display. There are flags everywhere. I don't think anyone needed to actually be told to fly flags. It just happened.

At 5:30 this evening we went to Anh Tần's house for dinner. His wife Tuyến and many guests were there, including Hoàng Lộc and a doctor named Nam. They said they are the "free chairmen," whatever that is, of an organization of people from all levels in society. Several people were professors, and there was a discussion about communism and revolution in the world. The conversation was entertaining, and they assured us jokingly that a revolution in the U.S. will come, maybe even in our lifetimes.

We saw three movies, one of people carrying supplies for the revolution, one of captured ARVN soldiers in Laos confessing, and one of the May 1,

1973, Hà Nội review of forces by North Vietnamese prime minister Phạm Văn Đồng.* I enjoyed the first film, *Con Đường Ra Trước (The Road Ahead)* the most. It had women, girls, boys, only a few men, all carrying, pushing, pulling, dragging munitions and supplies along, somewhere in the Delta. These films were all made before Liberation of course, and don't tell exact locations of things like bridges or villages.

Munitions were carried by shoulder, bike, water buffalo, pushcart, truck. At one point a cart topples over in a river, and they quickly surround it and right it. In many places there was nothing to hide behind, so they just ran across paddies and open fields. Helicopters sighted them and brought in bombers, and the photography was extraordinary, to see the bombs falling from the planes directly overhead. The movie was definitely not staged. We heard that among PRG photographers there was something like a 50 percent death rate. I believe it.

## MONDAY, MAY 12

This morning we all went to the Ministry of Foreign Affairs, after trying to attend what turned out to be a nonexistent cultural event at a local center. We waited a while outside to get in before we realized that. Then Keith and Sophie went to the post office to look for any mail that might have somehow arrived. But before they entered the post office, Sophie's over-the-shoulder purse that looks a bit like a camera bag was the target of two hoodlums on a Honda motorcycle. They came up close behind her, a strategy to make the victim move to the right, thinking someone is trying to pass. They grabbed her bag, but she hung on to it and went flying with it. The thieves fell over too, along with their motorcycle. Keith grabbed the purse from the ground (luckily it didn't have a camera in it) and slammed one of the guys on the head with it. Keith yelled, "Thieves!" over and over, but none of the people nearby helped, probably thinking that the hoodlums might be armed. Unfortunately, there were no cadres around. Sophie

---

* Phạm Văn Đồng was prime minister of the Democratic Republic of Việt Nam from 1955 to 1976 and then prime minister of unified Việt Nam from 1976 until he retired in 1987.

was hurt but not badly. The thieves got away. At about the same time, an Australian newsman had his briefcase stolen. He chased after the two guys, who were also on a Honda motorcycle, and a nearby soldier shot in the air, but they also got away. Our friend, photographer Jean-Claude Labbé, lost all his equipment too.

I got to the post office shortly after it happened and took Sophie home and helped clean her injuries. After getting her bandaged, I took a big city bus back to the Ministry of Foreign Affairs. The trip again achieved little. We learned we can each register as one of two things, social work agency workers or journalists. Sophie and Paul want to be registered as journalists, in order to be able to cable and telex, and they already have former press status. Paul will be bureau chief for WBCN-Boston, and Sophie will be a stringer for *Friends Journal*. Keith and Julie and I will be social workers, in order to be able to negotiate and travel.

Then, partly just to see if it was truly no-cost, I went to a dentist. It was professional and indeed free. Then back home we had a visit from the daughter of a former employee and her husband to ask if we could take their two young children out of the country and they would follow, secretly. That was a surprise. We couldn't of course, and wouldn't, and felt sorry that an architect and an engineer want to leave. But admittedly, rich and more educated people who made a good living before will begin to suffer more than they ever have. Probably they've already had several lectures at their places of work during their obligatory re-education sessions. And they don't like it.

Our close Mennonite friends Earl and Hiro came for dinner. Among ourselves, we felt free to discuss some of the poorer points of the new government as we see it, such as when some lower-level PRG photographers tried to "tough guy" CBS out of some of its earliest pictures of the liberation of Sài Gòn. A higher PRG representative intervened and told them to leave CBS alone. Some other North Vietnamese photographers asked our friend, Italian photographer and journalist Tiziano Terzani, for copies of his early pictures, in a manner he felt he couldn't refuse (presumably like our invitation to go to the police station), so he gave them prints and kept the negatives.

The PRG guys had told CBS that the pictures belong to the people of

Việt Nam. But for CBS, they don't. The CBS person told them that if the government would let the film be taken out of the country and to the U.S. first, he would send back copies later. That was not what they wanted. On many subjects, the PRG and foreigners are really on different wavelengths. I think they kept their film.

Paul told us about something that he had heard happened a day or two after Liberation. A student flagged down a bus in Gia Định, but for some reason it didn't stop. He shot his gun into the bus, killing an old woman. Some bộ đội soldiers saw it, caught him, and found out he was only pretending to be a student. He was actually a former member of the Thiệu Self-Defense Force militia, who were easily identified in the old government because they wore black, and they were known to terrorize people. The soldiers asked the people on the bus what they wanted done with him. They said to shoot him, and they did. That's the story, though we don't know if it's true.

## TUESDAY, MAY 13

Today Julie and Keith and I spent all morning, from 7 a.m. until noon, getting our first, temporary, official identification papers, an upgrade from the papers we got right after Liberation. A crowd of elbowing foreigners and half-foreigners, pushing and shoving, ignored the pleas of the unarmed soldiers to line up, to keep an aisle open. Unfortunately, with all the confusion, they didn't stick to their plan about who could and couldn't be processed today. They had announced that people born in Việt Nam could not be processed today, but those who shoved through apparently did get processed anyway. Lining up is not a strong tradition in Việt Nam.

Once we ourselves got inside, the officials gave us their full attention. They were remarkably pleasant and nice, especially considering the general rudeness of the applicants they'd been putting up with. One officer said he didn't know much about Quakers, but he remembered something about a boat trying to deliver medical supplies in 1966 or so. *(See "I Sailed on the Phoenix" on page 237.)* He was right, and it had indeed been delivering medical supplies. He said he studied English on his own so he could talk to his American friends and tell them apart from "American capitalists."

He asked about our work, our team members, and how we felt about the changes. He also asked how we felt about security in the city, noting that securing the city is the main job of the temporary military government, the PRG, and when it's done, the PRG would be replaced by a new non-military government.

Julie answered well, saying that though foreign journalists, being among the only good targets left, are having a lot of trouble with cowboys robbing them, people in Sài Gòn in general are relieved by the lower rates of crime and robbery. The officer seemed pleased that we knew this. We got our papers, thanked him, and left.

Later, Paul was sitting in a park reading a newspaper when a woman speaking pidgin English came up to him and asked him to read a piece of paper that she handed him. The paper said, in English, that she wanted freedom and couldn't live here and would he please marry her and take her away. It said that although she can't speak English, she'll try to be a good wife. Paul said he ripped the letter into four pieces and gave the pieces back to her.

We five (me, Keith, Julie, Sophie, Paul) just had a short team meeting about general subjects, such as how long to stay, what our roles are, how to keep busy, and how to be useful. If we begin to feel like a burden or embarrassment to the government or the people, we'd like to leave. But if possible, we still want to go to Quảng Ngãi first. As for negotiating for all of AFSC, that may be way off in the future. We hope it won't be a very long time before we can have contact with our main AFSC office in Philadelphia to coordinate efforts to establish a formal relationship between the new government and AFSC.

My language tutor Dung and a doctor friend of hers came to visit in the evening, and she told a funny story. She was the featured speaker at a forum attended by some two hundred young people. She was telling them the basic principles of the revolution, and noted that while she spoke they sat in total silence, perfectly still, seeming to not even dare to breathe. After her talk, she asked for questions. At first no one responded. She waited. Finally, one wary hand went up. "Can we really ask questions?" was the first question. She said, "Yes, of course." The next question was "You spoke a little fast and we couldn't memorize everything yet."

The doctor told about medicine in the north, which he's interested in although he's never been there. His accent is definitely southern. He said that as much as 60 percent of medicine in the north is herbal, such as IVs of coconut juice. (I find that hard to believe.) He said northern medicine works well and is locally available, not dependent on a foreign Western country. Back in Quảng Ngãi I did drink that northern medicine broth with beetles in it.

I have had another northern medicine experience in Việt Nam too. When I was five and a half months pregnant, my friends took me to visit a northern doctor in Quảng Ngãi, just for the experience. I was seated in front of a Dutch door, and a few minutes later the top part was opened by the northern doctor on the other side. She said hello to me and took both my wrists in her hands. Only the upper part of my body was visible to her. She silently felt my pulses on both wrists with her fingers for no more than a minute. Then she told me I was five and a half months pregnant, and it would be a boy. Right, and right.

After visiting some more, Dung and the doctor left, and the deaf woman from the house next door showed up with the daughter of the other woman in the house, who we always thought was the owner, but she isn't. They're having trouble because the actual woman owner has left the country, and the actual man owner, her husband, who didn't leave, wants to reclaim the house. The women who live there now say the man owner can't reclaim it because an original payment they, the residents, made in 1965 of 75,000 đồng was a down payment on buying the house. But the man owner says it was a deposit, not a down payment.

They said the owner knows that in the old government he would have had to pay the family at least a million đồng to get them to move out, but he has gone to the local revolutionary officials to get permission to pay them back only the 75,000 đồng down payment/deposit. At the present value of money, this is less than 10 percent of what the resident women originally paid. The women are having this argument with the man owner, and are also scared that the government itself will confiscate the house, since they can't formally prove their claim to it, and of course one of the two owners has gone to America. The government is confiscating houses of families who went to America, but what about when it's only the wife or husband and not the other? It seems to be a local decision whether or not to confiscate a house, because in some cases a relative is able to claim it, and in other cases not. The government is using the houses it confiscates as administrative centers or as housing for soldiers.

I forgot to mention yesterday the fifty or so open trucks full of soldiers, uniformly seated, rifles up, very disciplined and also friendly, coming into town at 10:30 a.m. There was also a truck hauling away a hulk of an abandoned vehicle. Over the past week, the damaged or abandoned tanks have been removed from the streets, and now traffic is relatively light.

We heard today that journalists may begin submitting applications for exit visas and may be able to leave in a few days, though we expect the government would like them to stay through the festival, May 15, 16, 17, and Uncle Hồ's birthday celebration on May 19. Apparently a plane full of Western journalists was flown in from Hà Nội, so perhaps others will be flown out on the same plane.

This celebration will be a holiday for a lot of NVA soldiers and a chance for those with family nearby to go visit them. Soldiers have been building a festival structure in front of the palace. Yến's family will stay home and hope for visits from relatives not seen for twenty-some years. She has real devotion and strength to tackle the hard struggle ahead, of raising the kids, running a local district, helping with re-education, of everything, without her husband. She's one of many, of course, who have lost loved ones, but it really stings now that there is peace.

## WEDNESDAY, MAY 14

The social changes are both subtle and dramatic. Everyone we meet looks forward to having one big country again, being able to travel to the north, to have friends and family from the north and PRG areas come visit them, and everyone looks forward to being able to travel by train. The old French train bed has been bombed and destroyed, and at places it's hard to even locate where the tracks were. But they're finding, fixing, and rebuilding it.

Keith and I had breakfast at a neighborhood noodle stand. A woman sitting nearby, obviously poor, said she has eight children and playfully offered me the youngest, which made him howl in fear. She asked me and a better-dressed Vietnamese woman eating nearby if we knew a way for her to have fewer children. We both said yes, and to wait until the new government is better organized, and for sure they'll give help free of charge. Yến has already said this will happen, that birth control will be available. Then a beggar woman approached us and said she needs food. We pointed out the revolutionary administrative office a few doors down and suggested she go talk to them.

The beggar woman said she is a northerner who left in 1954, but still considers herself a northerner. Her whole family remained in the north. Now that she can, she wants to go back. She says the climate is much nicer than here, much cooler. The mother of eight children is a northerner too, and says she will wait for a railroad, maybe in six months she hopes, because she can't pay bus fare. I hope the government will offer some free or almost free transport for the poorest people. It was a nice way to start the day, talking to two northerners who have lived here since 1954, when they fled to the south, and who sound, nonetheless, optimistic about the reunification.

A man we talked to last night said the PRG expected to lose as many as seven divisions in a battle for Sài Gòn, but in fact lost almost no soldiers at all.

Today we heard distressing and ominous news from Cambodia. People are arriving in Việt Nam as refugees from Cambodia. We heard that President Ford is meeting with the U.S. Security Council about a U.S. vessel "captured" by the Cambodians. That's all we know.

Bill Cooper, we learned, was picked up before we were ever questioned, when we spent the day being interviewed and missed Yến's memorial party for her husband. And Bill still isn't back. The officials came to his house and took his electric typewriter, perhaps to see if it's really a radio transmitter or something.

Today Anh Duy, who worked at our rehab center in Quảng Ngãi, came to the house. Keith and I weren't home so we missed him, but he brought lots of news to the others and they shared with us. He told them there's a doctor assigned to our rehab center now, which is very good news, and also a political officer. He said there are no more heads of departments, there are meetings regularly, and Anh Bích, our main medical practitioner, continues to work with the patients in the hostel.

He said that about a third of the staff have gone home to farm. Those who stayed did so out of dedication alone, because they have been receiving no salary or benefits. They get just two meals a day, or two cans of rice, and 50 đồng.

Julie said Duy is in great spirits, though he looks much thinner and seems a little odd. Duy told her that in Quảng Ngãi he walks to his village, brings back some vegetables, and sells them in trade for . . . one cigarette. He told her he wishes he had money to drink coffee and talk to the NVA soldiers in cafes downtown here in Sài Gòn.

He thinks that if we're allowed to go back to Quảng Ngãi it will probably be for a visit only, not to stay and work. He said our rehab center now treats soldiers as well as civilians. Civilians get first priority, northern and NLF soldiers next, and then ARVN soldiers. We're sorry we didn't get to see him ourselves. The others weren't sure if he'll be back.

Today I spent most of the day writing a letter that was outdated as soon as it was written. I noted how unarmed the city is, then went downtown and saw dozens of new tanks, anti-aircraft guns, cannons, and armed soldiers there. The news from Thailand and Cambodia is very threatening, saying that the U.S. is moving in marines to threaten Cambodia into releasing the supposedly captured U.S. ship, a merchant marine vessel, I think, called the *Mayaguez*.\* It makes sense for the PRG to take no chances, so their defenses are going up, anti-aircraft guns being strategically placed. This is probably the reason for the jets we heard this morning too.

Today's other news is the bigwigs are in town! All journalists are invited to a feast tomorrow night given by government leaders Nguyễn Hữu Thọ and Huỳnh Tấn Phát. Madame Nguyễn Thị Bình, a very important member

---

\* The "*Mayaguez* incident" happened between May 12 and May 15, 1975, shortly after the Khmer Rouge took control of the capital Phnom Penh. The Khmer Rouge seized the U.S. merchant vessel SS *Mayaguez* in a disputed maritime area. The U.S. recaptured the ship and attacked the Cambodian island of Koh Tang. The *Mayaguez*'s crew members were released.

of the Central Committee, is here too, as well as presumably most all other important dignitaries.* They're staying at various hotels downtown. Since Paul and Sophie are registered as journalists, they're invited to the feast, but we three "social workers" are not.

Internal politics took on a new aspect for us recently, as Hoàng Lộc's "student group" looks to us more and more like an unofficial and perhaps unwelcome organization. Today Anh Hằng, whom we met through Hoàng Lộc, asked Keith what he thought of Hoàng Lộc. Why? He didn't say. We really don't know enough about him, about either of them, and we didn't know them before Liberation.

This evening I stopped in at the office of the local official governing committee, just to get acquainted. I talked with the chairman, a man of about fifty-five, a northerner. Lots of people were there busily preparing for tomorrow's festivities, which for them will start at 2 a.m. as they parade to the palace. Why do festivities start in the middle of the night? Well, for one thing it's cooler. For another, maybe it's a celebration of the new safe feeling even in the middle of the night. Maybe it's to prove there's no curfew. Whatever it is, we don't plan to be there at 2 a.m.

We chatted for a few minutes about recent political developments, like the situation in Cambodia. A woman in the office said she knows the

---

* Nguyễn Hữu Thọ was president of the PRG and chair of the Advisory Council of the PRG. In April 1975 he briefly became prime minister of the Republic of South Việt Nam, and after reunification he was a national vice president. Later he was the acting president while also the mayor of Sài Gòn, renamed Hồ Chí Minh City. In later years he was vice president of the Council of State and chair of the Standing Committee of the National Assembly.

Huỳnh Tấn Phát was chair of the Provisional Revolutionary Government (PRG) before reunification and was prime minister of South Việt Nam from April 30, 1975, to July 2, 1975. Later he was deputy prime minister and vice president–minister of construction of Việt Nam.

Madame Nguyễn Thị Bình was minister of foreign affairs of the Provisional Revolutionary Government of the Republic of South Việt Nam and signer of the Paris Peace Agreement as representative of the PRG. After reunification in 1975, she became minister of education and later a vice president of Việt Nam. See Nayan Chanda, *Brother Enemy: The War after the War* (New York: Harcourt Brace Jovanovich, 1986).

American people have been against the war. She hopes I'll stay three more months to see the new society and economy really get underway, and that I'll then go home and tell the Americans what I've seen.

I told her that many of us definitely are and have been against the war, some men for the more personal reason of wanting to avoid being drafted, of course. She said imperialism is abuse of foreign countries without moral restraint, for power or money or both. I couldn't disagree. And now Thailand has threatened the U.S. with a suspension of relations if they don't remove the recently arrived U.S. Marines from Thailand. And the situation between the U.S. and Cambodia seems to be more and more tense.

# 10

# CELEBRATIONS

**THURSDAY, MAY 15**

Today is the first day of the three-day victory celebration all over Việt Nam. Then there is a Sunday, and then Hồ Chí Minh's birthday on May 19, so it's really a five-day celebration. This morning we thought the celebration was on Indochina time, so we arrived an hour late. We woke to a cannon salute and outside our flophouse door found part of the long line of vehicles in the parade review. We went to the main house to check with the others and heard the startling news that the U.S. has bombed some ships in a Cambodian port.

We learned later that this apparently happened despite the American crew from the "captured" *Mayaguez* ship having already returned to American territory. The incident is disturbing because that U.S. ship was way off course, so it looks suspiciously as if it was for espionage, or sent in to give the U.S. an excuse to attack or bomb. Ordinarily one would expect such an incident could be quickly and easily handled by the governments of the countries, but in this situation America really looks to people here like a power-hungry Napoleon or Hitler.

So that was on our minds, as well as news from Laos that due to disturbances and anti-Americanism, many foreigners are leaving Laos.

We took a cyclo downtown, and when we arrived we managed to get fairly close to the impressive reviewing stand erected in only three days in front of the Presidential Palace. It's a beautiful, well-made wooden structure with curtains and banners and doors, a huge painting of Hồ Chí Minh, fabric flags of different colors, and flags of both the north and the south (PRG). Most people had been there since 2 a.m. in the rain and the mud, under the strings of "Christmas lights" all over the square.

Lo and behold, ahead of us on the low bandstand we recognized many famous people. There was Madame Nguyễn Thị Bình, Madame Nguyễn Thị Định, Lê Đức Thọ,* Nguyễn Hữu Thọ, head of the National Liberation Front, Hùynh Tấn Phát, prime minister of the Provisional Revolutionary Government, and others.

It was remarkable and truly shocking to see them standing there, no more than ten feet from the crowd of citizens filling the huge square. The crowd of course included supporters of the old government as well as the new one, and yet these heads of government stood in front of all these people, outdoors, unarmed and unprotected. No guards stood with or in front of them watching the crowd, no bulletproof shields, nothing. The only precaution we saw were some temporary bomb shelters they had constructed

---

* Madame Nguyễn Thị Định helped found the National Liberation Front, was its first woman general, and was its deputy commander. She was a member of the Central Committee of the Vietnamese Communist Party. Later she was the first woman vice president of Việt Nam. She served on the Central Committee of the Việt Nam Communist Party and led the Women's Union of the Socialist Republic of Việt Nam.

Lê Đức Thọ was leader of the Vietnamese independence movement against the French. In 1948 he was sent to the south, where he became a leading cadre. After returning to Hà Nội in 1954, he became a powerful party leader behind the scenes as head of the Party Organizational Committee. He signed the Paris Peace Agreement on behalf of the DRV. He was awarded the Nobel Peace Prize with Henry Kissinger, but refused to accept it. Later he was standing secretary of the Secretariat and head of the Central Organizing Commission.

behind the stage against, we're told, possible American bombing, a real concern after the news from Cambodia and Thailand.

No one in Thiệu's government would ever have dreamed of being so exposed to the general public. This is a spirit of trust and fellowship, although we were saddened to learn later in the afternoon of the murder of two more NVA soldiers (about ten soldiers and cadres so far that we know of) in an outlying district. And they haven't been able to capture a single one of their murderers yet.

The event had very short speeches, then a military review. Passing the reviewing stand came women soldiers, men soldiers, soldiers with cannons, soldiers with anti-aircraft guns, soldiers with tanks, all traveling on trucks, tanks, surface-to-air missiles, then floats, student groups, civic groups, labor groups, Girl Scouts, Boy Scouts, and kids following along. The famous people on the bandstand lasted through several hours, smiling and waving and hugging old friends who came up on the platform to greet them.

Nguyễn Hữu Thọ made it a point to keep his hat off so people could see him, but through this kindness he suffered from the very hot sun. Unfortunately, the sun was eventually too much for them all, and the last groups in the parade didn't even get to see them. We enjoyed it and stayed until the end. Then we strolled around and had over an hour's conversation with soldiers and people outside the palace. Some Vietnamese women in Western clothes looked surprised that I was wearing an áo dài tunic. I didn't see it, but Keith said he "looked surprised" back at them in their Western clothes and they looked away.

A group of women Liberation soldiers in uniforms with helmets were sitting in a circle. They saw me walking by and grinned at me. I was thrilled, because most of the guerrilla PRG and NVA women are very shy. So I went over to them and we visited together. They're all from the north, have been in the Sài Gòn area for a few months, and expect in a few months more to be able to go home. They find Sài Gòn interesting, but are eager to go back north as soon as they can.

Then they had to go, and I stayed and talked with a very nice man soldier from near Huế. I asked why I didn't see more women soldiers, and he said not many came to Sài Gòn. I asked what most of the women soldiers do (not having thought to ask the women), and he said "lighter work" like nursing or radio communications. I told him I'd seen movies where women shot down airplanes. He grinned and agreed, and said there are just not many in Sài Gòn at this time. He wasn't exactly changing his statement though, just being agreeable. Of course, maybe only a few women shot down planes, but were featured in the documentaries.

I asked him if people are ever drafted or forced to be soldiers in the north or with the PRG. He said never, that they're all volunteers who join for varying lengths of time. We agreed that one reason the "puppet" soldiers of the south lost is they were drafted and forced to fight, as were many of the Americans, and if they don't strongly believe in the struggle, they won't have enough will to fight to win.

He mentioned that although Hà Nội was greatly destroyed in the 1972 bombings, there weren't as many deaths as there might have been because thousands of people, especially children, were moved out of the city, and because they had such good bomb shelters and tunnels. We talked about the U.S., whether it would dare come back and bomb Việt Nam again. He said no, impossible.

A local woman we met, whose husband is French, and whose brother just returned after thirty-five years in the north, walked with us to eat a delicious rice bowl lunch at a nearby stand. We went with her freely as if we were in a totally different country, without our usual concern of how it might look for her to be seen with Americans. She didn't seem to be thinking about how it might look to be with us, either. And of course more and more people think we're Russian, anyway.

She and others we chatted with at lunch were urging us to stay long enough to see how the revolution develops, not that we can leave yet anyway. One person asked if the Vietnamese government supports us, and I said no, and it shouldn't, of course, support us, because there are plenty of poor Vietnamese who need support more than we do. I said we don't have useful work anymore. They suggested we teach English, but I said that isn't very useful right now. So they said we should teach children, and I said Vietnamese can do it better. So they said stay and study a new skill and then use it!

Then Keith and I walked to a park to see the big guns the newspaper said would be shot off for the celebration. But we didn't find any. The front page of the same newspaper told everyone not to be scared when they heard airplanes, because part of the celebration would be MIGs and other fighter jets flying in formation low over the city. Maybe they announced this on the front page of the newspaper to be sure to avoid an incident like in Nha Trang, where the anti-aircraft guns apparently shot at their own planes, thinking they were ARVN. I didn't know the North Vietnamese even had MIGs and fighter jets, actually.

Keith and I, along with Yến's nieces Hồng Vân and Hồng Quân, went downtown from 7:30 p.m. until 10 p.m. to see the fireworks. The palace was all lit up and the park too, and there were lots of people. The fireworks went on for a half hour, high in the sky by the river, though they made me, and lots of other people as well, jump every time they went off, because it sounded just like the war.

Paul was one of only ten journalists, foreign and Vietnamese, who were invited to a reception at the palace with the dignitaries who had been on the reviewing stand. There were about a hundred people in total. He said Madame Nguyễn Thị Bình, the foreign minister, seemed to have the flu, but she still was very gracious and told Paul she remembered the Quakers. She asked Paul if he was the Quaker from the Paris International Quaker Center. Yes, he was. Astounding, impressive. I guess having a good memory for people and faces and events is part of what helps an individual go far in life and politics.

At 11 p.m. I came to the flophouse building and met Francesco, the Italian suitor of the landlord's daughter. This whole family seems to be in a dream world. They don't go outside, don't read the paper, don't talk to anyone. I asked Francesco if he had gotten his government papers yet, and he said, "The VC don't have a government yet, so I can't get papers yet." First I suggested he stop using the term "VC," especially when talking to officials. Then I introduced him to the existence of the PRG, how to get papers, and I told him about the parade this morning, which he of course hadn't gone to. He said he has talked to a few foreign press people, and they have told him the people are happy because there is peace and they can go anywhere. But he wants to know what the government will really be like. He said his understanding is that the PRG is a coalition government of all shades of political persuasion, while the north is straight Communist, the two parts never to be reconciled. I said the north is indeed Communist, or socialist, actually, and that Thiệu had lost his chance to negotiate, and that now Việt Nam will be one country. All the parts of the country differ from one another, but the north and south not more than, for example, Huế and Quảng Ngãi, both cities in the south. The conversation seemed to be a revelation to him. His girlfriend and her family must be remarkably uninformed. I suggested that he and his girlfriend go to the movies, for a start.

# 11

# INTERESTING CHARACTERS

**FRIDAY, MAY 16**

This morning we got up late and were greeted by the flophouse landlord himself, who solemnly took Keith aside and kicked us out. He said he has heard on the radio that buildings that were rented to military Americans will be confiscated, so he's sure his buildings will be confiscated, and he doesn't want to hurry the process by having anyone notice that we two Americans are still here. We don't like staying here anyway, so this is okay. Keith asked him to open the back gate so we can more easily move our stuff out. But he said he wouldn't dare, because the local administrative office is just across the street. He was petrified that they would see us coming and going. I've been inside that very office, actually, and I'm positive they've already seen us and know where we sleep.

Funny he's taken this long to kick us out, really. We've never liked him. He is very rich and paranoid and annoying. He told Keith he is a virtuous man who has been a vegetarian for thirty years. Virtuous, while getting rich by renting to the U.S. military and U.S. contractors, and putting up a sign in English that's still on a wall in the courtyard that says, "Please don't bring girls through this way."

We reached the main house alley, and a handsome, familiar man came up to me and shook my hand. Anh Duy! He said he's been walking all over the city, so I offered him the loan of our bike. He told us a rather elaborate story about a bike he had in Quảng Ngãi that a friend lent to an NVA soldier, and then someone stole it from that soldier. Duy says his friend now owes him a bike, but his friend doesn't agree, since it wasn't his fault the NVA soldier was robbed.

Julie had said Duy was much poorer but also much happier when they saw him just two days ago, but I couldn't understand it until I saw him today for myself. Duy said he more or less hitchhiked his way down to Sài Gòn from Quảng Ngãi, apparently enjoying it. In Sài Gòn he sold his watch for 18,000 đồng and bought a camera for 15,000 đồng. He's taking pictures of everything to take back to Quảng Ngãi.

Duy says that everyone wonders why we haven't returned, and at first they were sad because we didn't come back with money, of course. I guess we need to write again, clearly explaining the sequence of events that kept us from coming back and from delivering money. At least we have now told Duy, so hopefully he'll be able to clarify things for others. He asked about the Tết pictures I'd taken, and I told him I'll try to get them to everyone in Quảng Ngãi.

Duy told Keith about not having money to drink coffee downtown or smoke cigarettes. He said he could sometimes drink coffee, but only if he sold a few vegetables first. He was proud of that. I find it odd for him to be so concerned about coffee and cigarettes.

Almost his whole family has returned from the north, where they went in 1954. The Thủ Lộ refugee camp and settlement near our medical assistant Anh Mỹ's home are now flat, empty fields. The refugees have disappeared, have gone home. Unlike in Sài Gòn, the return to the villages was immediate and dramatic, right after Liberation.

Duy said Quảng Ngãi is prettier than Sài Gòn, has more signs and decorations. We joked that we should go tell the government to put up more flags and banners. He said that wouldn't help, that Sài Gòn will never catch up, because Quảng Ngãi was liberated first. There's that famous Quảng Ngãi revolutionary pride. Many famous Vietnamese revolutionaries are from Quảng Ngãi Province. People there are proud of what's generally considered to be the poorest province in all of Việt Nam.

He said people are studying to learn how to raise sugarcane, and the sugar industry will make Quảng Ngãi very rich in the future. Huge plows have been brought in and are clearing areas for sugarcane. Since Liberation he's heard of only two incidents of unexploded ordnance in Nghĩa Hành, an area that had a lot of military action. One death, one injury. So what about all the mines and grenades we know are there? The local military immediately after Liberation identified areas known to have seen a lot of fighting and closed them off. They're clearing out the explosives, locating and removing the landmines. Of course there are plenty of mines all over, and they need a lot more equipment to find and remove them, but at least they're trying to clear some areas.

I asked Duy how he thought it would be for foreigners, us, in Quảng Ngãi or on the bus ride north to get there. He said it would be fine. The experienced PRG people who understand PRG policies really know the difference between the American government and American friends, and it's the old South Vietnamese GRVN supporters who might misunderstand or might be resentful.

He said we would be welcome in Quảng Ngãi, especially since people very much want us to continue to supply the center, and they want us to go there to negotiate with the new officials. We know we need to set up some method of communication, and we have been trying to do just that. How can we continue to support the program? Right now we can't even connect with our home office in Philadelphia. In future, could AFSC send supplies to the rehab center? Could the center staff send a list of requests every so often? But by what means? How to communicate? Who will translate so the staff in Philadelphia will understand? Though they don't require many items from abroad, I hope AFSC and the new government can have an agreement so that AFSC can continue to provide some higher-quality materials that are not available here. Better quality means the artificial legs, the crutches, the wheelchairs last longer, and farmers who are amputees can work better and longer, which will matter more than ever now that there's no more U.S. non-military support at all.

Duy said there were trials, and he said his own uncle, a lawyer trained in Czechoslovakia, was a judge in the trials. In the whole province, only two people were dealt with most severely, by being shot to death. These two were well-known torturers from the Interrogation Center, known for their cruelty throughout the entire province and responsible for many deaths.

He said one person was jailed. That was Ông Triết, the chief of police for the province and cousin of our physical therapy aide Nguyệt. No one knows for how long, but for now he's gotten off easy. He's in a cell in his own prison, not in the Interrogation Center, which has been closed up. We've recently heard from other people who've come from Quảng Ngãi that he almost certainly helped organize, and profited from, burglarizing our house over and over again. And of course, we certainly weren't the only victims, but we were easy, since we weren't armed, and he would have known that.

Other people, said Duy, have gone to "reform study," and those who don't reform successfully go live in the hills together, for longer periods of time. The hospital doctors finished their period of re-education in about a month. Re-education will be very hard to explain to foreigners—how forward-looking it is intended to be. The idea is to separate the people from the rumors and propaganda they've heard for so long, and to educate them about the true policies and goals of the revolution. For how long depends on what their position was before Liberation. *(See "Re-education Camps" on page 251.)*

The idea is, for example, to educate doctors so that when they come back from re-education they won't take money from patients for better service or accept bribes for anything. Duy said that everyone in Quảng Ngãi now understands the policies. He sees much less change in Sài Gòn, and fears it will be a much more difficult task to re-educate Saigonese like our flophouse landlord.

Duy left, and later Mạnh Tường arrived and spent most of the day with us. We had a depressing enlightenment when Mạnh Tường said he has discovered that in fact the student group we've become so familiar with, led by Hoàng Lộc, is a fake, and Hoàng Lộc is a fraud. So how did he get newspaper clippings about himself? Maybe it's not his real name. I'm personally embarrassed because I think I may have mentioned him or written his name down as a reference at the Immigration Office. Maybe I should write a letter to correct that.

Mạnh Tường also said he has discovered that his friend Tùng, whom he has completely trusted, who drove the jeep when he came to get us right after Liberation, who was armed, was actually never a political prisoner, as he had claimed to be. He had been, instead, imprisoned as a common criminal. Of course, some common criminals became politicized in prison, but Mạnh Tường says he now doesn't know if Tùng has had anything but his own interests in mind since Liberation.

Well, it's not a complete surprise. We know we can't trust everyone, especially if even Mạnh Tường, an experienced, intelligent, anti-Thiệu Third Force supporter, was tricked. Many people are trying to maneuver to protect themselves, which of course is human nature. Mạnh Tường said another friend, named Thử, doesn't need a pair of crutches but won't stop using them, perhaps to pose as a military invalid. Everyone, said Mạnh Tường, has a scheme.

Also, Mạnh Tường brought a new version of Bà Hai's story of an NVA soldier accidentally running over a child. Bà Hai's story is the soldier who did it asked the mother how he could compensate for what happened, and she answered, "Only by my child living again." Another soldier then shot him dead. Mạnh Tường's story is the soldier then shot himself dead. It's become local lore.

In the afternoon we five and Mạnh Tường went to a movie called *Chiến Thắng Điện Biên Phủ (Victory at Điện Biên Phủ)*. It was a riveting documentary, with film footage of the battle from both sides, and movies of Hồ Chí Minh and Phạm Văn Đồng meeting in the mountains. There was a famous scene of Hồ typing on a typewriter at a desk, outside, near a waterfall. There were scenes of people cheering as French planes were shot down. There were images of fifty or so soldiers hauling a cannon by hand up a steep hill; then a spotter plane sees them (all caught on film!) and they redouble their already strenuous exertion while bombs fall around them. There are scenes of people running through fields as the fields are blowing up. Stunning.

## SATURDAY, MAY 17

I observed a nice interaction this morning. I passed a police station on Yên Đỗ Street, just outside our alley, and saw an old man come up to the fence, talk to someone within, and moments later a smiling soldier passed the old man a glass of water through the fence, respectfully, with two hands. Very different attitude from police in the old government, and a very different level of trust by the citizens.

This morning we discussed whether I should write a letter to the Immigration Office about using Hoàng Lộc's name as a reference. I'm not sure I did use his name, but I want to act first to say that using his name, if I did, was a mistake, that he's not someone I now trust. I don't want to wait and maybe be called in to explain the relationship. The group consensus was that I write the letter.

In the afternoon we went to a very nice photography exhibition, where many of the photos and books were actually Paul's and AFSC's. There were lots of people there we knew, including Hùynh Liên and other Buddhist nuns. Just for fun, I wore my peach-colored áo bà ba blouse, my black quần pants, my black-and-white Liberation scarf, my rubber déps (sandals), no purse, so I was dressed like a guerrilla. Our friends at the exhibition loved my outfit, and made me wrap my scarf around my neck "correctly" to look "perfect." They told me I was only missing a floppy hat, and those are now sold at the downtown market.

As we stood watching a singing performance and a dragon dance, a boy of about thirteen, with six hand grenades on his belt and an AK-47 rifle, dressed like a guerrilla, was quietly and gently trying to herd the noisy street children in the audience. He was trying to keep the children in a certain area so they wouldn't disrupt the performance. He is very young himself, but apparently an experienced guerrilla, and like so many of these guerrilla soldiers he is very impressive with his steadiness and maturity. The guerrillas are pleasant and modest. I can't explain it, but I can see it.

In the exhibition room I was told people couldn't locate me easily because I'm the same height as Vietnamese, while the other foreigners tower over the crowd. I'm five foot two, and this is something I particularly enjoy in Việt Nam, being close to the same height as most people, rather than short like back home.

I was looking at some pictures on the wall when a very pleasant young man came up to me. But before I go on, I must describe, for the sake of contrast, our usual situation, as indeed happened at today's exhibit several times. A voice says haltingly in English, "You are French? Do you speak Vietnamese? Oh! You speak so well! How do you like the revolution?"

But this young man asked me, in Vietnamese, "Where have you been soldiering?" He seemed actually serious. I laughed and told him I was only a fake guerrilla soldier, and I just wore these clothes today for fun. He liked that. The young man next to him was dressed in an NVA cadre uniform shirt with a Hồ Chí Minh pin on it, so I asked him, jokingly, if he was a real bộ đội soldier. The answer was fast, clear, and serious. Both really were guerrillas, had been for four years. I said, "Excuse me, but how old are you?" They looked very young, and in fact they are. They are both fifteen. Indeed, it's not uncommon. One ex-patient of ours who we sent to the Barsky Hospital was a guerrilla at age eleven, and a woman I met there said she was one at fourteen.

I asked this young man, named Tắn, how he had joined the National Liberation Front at eleven years old. He said he started by carrying letters and messages. I said his family must have favored Liberation, or did he join alone? He said the whole family always supported the revolution. He went from carrying letters to working with peasants and educating peasants (a twelve-year-old boy!) and then battling. These two and a third friend always worked together. All are fifteen years old now. They saw many people die and saw B-52 bombings. I said I understood that usually people knew when B-52s were coming and got into shelters. He said they always knew, but weren't always prepared and weren't always near a shelter. Their family homes are in Sài Gòn and their fighting was in Củ Chi, just barely out of Sài Gòn to the north. They said bombing there could sometimes be heard by their families in Sài Gòn.

## SUNDAY, MAY 18

Today I felt I accomplished something because I took care of the Hoàng Lộc problem. But first, in the morning, we tried a new breakfast shop where we had delicious phở and bánh bao. It kept us going until 2 p.m., better than our old place with its much more expensive breakfast of bread and butter. Bread's not very good anymore, made largely of rice flour with little salt, and butter is very expensive and considered "anti-revolutionary." We still spend money on fruit even when it's a bit expensive, for nutrition and our emotional happiness.

This morning we met Duy at the house again and he said he wanted to go to the Barsky Hospital with us. He's been hinting about us giving him money to go to a beach town, Vũng Tàu, for fun, but we wouldn't and haven't. His asking just doesn't feel right. We had been thinking of asking him to take some boxes of copper washers for the rehab center back to Quảng Ngãi, and we also considered asking him to accompany one of our patients who is here to Quảng Ngãi, but I'm afraid we don't quite trust him anymore. Julie was bemused recently when she gave him 7,500 đồng for his mother's bus ticket and two hours later he came over, drunk from, he said, 500 đồng worth of beer. We're wondering if somehow he's been corrupted by being here in Sài Gòn, by proximity to us, and by our invitation to make himself at home.

Keith and I and Duy went in the team car to visit our former patient Thắn at Barsky. I'd really been worrying about him, but he looked good, better than before, and he was sitting up and smiling. Another patient, Sương, looked good too, and she said she has her discharge papers already but not the means to get home. I said I thought we could lend her the money to get home, and she said she would appreciate that. In the thirteen months since she was injured, she's never met nor seen a picture of her thirteen-month-old son. She was unconscious when the baby was delivered. When she was first burned, I remember her husband thought it would be bad luck for the baby. Let's hope he feels okay about how she looks now with burn scars.

There is still no doctor there, so no surgery is being done. We're told doctors at the Bình Dân Hospital in Sài Gòn are very busy, have three shifts each twenty-four hours long, and surgeons are operating twenty-four hours a day. Sài Gòn is still definitely low on doctors.

We gave the two patients some mangoes and pomelos, and Thắn some newspapers. Then we went to the Immigration Office at the old police headquarters on Võ Tánh Street. It was noon, and the office had a sign posted saying it was closed. But I noticed the gate was open so I went in. The first person I met in the office invited me to sit down. I told him why I'd come. Then he left the room, and I was sure he'd tell me to come back tomorrow. But instead, an older man with gray hair, in uniform, came toward me, extending his hand to shake mine long before he reached me. He invited me to a back table in the now-empty registering room.

I told him I had come for two purposes. One was to clarify the members of our organization and where we all are living, and second, to clarify some names and provide some addresses of Vietnamese references for us. In this category, I said I wanted to cross out Hoàng Lộc, if indeed I had written his name on the list.

He carefully went over our names, positions, and locations. Then he carefully re-read the names and addresses of our references aloud. Then he wrote Hoàng Lộc's name on another piece of paper. I guess I hadn't written his name on my first list after all. I said that we recently learned Hoàng Lộc had lied to us. I said, "I had naively thought that after the revolution I could believe everyone, but it certainly isn't true. There are still many problems."

He smiled and agreed that there are still many problems, especially in Sài Gòn. I said yes, unlike Quảng Ngãi, which is of course a much smaller city and has fewer problems. He said, "Sài Gòn is indeed bad, but Washington, D.C., is worse." Then he added, "Imagine trying to organize New York. It would be terrible, impossible!" He laughed, and so did I.

We chatted a while, and then he thanked me for clarifying the names and addresses on my list and said my coming to the office was very proper and appropriate. I felt relieved. He said they will be getting in touch with us. He walked me to the door and shook my hand twice. This man was friendly and courteous and helpful. There was no twenty-minute wait at the beginning, like in the old days, to make you realize you should pay a 1,000 đồng bribe if you wanted to get in. We never paid bribes, so it was always difficult and time-consuming to accomplish things.

After lunch I went alone on a bus to a movie downtown called *Mở Đường Trường Sơn (Opening the Trường Sơn Road)*. It was as good as everyone had said it was. It began with scenes of tall, misty mountains and clouds, moving down to a well-hidden road through difficult mountain terrain. People were working, many or even mostly women, with long hair in braids, building a road. They had dynamite, makeshift wheelbarrows, and they hammered the road-bed stones by hand with other stones. One scene showed them putting trucks on a railway track by taking off the truck tires and putting them inside the trucks, then putting train wheels under the trucks, thus making them ride on the tracks like trains. Through tunnels and over suspension bridges—trucks as trains.

The photographer was very courageous, not only for his/her shots of the planes and bombs falling, but for the amazing scenes on the ground of people running to shelter, or shooting rifles at the bombing planes, or shooting shoulder-carried anti-aircraft missiles at them. One memorable scene was of a young man not running for shelter, but instead standing on top of an exposed hill, shooting his rifle straight up into the air at an airplane. Another scene was of a SAM missile being shot off and hitting a B-52, which crashed.

There were also happy scenes of people playing ping pong in the mountains, singing together, doing embroidery, cheering the first trucks coming through a new tunnel, finding a safe storage area for piles of ammunition. There were scenes of destruction, forests burning, newly built parts of the road being immediately destroyed by bombs, badly damaged bridges being quickly rebuilt. While fires were still burning, people ran out to clear away boulders and fallen trees to make way for trucks. One truck moved forward, on fire. One scene was of five gasoline barrels all on fire, and people rolling the barrels and hitting at them with cloths to put the fires out.

Watching these movies I realize what a feeling of community and of selflessness these people must have, to do these heroic things over and over and so often to sacrifice themselves. And yet there were volunteers for all the missions where death was probable.

# 12

# HỒ CHÍ MINH'S BIRTHDAY

**MONDAY, MAY 19**

Happy birthday, Uncle Hồ!

New newspapers are appearing in recent days. One is *Phụ Nữ Giải Phóng*, a women's Liberation paper. As for all the groups popping up claiming to be this or that, the authorities have said they will let them all surface, find out which ones are what they claim to be and which are fake, and at some future time make the fake ones register and become real, or disband.

After breakfast and a taste of the very hot morning sun on our walk to the main house, we got there to find a messenger, a woman on a bike, delivering a note to us. Yesterday we five on the team had talked about putting a stop to Duy's debaucheries—borrowing belongings, getting food and drink for free by saying he had no money when he did, or just not paying, and borrowing our bicycle and things in our house without permission. But before we saw him again, it turns out he managed to get himself arrested.

The note was from him telling us where he was being held in Chợ Lớn and asking us to come. Keith and I gathered some of his clothes from our house and began to go off in the car. But there was an unfamiliar car parked in the alley, blocking the exit, so we decided to push out the Lambretta, which hasn't been working well and is out of gas. We bought some gas and in the beating sun tried to push start it. No luck, and now a half hour wasted already. What a way to spend Hồ's birthday. Finally we took a cyclo motorcycle for 1,000 đồng. The driver had trouble finding the right office where Duy was being held. Eventually we found it, entered, and found Duy inside, sobbing uncontrollably. I had the sinking suspicion that he had lost our bicycle, and I was distressed over what that would mean. He would be held responsible, sure, but we wouldn't have our bike, and they're very difficult to replace right now.

The local chairman in the office told us what Duy had done, and it was more than his note had said. Duy's note said that he was arrested because he was drinking coffee after curfew. The officials say that at dinnertime he ate a dinner that cost 250 đồng and only paid 100 đồng. The food stand owner complained to the police, and the authorities took away Duy's papers, Sophie's sandals, which he was wearing, our water flask, which he had, and our bike. Then they told him to report to the office at a future time.

But then he managed to get arrested again right away, for being drunk and out after curfew. Different authorities arrested him the second time and asked to see his papers, which of course he didn't have. When the two offices connected up, they were appalled at his behavior. They said he told people he was a PRG cadre just arrived from Quảng Ngãi, and they were of course upset at how this sort of impersonation gives the real cadres a bad reputation.

He also apparently lied to officials in an interview and on a written statement about what he'd done. We asked the officials for our bike back. The man asked for the registration number of the bike. We said that in old Sài Gòn you didn't need one. He asked us to wait to get our property back until after the whole case is settled, which it isn't yet. On Duy's behalf we recounted his history of good work at our Quảng Ngãi rehab center, right up to the day we left. We said we could not take responsibility for him here in Sài Gòn and explained that we couldn't control his actions, and that we also no longer had responsibility for our program in Quảng Ngãi.

We suggested that after the case is settled he be sent immediately back to Quảng Ngãi, where the temptations of Sài Gòn can't have such a strong influence on him. At first they said they'll just release him along with our belongings, whether we were there or not, but Keith asked them to hold our belongings for us to pick up ourselves. Then they said they will notify us when we can come get him and our stuff.

In the afternoon we went to a student cultural performance at the Student Union at 4 Duy Tân Street, where Mạnh Tường's girlfriend, Qùynh Chi, and her ballet group were performing. The dancers were excellent, the musicians were pretty good, the singers were okay, but all the technical stuff was wretched. The amplifying system was distorting the music like a very bad tape recorder. Two light discs kept a group of young men busy trying to be artistic, alternately putting the performers into total darkness and shining bright lights so everything was lit except their faces. Now and then the fluorescent light switched on. For the first part of the show the electricity was faulty and lights and microphones would go off and on.

The songs and dances and dramatic skits were historic and about liberation, mostly from the Chinese and the French. Usually, the victors were danced by women, I think more because they're better dancers than because they're women, in this group. The audience was very enthusiastic. I enjoyed watching Qùynh Chi because I know her, and she's a beautiful dancer. Yến's nieces Hồng Vân and Hồng Quân, who sat with me, are very impressed with Qùynh Chi and find it very romantic that she is Mạnh Tường's girlfriend, with her being a ballerina and he being a polio survivor who walks with crutches and braces. They mentioned that Qùynh Chi's mother is definitely against her relationship with Mạnh Tường.

We also saw a good photo exhibit upstairs there before the performance started. There were scenes of Hồ Chí Minh, his funeral, children sobbing at a gathering with Phạm Văn Đồng over the death of Hồ. That was the most moving photograph. That's what we did today on Uncle Hồ's birthday.

## TUESDAY, MAY 20

Who should appear at our door but Duy again, saying he'd been let out of the police station and told to go back at 4 p.m. to get a special stamp on his temporary papers. He said we could go collect our things now. He had supposedly come to our house to pick up his towel, but within minutes of arriving he went to the kitchen, asked Bà Hai to feed him, and got her to make him coffee too. But at least he wasn't being secretive about it.

Before he left, I called him outside to the front porch and talked to him privately. He said right away, "You'll tell me to go back to Quảng Ngãi, right?" I said yes. I told him he should stop begging and acting poor. We had given him money, which he said he needed in order to buy his mother's bus ticket home, but instead he had bought himself beer. He explained the beer by telling us his mother had left him with some money, but a few days ago he said he had asked her for more money and she wouldn't give him any. He doesn't even seem to know he's lying, poor guy. I guess he keeps confiding in us and listening to our advice because we try to support and help him, even though we're not succeeding.

About an hour after he left, Keith and I went back to the same office so we could get our bike, sandals, and water flask. In the office we found a man we'd seen there yesterday. We said we'd come to pick up our things. He looked at us oddly and didn't answer. We explained that Duy had just been to our house and had told us our things could be picked up, and so we were there to get them. We said Duy had told us they had investigated him, called Quảng Ngãi, and had then released him, and he was to come back to get a stamp on his identification papers. Well, apparently none of it was true. The official said Duy had actually run away last night from a different office where he was being held, and he had not come back. We were astonished, though I guess we shouldn't have been.

Then he invited us to sit down and he asked us a lot of questions. After that, he asked us to talk to someone who seemed to be the head of the office, and who was rather angry about the whole thing. Apparently Duy had either climbed a fence or left on the premise of going next door to eat dinner at around 8 p.m. and never returned. They had never locked him in a room, but they hadn't expected him to leave. His camera and our three items are all still impounded and will be until he comes in to talk to them. How do we get into these fixes? Good grief! Bill, the fake Hoàng Lộc, and now Duy.

The officer asked for our ideas of what to do about Duy. We explained that we felt, but weren't sure, he is mentally ill and not an intentional criminal, and he should first take care of his responsibilities toward that office and then be sent straight to Quảng Ngãi, where people who know him can help him. He asked us to "keep" Duy next time he comes to our house, if he does, and to bring him in. We said we didn't see how we could force him if he refused. The officer said to go out on the street and call the nearest bộ đội soldier. We tried to explain how funny that would be for two foreigners to walk up to or yell for soldiers on the street somewhere, and to then ask them to arrest a Vietnamese man we say is "bad." He said to have the soldiers call the district office at Quận 10, or to make the call ourselves. But we don't have a phone. He gave us the phone number and said to just go to any office and they'll call. But there are no offices near us.

We dropped it there, it being useless to discuss it more. If he had given back the bike we could maybe get to a soldier or an office more easily, but without it, it's a long trek. But we'll try to bring him in, for his own safety and also for our reputation. This is getting very embarrassing.

But two nice incidents also took place today. One was meeting three NVA soldiers and a younger brother of one of them, who came to see Sophie and Paul and overlapped briefly with Duy before he left. Keith had actually mentioned in our interview with the official that when Duy was at our house earlier today, there were also three NVA soldiers visiting with us right in our living room, and that if we had known Duy had left their office without permission we could have asked them to help us get him to turn himself in again. I think the official found that story completely unbelievable, that there were three NVA soldiers who were friends of foreigners, especially us, who by now surely they have to be suspicious of, with all this runaround with Duy!

The soldiers are Anh Hùng, Anh Quân, and Anh Thúy. They're all from the north, working as journalists now. We asked them silly questions about becoming soldiers, and they laughed but answered. I asked if everyone has to learn how to shoot a gun. They said no, not administrators, for example. We asked how one gets to be a soldier, and they said you just have to be strong and persevere. They said when they first started carrying heavy weights and walking long distances they were dead tired, but later they got used to it. I asked if people were allowed to join on the basis of their understanding and support of the revolution. They said almost everyone was welcome at the beginning, but if they later showed they didn't want to fight, they'd leave, and they pointed out that some did chiêu hồi, meaning they came over to the GRVN (South Vietnamese) side.

I asked if every bộ đội soldier has seen major battles. They said yes, definitely, B-52 raids and other horrors. They said ARVN soldiers would never survive conditions that the North Vietnamese soldiers lived in. Sometimes they had to battle on for three days with no food, because the fighting had cut them off from their food supply.

We admired one soldier's rubber sandals, much nicer than our own, with thicker soles. He said they last two to three years with constant use. He pointed out something we hadn't noticed and had never seen before. The tread is identical to the tread on an ARVN boot. Clever! The sandals are manufactured from rubber, not made from old tires like ours, and have that special tread on the bottom. That way, even hundreds of soldiers could walk and not worry about leaving footprints, since ARVN soldiers couldn't tell the difference between their own boot footprints and these. I asked if bộ độis themselves can tell the difference, and he said yes, if they look carefully. The toe area isn't quite as broad as a boot.

He mentioned that sometimes they hung buckets of human excrement in trees to attract heat-seeking missiles and to avoid the missiles themselves. He told of various guns the NVA invented, made intentionally slightly larger than similar American guns so that their guns could use the smaller American ammunition, but the American guns could not use the larger NVA ammunition.

We went outside to take pictures. They said they send pictures home, and their families write letters saying to send photos of their entire bodies, so they can see that their sons still have their arms and legs. I told them that with a good artificial leg you couldn't tell the difference in a picture! Everyone laughed. We took pictures of us in their floppy hats and helmets, with them, in various poses. It was fun and relaxed. Paul said that when they first met Hùng he gave them a real grilling, but now obviously he trusts Paul and Sophie, and therefore us.

The other especially nice incident today was that Keith went to a camera store we go to, owned by a man named Anh Cơ, to pick up some film (belonging to Duy, still trying to help him). Anh Cơ told Keith that before

Liberation he had had a two-hour talk with me that was extremely important to him, and he wanted Keith to thank me. Anh Cơ told Keith that our long conversation was about whether people like him should try to go to America to avoid the Communist takeover. This was during all the evacuation panic. He had wanted me to help him leave the country.

I remember the conversation but didn't know it would end up being important to him. I remember he had started by saying, "Will they kill us all?" but toward the end he asked, "Do you think I'll be able to continue my work, to keep running my shop?" At one point his phone rang, and the person on the other end asked him if he knew of any way to get to America. I heard him answer that there was an American in his office right then saying it was safer to stay than to join the mobs trying to evacuate. Toward the end of our conversation several women came in, repeating the common questions, "Will they kill us all? Will they tear out our fingernails if they're polished?" But by then apparently he had decided those questions were rather foolish.

So today when he saw Keith, he told him he wanted him and me to know that he stayed and he's happy about it, and that it's partly because I helped him remain calm.

## WEDNESDAY, MAY 21

I was thinking about the remarkable difference between pre-Liberation ARVN soldiers and the PRG soldiers who have taken over. Hearing that NVA soldiers have been killed since Liberation, I was thinking, why don't they wear bulletproof vests or flak jackets to protect themselves? Then I remembered how I used to feel walking past unsmiling soldiers carrying rifles, bayonets, with heavy helmets, in flak jackets and wearing boots. It was a sight that made people feel uncomfortable and threatened, not safe.

I think about today's soldiers, men and women, in their loose green pants and shirts, loose floppy hats or light cane helmets, rubber sandals, and that's all they have. Many are unarmed, and they're mostly just doing normal things like buying food in the market or driving with children on Hondas or bikes, or chatting with people. The attitude of these soldiers now is like the attitude of their leaders on the bandstand who stood unprotected in front of all of Sài Gòn. If they wore flak jackets it would be like saying the people are the enemy.

This is the same as how they draw a distinction between the U.S. government and the U.S. people, and similarly between the Sài Gòn hoodlum cowboys and the Sài Gòn people. It is certain that these soldiers are perfectly capable of arming themselves and making an armed city, but their commanders don't want them to. They actually seem to want to win the people over rather than dominate them.

Keith and I walked to our official phường (ward) headquarters way up on Kỳ Đồng Street to update our household form but found it very crowded, so we took a cyclo to the larger headquarters on Lê Văn Duyệt Street by Tứ Xuyên to do it there. On the way, we passed a drink stand that had two beautiful imported batiks hanging as curtains, clearly looted from a rich house.

My guerrilla-style rubber sandals seem to have helped us get the cyclo ride at the correct price. The driver seemed mildly intimidated by . . . my shoes! No wonder people believed Duy when he said he was a cadre, if someone can be intimidated by rubber sandals on a foreign woman's feet.

In the evening we had a team meeting in which we discussed the next few weeks or months. Paul suggested an attitude for us all to consider, that we say we want to leave Việt Nam as soon as it is convenient for the government and we can get on a flight, in order to return to America or Europe to tell people there the truth of the situation here. That's a positive reason for leaving, and a positive statement to give the government here. We like this idea.

Until now we've said our plans depend on what the government decides, but in fact, if the government decides we should leave, it would be much more pleasant for us to have decided it ourselves beforehand. We all agree that we don't think we're going to get permission to go back to Quảng Ngãi, and without some sort of work, besides observing and reporting, we might as well look ahead and plan to leave. Besides, we will run out of money and have no way of getting more. Relations between the U.S. and Việt Nam are severed, so AFSC has no way of sending any sort of money to us, and even if they could, dollars would have no value right now. Even the value of Vietnamese money is unstable.

Paul said that he's becoming somewhat reluctant to ask meaningful questions of government officials or even bộ đội soldiers, for fear of appearing suspicious. We all want to keep what we think is still our good reputation. I guess if I were the government, I might not want us back in Quảng Ngãi, perhaps because of such simple things as there not being a lot of food, or a place to stay. I wouldn't be surprised if they think we would require special transportation, even protection, and this would be a bother and an expense. The authorities certainly don't understand that we lived much like Vietnamese in Quảng Ngãi. We could stay anywhere, eat anything, travel like Vietnamese, and we definitely wouldn't want special protection. But they generally think we lived like the USAID and CIA officials in their big compound with armed guards and private planes and so on, despite what we tell them.

We've learned that the widow of Nguyễn Văn Trỗi,* Phan Thị Quyên, is to be a regular columnist in the new newspaper. Today's edition has more local news than previous issues. There's a front-page article on hoodlums still murdering and robbing. It says the local people of the area caught two armed robbers and detained ten drug users and thirty prostitutes, and all will be participating in re-education. It says as soon as these people understand the meaning of the revolution, they can return home.

It says all former soldiers, police, and government workers will receive the same benefits as everyone else, including free rice right now. As of today the government has helped three hundred families go home to wherever they came from before they became refugees. Each family gets fifty kilos of rice and bus or truck fare. It says six thousand more people have signed up for assistance so far.

---

* Nguyễn Văn Trỗi was a member of the National Liberation Front. He attempted to assassinate American defense secretary Robert McNamara in Sài Gòn in 1964. The South Vietnamese government killed him by firing squad when he was twenty-four. To the end, he defended his actions as patriotic, and he is considered a martyr. His last words were "Long live Việt Nam."

# 13

# DAY BY DAY

**THURSDAY, MAY 22**

This morning we had a pleasant visit from a British fellow named Peter Wiles who works with International Union for Child Welfare, an organization based in Geneva, Switzerland, that has provided aid to children almost exclusively in the north. His organization asked him to stay in the country to negotiate an arrangement with the new government. But, like us, so far he has accomplished nothing.

He told of having his camera stolen, and then he found it at the black market. He asked local red armband student police to get it back for him, and they did, but they asked him for some money to compensate the woman who had been trying to sell it, to make up for what she would have gotten selling it to someone else. He did not want to comply, but in the end he gave her some money, which saved face for her and got him back his camera.

Earl Martin, our MCC friend from Quảng Ngãi, said there are still sound trucks going around the black market area telling bộ đội soldiers not to buy anything because they'll be cheated, but there are still lots of them shopping there anyway. We chatted a bit with Earl today, and he said he is hoping to stay in Việt Nam if possible, as we were also hoping to do until we had our team discussion last night.

Julie and Sophie and I went to the Quận 10 police station again, and I went in alone to give them an address we'd found, of Duy's uncle. I met a man I've met there a few times before. He's friendly, smiling, and has four gold teeth. I gave him the address and said that we had waited for Duy at our house, but he hadn't come. The man listened to me, smiled some more, and said, "Please remember we didn't ask you to look for Duy." I said we didn't actually go looking for him, but we felt very bad about the whole situation and wanted to help.

Then the man took advantage of the more informal situation of Keith not being there, and me being alone, to ask me some personal questions. He asked what we're paid. I explained that we're volunteers. He asked how much money we spend to live on. Not much. He asked where the AFSC organization money comes from. Donations, contributions. Then he asked the usual questions people in Việt Nam always ask. Normally this is done when you first meet, to ascertain who is older, who is younger, and what to call each other based on that.

He asked my age, when we will go home to visit family, how long we've been married, do we have children, and if not, when will we. I felt he had held in his curiosity until now, when he had an opportunity to satisfy it. And of course I was happy to oblige. I answered him according to Vietnamese custom, telling him we had had a son, but he had died. I said we hope to have more children. I do hope, but not too soon. We will have to wait to see if it's even possible.

We also talked about sandals, and I said ours were precious because before Liberation, few foreign people had any, but we did. We talked about the special tread on the bottom of some sandals (not ours), and we each took one off to examine them. His were notably superior, being made from a mold and mine from an actual truck tire. But his did not have the ARVN boot print sole on the bottom and I teased him about that, and he laughed. He asked how many vehicles Keith and I have. I said only one bicycle, the one he knows about. He said not to worry about the bicycle, that it's carefully locked up, and when this problem is resolved it will be returned. I was sorry that despite this nice conversation, I still couldn't get it back!

## FRIDAY, MAY 23

Keith and I went off to see our friend, Buddhist head nun Hùynh Liên, and the other nuns at the orphanage. I decided the first Vietnamese name I've thought of that I'd really like to name a child is her name, Liên. It means lotus, reconciliation, and it's the name of all the Buddhist nuns, because Buddha sat on a lotus. Hopefully I'll get pregnant again when we get back to the States.

We talked for several hours and Hùynh Liên invited us for lunch. She said with a twinkle in her eye that now the nuns will have to get some land and learn to grow rice. I said that that's against Buddhist vows for Mendicant "begging" nuns. She agreed, but giggled in her way and said that in future people won't be able to beg, not even monks and nuns, so they'll have to work, because other people won't have extra to spare. She said she's rather looking forward to it.

The Mendicant nuns have always been actively working for peace, against the Thiệu regime and for the Third Force option, a compromise among all sides, which of course didn't happen. She said she's not afraid of the new government and the withdrawal of all American aid because for the last thirty years she's only had one meal, a bowl of rice, per day, so how much less could one have and still live?

Another visitor teased her about being such a rich beggar, since people bring them food every day, build the pagoda, buy them gas, volunteer, because the nuns can't have money. I said, "If a person is really bad, but gives things, do they gain merit?" "Oh no," she laughed, "but we take their offerings anyway, and we tell them if they're good they'll get merit. But the person must live a virtuous life, since self-satisfaction cannot be bought."

She said they're only poor nuns, but some of the Buddhist monks who accept money are very rich, used to fast living, and they have big cars and good food. I think she enjoyed the idea of them having to work in the future.

She asked a lot of sophisticated questions about life in America. She asked about people with, as she put it, red, black, brown, white skin. She asked why people eat food that comes in cans. And she asked how people can grow food in places with snow.

We talked a bit about the half-Vietnamese children and how they and their families are discriminated against. But in America, she said, she understands that many people are a mixture of races and backgrounds. She thinks there's no racism in America. She asked Keith about life in Africa too when she learned he had volunteered in Ivory Coast with the Peace Corps before coming to Việt Nam. She asked which is the happier place to live, Việt Nam or the United States. Keith answered diplomatically, saying that if more Americans had attitudes like Vietnamese have, it would make America a nicer place to live than it is now.

After lunch we went back to the house to hear the heartwarming story of Anh Duy's ... capture! Sort of. In the morning, Julie and Sophie had driven to Barsky Hospital. As they got out of the car, who should approach them from across the street but Duy. He asked Sophie for money to pay for the breakfast he had just eaten, and asked Julie for 10,000 đồng to go to Quảng Ngãi. He certainly seemed disturbed. Julie took him by the arm, paid 130 đồng for his breakfast, and said firmly, "Now you have a responsibility to us and now we're going to the station to turn you in, and to see about our bicycle." He tried to talk his way out of it, saying he'd better be going, but Julie was firm, and he went with her to the station.

At the gate, Julie found herself shaking, with her heart pounding, in this very odd situation of an American taking a Vietnamese to the police. She asked at the entrance to be allowed in, and introduced Duy. A young guard standing outside at the entrance said, "Oh yes, you're the guy who impersonated a cadre, aren't you? And you ran away." He chatted like that and Julie got more and more tense, hoping Duy wouldn't leave. Finally they got into the building, but moments later Duy went out on the street again. Julie tried to impress upon the guard that their "guy" had indeed already run away before, just as he had said. They retrieved him and took him into a back room, and there a very confused police officer stared at the two American women and couldn't really focus on what they were saying. So they excused themselves and went back to Barsky, saying they'd return later.

In the afternoon I went to visit Phương-Hằng's sister Bình. She's interesting and smart, and I enjoy visiting with her and all the family. She told me a very sad story about a man she used to work with who before Liberation was very scared, but afterward he found out that his own brother was a high official in District 1 and felt reassured. Somehow her colleague got a job confiscating houses whose owners had left. She said he was working together with another man who introduced himself as having been a secret cadre for a long time. One day they found someone was living in a house they were about to confiscate. The "cadre" was very rude and kicked the person out in a manner Bình's colleague felt was unacceptable. He was, somehow, senior to the "cadre" and told him he didn't want to work with him anymore and that he should leave. The "cadre" left but was angry, and came back a few days later and shot and killed him.

Bình hadn't yet thought about the cadre maybe being a fake, but I told her about our own experiences with fake cadre Hoàng Lộc, and she realized he probably was an imposter. I told her about him and also about Duy, our two main embarrassments. We talked about the difficulties of changing a police state into a non-police state, while still needing to control the violence but with few visible police on patrol. She said she's in favor of the solution of "killing killers on sight," as she put it.

We talked about the new newspaper *Sài Gòn Giải Phóng* ("Liberated Sài Gòn"). She worked for the Sài Gòn Press until a short time ago when over a hundred people were laid off. She said this new newspaper isn't really reporting; it's just making announcements. I agree. She feels as a journalist that it's a mediocre paper. People won't read it because it's boring, especially for intellectuals. It is indeed rather boring, more simply written, which I appreciate because its simple language is easier for me to read.

She said some Japanese journalist friends of hers have been told that they'll be allowed to stay, but only one person per newspaper or wire service. And their interpreters must be approved by the government. She said her friends don't like this and may leave. I suggested they spend some time studying Vietnamese so they won't always need interpreters, and she thought that was a good idea.

She had been very hesitant when Liberation took place, even though her parents are progressive and her father had been a political prisoner long ago. Now Bình is watching the changes, good and bad, paying attention, and is planning for the future. Her extended family is considering moving to Lâm Đồng near Đà Lạt to work on a friend's tea plantation. Or maybe more of the family will move to Sài Gòn.

Bình is wondering whether her sister Phương-Hằng will try or be able to come home from America. She's been in the U.S. since December and might want to come back now because of what's happened, or she might want to stay there. I doubt she can return, at least not soon, since her passport isn't valid, having been issued by the previous government. Our visas for being here are also, of course, no longer valid. There are no diplomatic relations between the two countries, and no one knows when they may be established. *(See "How I Came to Live in America" on page 228.)*

Bình said her father told of dozens of former police and military officers being taken far off to a secret place in the mountains for re-education, but many died on the way, from malaria. She felt that story was quite suspicious, saying that people don't usually die suddenly of malaria. It is also rumored that in Tuy Hòa a lot of bad people from the previous government were killed. She pointed out that Tuy Hòa is a particularly strong revolutionary province, like Quảng Ngãi, and right now each province is pretty much autonomous, so she thinks it might have been a local decision to order those killings.

The paper today has a photograph of two young men on a Honda who were shot dead after stealing a watch as they rode by the victim. We doubt this has happened often—the shooting, not the stealing—but the government wants people to see the photo and be scared and stop thieving. It's pretty rampant now. The government has made announcements, posted notices, published pictures, and now it's publicizing punishing criminals with death, in an attempt to control crime.

We went to dinner at the Mennonites' house. Max Ediger told us that on April 30, right before Liberation and during the mass looting, some armed and intimidating ARVN Self-Defense Force soldiers came to the VNCS guest house and insisted that the only person who was there, the cook, open the gate. She called some ARVN soldiers over to stop them from coming in and looting, and they did make them leave. But later that day, the same Self-Defense Force soldiers came back, blew the gate apart, tore the house apart, tore the cook's own little house next door apart too, and pushed her out onto the street. Max and the others were furious when they learned about it, but there was nothing anyone could do and the soldiers were never found. I wonder where they are now. Impersonating cadres, maybe?

## SATURDAY, MAY 24

Where do we stand? It's been three and a half weeks since Liberation here in Sài Gòn. Today we got our first mailed letter from anywhere, from our Philadelphia AFSC Indochina Peace Program director John McAuliff, who is in Hà Nội, a guest of the Việt Mỹ (Vietnamese American) Organization.* He says the PRG in Hà Nội told him we here in Sài Gòn would be "pushing" for the Logistics office to release our shipment, and that we'd be asking where to go in order to negotiate for this to happen. Well, yes, we certainly have been trying to release our shipment and trying to figure out where to go to make this happen. As for "pushing," we haven't found any effective way to do that.

We can't tell when the letter was mailed, and in it he didn't tell us how long he'll be there, where or how we can reach him, or who at the Việt Mỹ office we might attempt to contact. He of course can't know how hard we've been trying to find anyone to negotiate with about our Quảng Ngãi program, our stuck shipment of supplies, and establishing a relationship between the new government and AFSC.

We regularly try to make and maintain contact with people and get information, but negotiating is an entirely different thing. We have no power and no authority to make anything happen. We are guests in a country run by a new government, and we barely have any status, except nominally as social workers and journalists. We have a sensitivity from being here that well-meaning, very knowledgeable outside people just can't have. We don't want to bother the government in order to help it. We feel it's not productive, not appropriate, not our place. We can "push" but can't insist.

Latest news on the embarrassment front. Now not only are Bill and Duy being detained, but we've just learned that our other embarrassing acquaintance, Hoàng Lộc, has actually been arrested, for illegally confiscating a

---

* Two AFSC staff members, John McAuliff and Bill Jeffries, and representatives from the Indochina Peace Campaign (IPC) arrived in Hanoi on April 30, 1975, the day the war ended. AFSC worked closely with IPC, an organization founded by Jane Fonda and Tom Hayden, part of the Coalition to Stop Funding the War.

house, inviting bộ đội soldiers to live with him there, and then inviting rich people to come over and "contribute" money to them. What nerve. Another bad reputation–maker for the government. But now he's been stopped.

Today Sophie managed to send off a cable to the U.S., so we might get communication from AFSC in Philadelphia in a week or so if we're lucky.

I went downtown on the bus (price rose 10 đồng) and found the post office closed, so I couldn't access our post office box. Turns out the post office is on old Sài Gòn time, for some reason. I bought stamps from a boy at a stand, mailed a letter to our rehab center receptionist and close friend Chị Mai in Quảng Ngãi, and I enclosed a stamped return envelope. Some PRG soldiers there asked me if I knew if they could buy a stamp with one piaster. They thought one piaster was one sou and that that was one South Vietnamese đồng. (I don't know anything about the value of piasters and sous.) I learned from them that the largest money in the north is a 10 đồng bill. Here it is a 1,000 đồng bill. So no, one piaster wouldn't be enough. We all laughed at this confusing conversation, and they bought their stamps at the price the boy was asking. I wonder how they make up for the loss in value of their currency.

I went to a photo exhibit called "Women in the Revolution" at a former art studio near the cathedral circle and Tự Do Street. It was an interesting exhibit, and they asked me to write something in their guest book. I wrote a short paragraph, including, "I myself am an American and I am proud to be defeated so Việt Nam can have peace."

## SUNDAY, MAY 25

It's the Buddha's birthday. We went to the main house for a special Sunday breakfast of real butter and bread and eggs, but there was a visitor, so to be polite we ended up just nibbling on the food and drinking coffee with him. The visitor turned out to be a very special person, someone I had known of but never met before. It was Ba Minh, my language tutor Dung's husband. I've heard of him since I first came to Việt Nam and met Dung, but he hadn't been home here in Sài Gòn for three years, until April 30, 1975, when he walked in along with all the other NLF and PRG soldiers.

He told us that when our AFSC program's previous Sài Gòn representatives, Peggy and David, hadn't been here very long, he asked them to take him to a place near Cần Thơ, where he got out of the car and said goodbye to them on the side of the road, went through the trees, and joined "the other side." He said Peggy and David, or just David (he wasn't sure if they had both been there), hadn't realized what they were doing for him. Since then, Dung has gone to see him a few times, but he hasn't been able to come home. Dung had told him about us, and today he did us the honor of coming to visit us, so we could finally meet each other. It was a double honor because it was his only day off from the work he is doing now, which is writing.

He is soft-spoken and self-effacing, and doesn't seem to like to talk a lot about himself. He has written poetry and stories and articles. I asked if he thought some North Vietnamese or some NLF guerillas were disappointed to find that some Saigonese still want to fight, even though the Americans have left. He said no, he felt all those who came into Sài Gòn were briefed beforehand and knew what to expect.

At about 11 a.m. he had to go, and we went off to the Buddhist monastery for a birthday party for the Buddha, with our own small offering of sweet bananas. While there, we attended a women's meeting upstairs at the pagoda, led by Huỳnh Liên. In attendance were some important people, including the very famous Madame Ngô Bá Thành.* Everyone was in excellent spirits. Three women had their heads shaved behind the altar in honor of the occasion, to practice religious devotion and humility. *(See "Việt Nam's Religions" on page 252.)*

Huỳnh Liên and Ngô Bá Thành acknowledged us and proclaimed that we are helpers in bringing about the victory of the Vietnamese people. It was a party, so we were asked to share something. Sophie and Julie came up with a great song about Hồ Chí Minh, and I gave a one-minute speech. Keith and Paul, being men, didn't speak.

Later, there was some serious discussion of the merging of all former

---

* Ngô Bá Thành, previously footnoted activist and prominent Third Force Leader, also was the head of the Committee of Women for the Right to Life, an anti-war organization. After reunification she became a member of the National Assembly.

Third Force groups into one or a few larger groups. This would include the Buddhist group, the Catholic group, and various political groups, including the one Madame Ngô Bá Thành has been active in. Sài Gòn now has two national women's groups offices, one on Hồng Thập Tự Street, the other on Yên Đỗ.

I said that people in the U.S. will ask how Third Force members feel about the Provisional Revolutionary Government taking charge, rather than having achieved a compromise solution. Hùynh Liên and Madame Ngô Bá Thành said there is no more Third Force now and everyone is part of the victory, and we shouldn't say Third Force anymore. That was a necessary tool, but no longer relevant. Some people, they said, were Third Force, while others who said they were Third Force were NLF but didn't dare say so. Now it doesn't matter, there is peace, and it's time to unite and rebuild.

After the meeting, the nuns insisted on setting up a special lunch table just for us, since we had missed the luncheon before the meeting. We five and Madame Ngô Bá Thành, Hùynh Liên, and another Third Force activist named Father Tư sat and ate together. Hùynh Liên teased Father Tư about whether he could stand to eat their vegetarian food. She's really funny. I remember our conversation the other day when she said she would hate to live in a fifty-story building in New York City, or experience other "glories" of American civilization.

After we left the monastery I went to visit the film developer Anh Cơ in his camera shop. He has lost all his regular clients: U.S. banks, Esso, IBM, American Express, the *New York Times,* and more. He has lost his monthly $140 U.S. retirement check from USIS (United States Information Service). But he says he doesn't mind being poor all that much because now he won't have to pay huge bribes for schooling his nine children and to keep them out of the army. He has two wives and nine children in one house. I wonder what will happen with that. His father had five wives, he says. I'm pretty sure it can't be legal.

He has two bicycles and told me a story about them. One he bought for 1,500 đồng just before Liberation. He bought the other one for 300,000 đồng. I asked him how that could be. He said last year he paid a bribe of 300,000 đồng to get his son into the air force. The guy didn't get his son in, but kept the money. So the film developer threatened to expose him for corruption. Then the man gave Anh Cơ a bicycle, valued at about 40,000 đồng then, and said he'd try to give more money back later. But he never did. So Anh Cơ says he paid 300,000 đồng for the bicycle.

He said he used to have a huge salary of 500,000 đồng per month, but he spent it all on bribes. He doesn't even own his own house. He's a really nice man, easy to talk to, and his English is quite good, of course, since he worked with Americans.

Before I left he shook my hand and said he is excited about helping build the new Việt Nam. As his teenage son walked through the room, he said that now all his sons will help build the new country too. No more lazying around the house while their father feeds them, he said, making sure his son could hear. Before, they couldn't work because they had papers saying they were in school. Now they don't have false papers and can actually go to school, for free, or work, as they like.

In the evening we walked around the corner to the movie theater. The cashier had gone home early because there were so few people watching the show. We went right in and saw a movie on the life of Hồ Chí Minh. Well-known people were in the film including Mao Tse Tung, Chou En Lai, Tito, Nehru, all embracing Hồ on the eve of Vietnamese freedom in . . . 1945. Thirty more years until 1975.

# 14

# TIGER CAGES AND POLITICS

**MONDAY, MAY 26**

There have been airplanes flying these last few days and again today. They sound like DC-3s. The journalists who were trying desperately to leave finally left, day before yesterday. The only news report that we heard was from one saying they were well treated here. We have heard nothing about it on BBC yet. We found out today's planes are carrying a lot of Japanese journalists who are leaving.

This morning Keith and I stopped in at Father Chân Tín's for a chat. We asked him what he's been doing since Liberation, after he spent April 30 in the airport bunker with North Vietnamese diplomat Phương Nam and the rest of the delegation from the north. Father Chân Tín said that since Liberation he's been mostly helping with released prisoners. He sees his future role as helping the former three sides (Third Force, NLF/PRG, North Vietnamese government) of the anti-Thiệu and anti-American side of the war all become one.

He personally doesn't feel there will be discrimination against Third Force leaders like himself who cooperated with but also resisted the former regime. He gave us a paper published by Father Trần Hữu Thanh, a former staunch anti-Communist, who at the same time was a leader in the anti-corruption campaign that contributed to the final defeat of Thiệu.* Father Thanh is now working with Father Chân Tín for reunification and reconciliation. In the paper, he said the people were victims of lies and propaganda. Now, he said, he sees that socialism is very close to Catholicism. He tells his followers to join in the revolution, join in the policy of reunification.

Father Chân Tín mentioned that he had heard that some political prisoners were killed in Kontum, but he had no details. He said there also had been a plot before Liberation to kill all the prisoners in Côn Sơn Prison, but a captain on the island and some police officers there, all from the Thiệu government, bravely refused to carry out that order.

He said that in Sài Gòn at least six to seven thousand common criminals broke out of jail along with political prisoners while the latter were being released. The PRG did not want this to happen, but it did. Now everyone has a fresh start, intentionally or not. Many prisons are now closed, but if the recent rise in crime doesn't let up, I assume they'll re-open them. After all, what will they do with Hoàng Lộc?

At the main market today both Sophie and Julie had their purses slit, but nothing lost. Those thieves are taking big risks, considering today's newspaper accelerated to showing a photograph of a public execution of an armed robber, and a crowd of people watching and appearing to agree with it. The people at the market, discussing theft with Julie and Sophie, said that last Friday a thief was publicly executed there. We have no idea if these cases we've heard about are the only ones, or if there are many others. Definitely the newspaper is a tool to disseminate information that the government wants publicized. They're trying to convince thieves that they will be punished, but without setting up a system of secret police or having a stronger police presence, will it work?

These days people can complain about the government, can complain

---

* Father Trần Hữu Thanh, a leader of the anti-Communist Catholic movement and an influential political figure in the South Vietnamese government for decades, participated in planning, with air force marshal Nguyễn Cao Kỳ, a coup attempt for around April 10. The goal was to remove Thiệu and replace him with someone less corrupt who would continue the fight against the Communists.

about the newspaper, can stay out until late at night. They aren't afraid that their neighbors are secret police. They are beginning to trust that when a person is arrested, he or she won't come back to get revenge. Most investigations are almost painfully carefully done, as Keith and I discovered today when we checked in with the local phường administrative office about whether we need to register a change of address before moving into a new room we've agreed to rent.

The man in the administrative office, who was obviously local by his accent, heard our reason for coming and said he didn't see any problem, only that the landlady should come to the office to list the names of people she rents to. But then a higher authority cadre with a northern accent intervened and said we have to write a paper explaining who we are, what we want, why we're here, and so on. And he said we certainly cannot move in tomorrow. Bureaucracy!

We're noticing that now people don't stay out quite as late at night anymore. There's an increase in crime, or at least in reports of dealing with crime (via executions), and by 11 p.m. Sài Gòn time streets seem quite empty. In the daytime, there are lots of people.

Our afternoon visitor was a man named Anh Thạch, an English-speaking financier, some sort of business or economics expert, who studied in California for four years. He had a lot of interesting things to say. I asked his opinion of our present intention to leave Việt Nam soon. He said we should try to stay until we hear something from the government about its relationship with AFSC. He feels the government would like foreign aid, but hasn't the facility to organize it yet. But even if they eventually approve AFSC aid, will the U.S. government establish relations so the aid can be delivered?

He mentioned that people have forfeited education for twenty years now in order to fight, and the National Liberation Front soldiers in the south have not only lost huge numbers of talented people who have died, but those who survived have not had time or opportunity to get much education. Therefore there's a lack of sophisticated officials in the new local governments. Yes, I think we've noticed that.

Anh Thạch talked about the U.S. evacuation of refugees. He and many other friends have asked about the fate of Vietnamese who left in the panic but may now or soon want to come back to Việt Nam. We of course have no answers. We discussed the radio reports that some Vietnamese would have to remain in refugee camps in the U.S. or elsewhere for a long time. I wonder how the American public is responding to the people who arrive there, especially if they're not adorable babies, but rather ordinary adults, military officers, ex-secret police, Sài Gòn "cowboys," and more. Are they welcoming them? Or is this evacuation an American miscalculation?

Anh Thạch says he knew of pilots who had prior arrangements with the U.S. to fly their planes out of Sài Gòn to Thailand. Their families were flown out some five days earlier, and this essentially blackmailed the pilots into following. He said many doctors were picked up at their homes in buses and taken to the airport, receiving first-class treatment. Anh Thạch has of course lived in America, and he believes these doctors will get good jobs in general hospitals in poorer areas of big U.S. cities, since those positions are the least attractive and lowest paid, and it's hard to find U.S.-trained doctors to work there. That's what he thinks, but I disagree. I don't think their medical credentials will be recognized in the U.S. at all, and they will be unhappily surprised.

Anh Thạch used to receive 80,000 đồng per month from the previous government in his job in the Land to the Tiller program,* which he said USAID set up and funded. He said that in the program, the government paid wealthy landowners for some of their land, half in U.S. dollars and half in bonds, maturing after ten years. But the government soon found this to be a very expensive proposition. So, with USAID help, they set up a divestiture program that let people use their bonds before maturity to buy into newly divested government-owned companies and businesses. Anh Thạch said it didn't look good that the government directly owned companies (it didn't look like capitalism; it looked too much like communism), so making them privately owned looked better.

The biggest companies, like Air Việt Nam and the water and power company, remained government-owned, and the U.S. advisory organization was angry because while they knew these businesses were making a profit, they

---

\* The Land to the Tiller program was a land reform program and strategy to attract peasants sympathetic to the National Liberation Front over to the Sài Gòn government side. It ran from 1970 until 1973, financed by the United States, but was not very successful. In 1975 the new government instituted more expansive and successful land reform. See Jeffrey Race, *The War Comes to Long An* (Oakland: University of California Press, 2010).

also knew that income, in the form of investments or taxes, never left the businesses, meaning that the business executives and their collaborators in the government kept the profits. On the books it said the money went into advertising or re-investment, or a similar category.

Thus, partly through American attempts to "privatize," to change how the government operated and appeared to operate, came the fall of the government. The U.S. poured in more and more money, and the high-up people took more of it, and the government's dependence on foreign investment increased rather than decreased. So when the U.S. pulled out, many businesses and programs collapsed.

Both Anh Thạch and another visitor, a university-educated man named Lòng, told us about salaries for civil servants. This is a temporary subsistence-level figure, they said, that they hope will rise. The most valuable workers will get 23,000 đồng per month, the wife (that's the word they used) gets ten kilos of rice and each child gets five kilos of rice. This is really high pay, considering. This scale is for Sài Gòn and Gia Định only, where the cost of living is high.

They said there's a scale of four levels: Level A gets 23,000 đồng, Level B gets 18,000 đồng, Level C gets 14,000 đồng, and Level D gets 10,000 đồng. Thạch himself, who used to get 80,000 đồng, is now classified as Level D, because his work is non-essential, so he's down to 10,000 đồng. I asked him if he had saved money from his former high salary. He said he did, but it's in the bank, and the bank is closed and no one knows when it will re-open or what the money will be worth.

Lòng pointed out that cadres make only 40 to 60 đồng per day and get eighteen kilos of rice. That's barely enough to get fuel for cooking, much less to buy vegetables to cook. But he said all cadres just got a raise to 200 đồng per day. I'm not clear who is included in the category of cadre.

Lòng is probably in his late thirties and has been active on what he calls the Committee on Prisons, which was formed in 1970 when new facts about conditions in Côn Sơn Prison were just coming to light. It was in that year that Don Luce and Augustus Hawkins discovered the "Tiger Cages." Former prisoners, including some who had been kept in the Tiger Cages, testified aloud at a "secret" meeting about their treatment in that prison. *(See "I Helped Find the Tiger Cages" on page 232.)*

From then on, they developed channels for receiving and sending information and documents about prison conditions. We asked how they managed to get their hands on so many informative documents, and Lòng said all sorts of people on many different levels helped.

On Côn Sơn Island, Lòng said, there was a captain and many members of the police force who were against the imprisonment of political prisoners. These very people put down a plan to pour gasoline on the political prisoners and use hand grenades to blow them up, there in prison. And they themselves, the captain and the guards, are the ones who opened the gates and let the prisoners out in the end. This is the same story Father Chân Tín told us, but with more details.

Many national police helped smuggle information and documents out, and not for bribes, but just because they felt outrage. There was real solidarity among the prisoners, and some of it must have affected the guards. Many people became police and guards just to avoid being drafted into the army, anyway. Lòng said there were people in lots of offices who would also help. In the prisons themselves, often the "common criminals" were allowed to do jobs of responsibility, including caring for the files of political prisoners. They (experienced thieves in many cases) stole lots of original documents and smuggled them out. They also helped smuggle out letters from prisoners.

Lòng said some of the people on the Committee on Prisons had actually been NLF members for a long time. Before Liberation, of course, it would have been risky to share that sort of information, so no one knew for sure who anyone else was or what they believed or what cause they supported, if they did.

Lòng said that during the last five years the committee has regularly held meetings at his house, but they've never been discovered and he was never accused. At least twenty people, mostly students, were arrested and sometimes tortured, but not one of them ever told where they met, and that's why his house was never raided. Most of them, he said, told interrogators the committee members met at Ấn Quang pagoda, though that wasn't true.

When people, especially students, went to join the NLF, as many did, they never saw each other's faces. They always, even when eating, covered their faces with their scarves. The goal had been that those who planned to work in Sài Gòn must not be able to recognize each other, so that if they were arrested and tortured they wouldn't be able to identify anyone else. But after Liberation, some said they could always recognize others anyhow. One said, "Even though you wear new clothes, they're the same style as your old ones."

At Côn Sơn Prison, at the end, the island officials took off in two boats. But the PRG navy went after them and brought one boat back. The director of the prison got away, but the head torturer is now in the Côn Sơn Prison. However, he's not in the Tiger Cages. No one is. They're not being used.

Lòng told a story to add to all the shivery tales of lovers being separated for decades. A new man at his bank is a southerner who just returned after twenty-three years in Hà Nội. He was only a poor peasant in the south, but in the north he worked in a bank, and he is now down here reorganizing the bank. He is strictly self-disciplined and cannot leave his post without permission, he says.

One day Lòng was invited, as part of the Prison Committee, to go to the beach town of Vũng Tàu to meet the prisoners returning from Côn Sơn Prison. Lòng informed his bank that he wouldn't be at work for a few days. When he told his new, highly self-disciplined banker colleague why he'd be gone, that man asked Lòng if he would do him the favor of looking for his wife, who was a political prisoner at Côn Sơn Prison, and he told Lòng her name.

Lòng was pleased that when he went to Vũng Tàu he was able to locate the woman. She was very surprised and asked how he knew her name. He told her that her husband had asked him to look for her. She began to cry. She said she was so happy her husband knew her name, because that's her prison name only, and it meant he knew her prison name and had been following her whereabouts in prison from far away, for all this time.

She had been arrested in Sài Gòn in 1969, after years of working with the NLF. She had news of her husband for the first time that year, right before her arrest, but hadn't seen him in person, nor heard about him or from him, since 1954. And now it's 1975 and her husband couldn't come see her himself because of his job, and she was told she has to remain in Vũng Tàu for two more weeks to regain strength and recover from prison, and also to attend political classes. (At first this period was going to be a month, to help the prisoners inform the rest of society about their ordeal, and also to get them help finding jobs, but the officials cut it down to two weeks.)

Then the released prisoners would be returned to wherever they'd been arrested, so she, luckily, was returned to Sài Gòn. They were given jobs "fitting their abilities." If she had been released to somewhere else, she and her husband would have continued to not see each other for an even longer time. It doesn't seem fair that they're held to such strict discipline, while civilians in newly liberated areas, like Duy (and for that matter, us), have lots of freedom. Now he and she still will live separately for another ten days, but then they will live together. And since she was released, they have managed to see each other once.

Imagine all the wives and husbands who wanted to go north or south for the last twenty years, but could not. So now there are couples beginning only their second year of married life at age forty, after they were married some twenty years ago. And here we feel we've been away from Quảng Ngãi for a long time. How selfish and short-sighted of us.

Lòng also told of a refugee boat that just arrived back in Việt Nam today after being refused entry at other ports, especially by its destination port, Singapore. Lòng met one man from the boat who came to Sài Gòn, who said he doesn't know where his wife and kids are. He worries that they might have gone on another boat to somewhere.

That reminds me of a similar story Earl told of a friend of his from Quảng Ngãi who said his family was last seen getting on a boat at Phủ Tọ during the panic, while the friend came to Sài Gòn. And once his house was empty it was taken over by the new government. Earl said his friend and similar refugees are being taken care of by a Catholic priest here, and there's no information about his family.

Lòng complained of how slowly everything is decided at all levels in the new government, at least in his experience. He says no one person ever makes any decision, no matter how small. He was talking mostly about economic decisions. Everybody must agree unanimously, not just a majority, before a decision is made, and the process must be slow, with a lot of respectful discussion, to avoid conflicts or bad feelings later.

# 15

# ADJUSTING AND ADAPTING

**TUESDAY, MAY 27**

Keith noticed an announcement on a wall about hygiene, calling on Sài Gòn citizens to be kind to their protecting forces—the cadres and soldiers. "Always give them boiled water and cooked vegetables. Show them where the bad water is. Don't expose them to illness, especially plague and hemorrhagic fever. Show them how to use machines such as washing machines so they don't break them." The sign is addressed to Sài Gòn civilians, not a warning to the cadres and soldiers themselves that might have said, "Beware of Sài Gòn water and vegetables! Don't eat anything anyone gives you!" Such a positive attitude.

This morning we had a visit from Anh Yên, a man Keith met at Vạn Hạnh Buddhist University after Liberation who introduced him to another man, named Sáu Xíân Tín, who is the military head of Regions 3 and 10. Sáu Xíân Tín took quite a liking to Keith, which feels like an honor since he's probably one of only five or so people of his high position in the whole city.

Anh Yên told us another version of the story of the bộ đội soldier who ran over a child. He said the child was a twelve-year-old boy. After the accident, the soldier driving the truck talked to the boy's mother. She said the only terms for her were for the soldier to die. A crowd of local people disagreed and tried to convince her that another death was senseless, but she persisted. So the soldier chose to obey her wishes and stood still while an officer shot him dead. This story now has many versions, and I have no idea which, if any, is true.

We asked Anh Yên when he thought the political government would take over power from the temporary military government. He said they're already all in power—didn't we know? Then he named most of the various ministers of ministries, knowing them by heart. Madame Nguyễn Thị Bình is minister of education. Minister of health is Madame Hòa. He said the military sticks strictly to military/security affairs, while decisions on policy, administration, all forms of government, are made by the political Provisional Revolutionary Government. He made a distinction between the PRG and the "military government," while we thought they were two names for the same thing.

Today Paul met the director of UNICEF, who said he was told by whatever ministry he went to that it would be most useful if he would come back in "a few months" to negotiate about UNICEF offering aid. Therefore most of their team members are leaving for now, with one or two staying on. Those who are leaving hope to be back in a few months. UNICEF, of course, has a long history of giving aid, is international, and is trusted. Well, if the new government is rejecting, even temporarily, UNICEF aid, why would they care about our AFSC aid? The only reason I can think of is because it is from an anti-war American civilian program. We feel this is another sign that our chances of staying and doing anything useful look dimmer and dimmer. We still await a cable from AFSC in Philadelphia, but nothing yet. It seems like it's been a long time, now at the end of May.

We finally handed in our paperwork to the district office about renting a new flophouse, with no problems. Luckily it was the local man we'd met yesterday who came out and took the papers, not the more bureaucratic uniformed northern cadre we'd met at the same time. He asked for photocopies of our ID papers, and said that by the day after tomorrow they will have checked out the "security" of our new room, to make sure everything is aboveboard. That's what we want. We don't want to move into a confiscated building or one with any complications.

Before I turned in those papers, while I was standing in the office waiting for Keith to arrive, I was watching a funny-looking man in pointed black shoes and huge rose-colored sunglasses, holding some papers he apparently wanted processed, same as I did. For no particular reason, I thought to myself he might have formerly been a secret cop. Also in the office, sitting in a chair, was a young male cadre armed with a pistol, but in plain clothes, with plastic sandals and a red armband, apparently a sort of receptionist. I'd been looking at him and at the other guy, back and forth, wondering to myself how one might be able to tell a real cadre or bộ đội soldier from an impersonator.

Anh Yên had recently told us that Sáu Xíân Tín, by himself, caught eleven fully uniformed bộ đội soldier impersonators who had taken the uniforms from dead bộ đội soldiers. He caught them because people reported that they were demanding money from people, and once their names were investigated they proved to be names of dead people. Like Hoàng Lộc, there seem to be a lot of selfish and corrupt people here. Like everywhere, I guess.

In the evening we had a nice visit with Hồng Vân, Yến's niece, who is a medical student. She said many of her med school professors tried to but couldn't get out of Việt Nam in time. They're very rich and very miserable. She wonders what they'll do now. We chatted about medical care in general, and she mentioned that she's seen many cases of severe anemia caused by overuse of chloramphenicol. Doctors prescribe this for all sorts of ailments. Vietnamese tend to like to be given medicine at a doctor visit, and many later return for more medicine. This over-prescribing helped doctors make a lot of money. If the new government really changes this system, it will be very difficult to convince the patients that they don't need the pills and injections they believe in.

Did I mention before how our Yên Đổ main house owner left Việt Nam? He told his wife he was going to work, and he just never came back. When she looked for him, his friends said he went with a U.S. evacuation. The lease for our house, it turns out, is in his name only.

## WEDNESDAY, MAY 28

In the morning Anh Tuấn, who worked with the New Zealand Barclay Quakers, came to see us. Before Liberation we had written him a paper stating who the Barclay Quakers are, so people would know he didn't work with an American organization. English-speaking program, yes, but from New Zealand. He came back today to thank us for "easing his heart" and said he's very glad he stayed and is pleased with the revolution. He said he no longer has much money, but it doesn't matter because he did his last buying splurge on a wedding dress for his fiancé.

He said he has attended five weddings in the last five days. He said they took place, one, because at last there is peace, two, because it's cheaper now than before, and three, because no one knows what the future holds. He is very impressed by the sacrifices made by the bộ đội soldiers and the cadres, and says he feels inclined to follow their example.

We went to the Logistics office again today, to ask them if they would send our two cartons of copper washers up to Quảng Ngãi with our shipment. But we learned only that our shipment of medical supplies isn't going anywhere. Still. Again. Apparently they're going to open and check everything in the shipment. They're going to open all shipments that are stuck there, not just our fifty-four crates.

We stopped at the police station and got a promise for our bike to be returned tomorrow. Julie and I had a nice chat with two soldiers. We noticed a lot of signs for bikes for sale, though the price of gas for motorcycles and motorbikes is going up and up, so how can people be selling their bicycles? I guess some people need to. And theft of bikes is also increasing. Bikes are now being sold with receipts so owners can prove that the bikes are legally theirs, if anyone asks or if their bikes are stolen and recovered. I wonder, though, how anyone would know if the receipts are valid.

Keith and I visited Anh Phong and his family. We met him when we met Sáu Xíân Tín. They invited us to stay for lunch. They said Sáu Xíân Tín is busy these days because his wife just had a baby. They added, by way of explanation, that he came home for a secret visit last year from being with the National Liberation Front. This newborn baby is eighteen years younger than its only sibling.

Anh Phong pointed out that with South Việt Nam's old economic dependence on the U.S., if the U.S. had decided to cut their aid one day, the government would have collapsed and people would have starved and suffered. Well, they did cut aid one day, and the government did collapse. People have suffered.

## THURSDAY, MAY 29

This morning we went to the Foreign Ministry to try to begin proceedings to register as an official organization. As usual, the first visit produced a second. We were told to make a formal request in writing, and that as yet there is no form for or policy decision about the matter. We also want to find out the general rule for travel, and for taking our undeveloped Kodak color film out of the country. We've heard from several sources that undeveloped film is being confiscated at the airport. We would develop it here, and we do develop black-and-white film in Sài Gòn, but the chemicals for color are so old the color slides turn out almost black and white.

Then off to District Office Quận 1 to turn in our paperwork to rent a new room. Yes, again. That's the third quận we've been to now. We thought we had accomplished this at the phường level, but later were told we needed to do more. The phường level passed it on to the higher quận level, and apparently there are various quận levels, and it keeps being passed along. It's very hard to be patient with all the paperwork. The answer will supposedly come tomorrow afternoon.

Then I went to our friend Nayan Chanda's Reuters News office on the park near the Presidential Palace. I'd never been there before. Nayan covers political and economic changes and events. Recently he has been covering workers taking over ownership of the factories and businesses, pre-revolution anti-Thiệu organizations merging with PRG organizations, and other details of the organizing of the new government.*

The important changes in Việt Nam are not the spectacular ones. The country people are joyful the war is over so they can go back home. The same is true for all the people in refugee camps (many of whom were those same country people, of course). Sài Gòn surely has the greatest number of people against the new government, and considering that, things are going pretty well.

The most exciting part for me is people's attitudes. A friend of ours

---

* Nayan Chanda, journalist, remained in Sài Gòn after April 30, 1975, and documented what happened, as well as Vietnamese history, in his book *Brother Enemy: The War after the War* (New York: Harcourt Brace Jovanovich, 1986).

complained that things are too slow, too annoying, but grinned broadly at having no more salary, though he still has a job. Why would a newly poor rich person grin about his new condition? Well, it's new, he's just like everyone else, he's not going to die of it, there's peace, and he can travel and live without war. And a few days later he even began to receive a very small salary.

Today we saw Anh Quang, whose wife, Tiến, worked with AFSC. He is Cambodian and an electrical engineer, trained at the Soviet Institute of Technology in Cambodia. He said he encouraged his family to stay here when they were making plans to leave, before April 30. He told them life in France would be even harder than here. But he is very disappointed to see in his local phường district office that the same officials as in the old regime are back in their same positions somehow, and are stealing rice and exploiting people just as before. He doesn't know why they're there, and he's trying to figure out what to do about it.

Paul was present when Nayan Chanda was interviewing the Vietnamese manager (after the French manager left in the evacuation) of the Hotel Continental. The manager said the NVA soldiers staying there always come to the desk before they leave, and pay full price. They never complain or drink or fight or have prostitutes, and he's very impressed. They're very polite and always make a point of stopping to talk with the workers in the hall and at the desk, the fifty-five- and sixty-five-year-old "boys," as the Americans and French called them. But the other day several of the soldiers told him they found the drug addicts and prostitutes who were hanging out in the hotel unpleasant and that they bothered them. The soldiers said they were requesting, not ordering, that if the manager wished to follow up on it, he could visit a local administrative office and that the local soldiers would help move the people to somewhere else.

The first time the manager went to an office to see about it, he couldn't meet the right people for a few days. The soldiers didn't say a word during those days. Later he did find help moving the people, and now the situation is much more pleasant for all.

The manager also told Nayan and Paul that there's now a workers' committee in charge of running the hotel. Once it was formed, he offered his resignation but was asked to stay on. A hotel janitor is the main secretary of the committee. None of the workers is known to be active politically, but of course they notice the difference between these soldiers staying in the hotel now and some hotel occupants of the past. The manager told Nayan about the French and English staying there back in 1954, laughing and brawling, drunk and sleeping with prostitutes. He's very pleased with the change he sees now.

Today's newspaper reads, "We oppose reactionary depraved arts and letters. Patriotic songs and culture are being printed. We do not burn books, because we are a civilized people. These are the words of a representative of the government." This notice follows misunderstandings of the last few days when over-zealous students have been collecting books and burning them publicly. Some have been collecting and burning all books written in English. The government is trying to stop this, according to the newspaper.

The author with flags of the Democratic Republic of Việt Nam (North) and the
Provisional Revolutionary Government (South), 1975

Claudia Krich and Keith Brinton, 1975

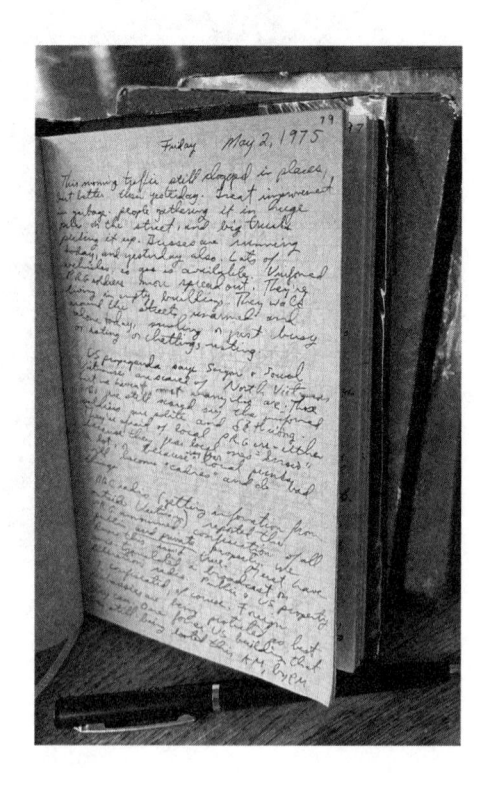

The author's Sài Gòn journals, 1975

Chị Mai (Nguyễn Thị Mai, Khưu Thị Hồng), 1974

**RICHARD WARREN THOMPSON**
( 1949 - 1973 )
I have always known
That at last I would
Take this road, but yesterday
I did not think that it would be today.

Narihira, 9th c.

Ngày đã biết tôi sẽ không ở lại
Tôi sẽ đi dù chưa biết đi đâu
Nhưng tôi sẽ tiếc thương trần gian mãi mãi
Vì nơi đây tôi sống dù vui sầu.

Bùi-Giáng.

Rick Thompson's memorial card, 1973

Chị Mai's false identity card on display at the Vietnamese Women's Museum in Hà Nội, February 2023

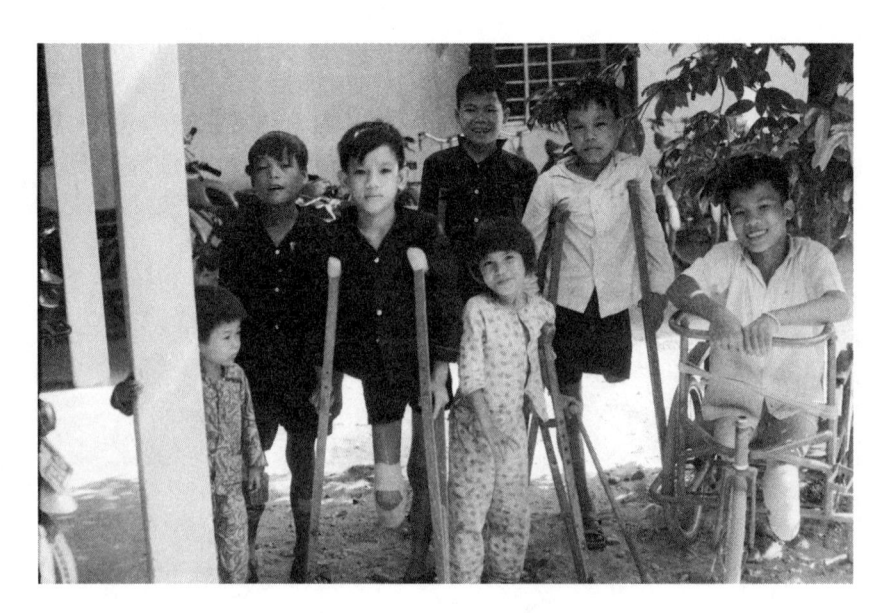

Young patients at the Quảng Ngãi AFSC physical rehabilitation center, 1973

*Left to right*: Claudia Krich, Paul Quinn-Judge, Julie Forsythe, Keith Brinton, and Sophie Quinn-Judge, May 1975

A North Vietnamese tank on the street in front of Vạn Hạnh Buddhist University in Sài Gòn, where students collected weapons, ammunition, and uniforms and issued new identity cards to South Vietnamese soldiers, April 30, 1975

Pedestrians and vehicles in Sài Gòn navigate around a South Vietnamese tank that had knocked down a power pole, April 30, 1975

A huge traffic jam in Sài Gòn the day after Liberation, May 1, 1975

Children play in the wreckage of a small spotter plane that crashed on a Sài Gòn street, May 5, 1975

South Vietnamese soldiers shed their uniforms, turned in their weapons, and registered as unarmed civilians at Vạn Hạnh Buddhist University in Sài Gòn, April 30, 1975

North Vietnamese soldiers arrive in Sài Gòn, May 1, 1975. (Courtesy of Paul Quinn-Judge)

A National Liberation Front cadre, center, walks with two friends in Sài Gòn, April 30, 1975. (Courtesy of Sophie Quinn-Judge)

Young local men chat with North Vietnamese soldiers camped in a park in front of the Presidential Palace in Sài Gòn. The soldiers' laundry hangs in the background, May 1, 1975. (Courtesy of Paul Quinn-Judge)

*Left to right*: Claudia Krich, Julie Forsythe, and Sophie Quinn-Judge with North Vietnamese soldiers in Sài Gòn, May 1975. (Courtesy of Paul Quinn-Judge)

The crowd at the victory celebration at the Presidential Palace included North Vietnamese soldiers, May 15, 1975

Dignitaries at the three-day victory celebration at the Presidential Palace in Sài Gòn. Left to right: Lê Đức Thọ, Huỳnh Tấn Phát, Madame Nguyễn Thị Bình, Văn Tiến Dũng, and Nguyễn Văn Linh, May 15, 1975. (Courtesy of Paul Quinn-Judge)

Women and girls at a meeting in Sài Gòn a few days after Liberation crowd around the author to ask her questions about the new government, May 3, 1975

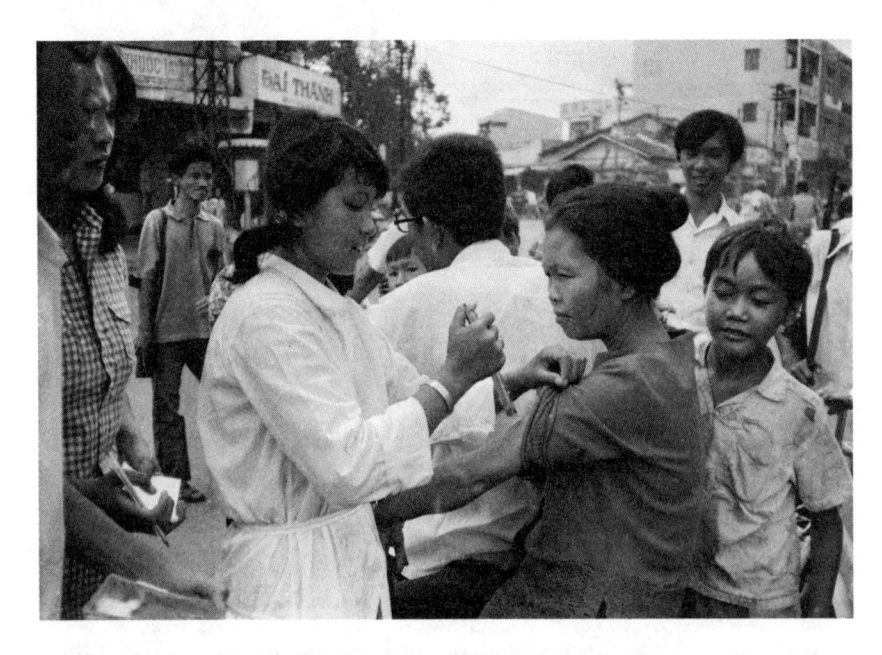

People line up at a medical roadblock in Sài Gòn for immunizations to protect them from cholera, plague, and typhoid, May 30, 1975. (Courtesy of Julia Forsythe)

The author's language tutor Yến and her children, 1974

Bà Hai, left, and Chị Mai pose with borrowed North Vietnamese helmets, June 14, 1975

The author's language tutor Dung, center, with her sister Thu and her husband, Ba Minh, June 15, 1975

The author writes in her journal on a Sài Gòn street corner, 1975

# 16

# IMMUNIZATIONS AND RED TAPE

**FRIDAY, MAY 30**

This morning as we walked to the main house we ran into a medical roadblock. They were stopping all pedestrians and all two- and three-wheeled traffic (most of the traffic these days) and giving everyone immunizations. There were teams of four people working together. One used cotton dipped in alcohol to clean the arm, another used an alcohol swab to clean the injection gun and then give the shot, a third pressed cotton on the arm after the shot, and the fourth sat with other people at a table writing down names and issuing proof of vaccination certificates.

There is no needle. It's a shot gun—safe and sanitary. It's one shot that immunizes against three things—cholera, plague, and typhoid. They injected young and old alike, but only with the person's permission. From what I saw, everyone was eager to get the shots. We were told that almost everyone is getting immunized for the first time. We saw young children, old people, rich women in áo dàis, poor people pedaling cyclos in ragged shirts. They all grinned at this peculiar roadblock. There were lots of kids enjoying the show.

One guy motioned to me and Keith that we could get shots too, but we said we'd already gotten ours. But Sophie and Julie did get them, out of curiosity. They said they could hardly feel them. They suggested maybe everyone was getting children's doses, or maybe the shot gun makes it not painful, or both.

Giving the shots are medical workers from the nearby Tan Định Clinic, where there is a special immunization room. They told us they can immunize about six thousand people per day with these roadblocks. There are twelve roadblocks throughout the city. One person working there was an NLF guerrilla nurse who gave shots so fast I could barely snap a photograph.

This particular health education is easy, because even though country people like we know in Quảng Ngãi believe in and use northern medicine, with herbs, compresses, and my favorite drink made of beetles, they also have great faith in Western medicine, pills and especially injections. And it certainly looks like people here in Sài Gòn feel the same way.

Earlier this week we tried, again, to send two short cables right from the post office itself. The person at the counter said she would try but did not think it would work. But they do seem to have gotten through, because today's highlight was our receipt of a cable direct from AFSC in Philadelphia. The cable said a draft agreement with AFSC and the "Mini Sante" (Ministry of Health, probably) was written in Paris and carried to Việt Nam back on May 9. It said to contact the Ministry of Health and someone named Trần Thị Minh in the Foreign Ministry. Per the agreement, the government would pay salaries at our rehab center, would assume ownership of all AFSC supplies, and AFSC would continue to send in supplies and would make visits every six months. Also, the present team (us!) would be able to travel to Quảng Ngãi now for a visit. Sounds great, wonderful, amazing, but we see no signs here that this will really happen. Nothing's moving, including us, or about to move, as far as we can tell. Paul went to talk to his friend Phương Nam and told him about our cable. His unofficial response was that "if we were able to receive it," then there probably is in fact such a document, and it's being honored. Well, we can hope.

Keith went down to the quận level district office about our room to rent, and believe it or not, the "issue" was kicked to the Immigration Office, where I'll try again tomorrow. This is getting more and more absurd. I thought the old government had red tape. But I guess we can be glad this one has only one speed for everyone. Slow, very slow. At least bribes apparently don't hurry it up any. But tomorrow we must move out of our present flophouse.

Bad news. At noon Paul went to see Lòng, who had delivered the message to his colleague's wife. When Paul went to his house he discovered it has been confiscated, and the reason given was that the owner had fled to France. But in fact the owner has lived in France for decades. Paul went to Lòng's office and found out Lòng has been arrested for resisting giving up the house and everything in it. Apparently the district office head is corrupt and wants it. Father Chân Tín was contacted and is now trying to act as an intermediary and straighten it out, but it will probably be as slow as everything else, and in the meantime, where will Lòng and his family live?

The news on the radio today says USAID workers are leaving Laos in large numbers. I think they've already left Cambodia. Meanwhile, the U.S. government expresses great concern about the remains of two thousand or so deceased Americans in Việt Nam they say they want to recover. Is this an attempt by the American government to come back? Is it a way to pressure Việt Nam? And imagine how many remains of Vietnamese have yet to be recovered, many more than two thousand. But right now there are too many other things that must be done before anyone can mount a large-scale search for victims' remains.

Nayan was late for dinner with us because he was writing a story about the government telling the people of Sài Gòn "Please don't swindle the cadres." Nayan drew a contrast between the extreme apprehension the Sài Gòn population felt before the change of government, fearing their throats would be cut and that they would be tortured, and the present state, where if anyone should be apprehensive and worried it's the cadres themselves.

There was also a letter to the editor in the paper today suggesting that upstairs tenants should stop throwing their trash out their windows for the downstairs tenants to clean up. Very appropriate, from our own personal observations.

## SATURDAY, MAY 31

In the morning I won a battle for the flophouse. Me versus a mighty, low-level civil servant. I got up very early and rode the bicycle (which I forgot to say earlier we finally got back) to the end of Võ Tánh Street to the now-familiar Immigration Office. There were long lines of Chinese nationals waiting very politely to register. Another day when we were here there were a lot of French and Indian people, and they were very rude, pushing and shoving. Today it was calm and orderly.

I walked up to a young woman in high heels outside the gate to show her my papers and to find out where to line up to go in. Julie had met a very unhelpful young woman here, and I hoped this wasn't the same person. I told her I needed someone to approve our moving to a new room. She said this could be difficult but she'd look into it and that I should come back later. Of course come back later. This might definitely be the same young woman Julie had to deal with.

I also asked her if we need permission now to go to Biên Hòa for the day. She said everyone needs permission for everything. I asked where to get permission, and she said, "There," pointing to the office, "but later."

So I went back downtown to the Foreign Ministry to submit our two more important written requests there. One was a fairly long paper describing AFSC and asking to be officially registered as an organization. The other was a shorter paper requesting to be able to send cables on our credit card, payment collect. We have learned that the only and proper way to achieve anything is by writing "đơns," or written requests. These were our attempts at writing formal, correct đơns.

I had luck in the Foreign Ministry. I went into a room and met an older cadre. The older ones are invariably the nicest people, and the newly revolutionary students the worst. He asked me where we were registered, where we are staying, and other details. I told him about the cable we received from AFSC in Philadelphia. He asked how long we plan to stay, and I told him we plan to leave pretty soon. He asked if we had applied for exit visas and if we needed any help with that.

While talking about sending cables, he asked if we have a radio transmitter in our house, and said that if we do we must declare it. I said we don't, and we never paid or bribed anyone to use theirs, either. I meant that as a joke! He responded very seriously that now there is no more bribe-paying. It's impressive how they always answer seriously, and start from first base. He didn't take it for granted that because I spoke of bribes I was against them. He listened to me carefully and asked relevant questions, and I really should have known better than to joke.

Then I went back to the Immigration Office. The same young woman at the gate told me she had asked other people and had learned that no one could help me, period. I told her that that wasn't really an answer. She said they've never had a request like this before, and they hadn't yet set any policy about it. I said I didn't imagine they *would* meet this problem often, since there aren't many foreigners left, and among them, few would be moving and even fewer would think to ask the government's permission first, as we'd been told to do. I asked her where else to go to receive a higher decision, since saying they hadn't decided on the decision wasn't a decision, as far as I was concerned. I told her I would just wait outside the gate until someone in the office who was free could help me. She said, "I'm as good as all the cadres here, and anything I say is exactly what they'll say too." I just dạ̣d (a polite sound a bit like a short, low grunt that acknowledges that the other person is talking) and stood waiting.

She went to a young male cadre guarding the gate and relayed the story of my obstinacy. He came over and parroted her words, though much more politely. I asked him if I could just throw away the papers and move in, since there was no precedent. He said he didn't know. So I waited some more, knowing that at the very moment Keith was moving us out of our old flophouse. So here I was asking if it was okay to move into the new place, which we are about to do regardless.

Then miraculously a man in his mid-twenties or so, in a white shirt (not dressed like a cadre), with a southern accent, walked toward the office from outside the gate and came over to me. He said, "I saw you waiting here and wanted to see if I could help you. What do you need?" He was gentle and pleasant, the way the cadres generally are. I showed him my paper and began to tell my story. He motioned for me to come back inside, but the young woman came over and elbowed me back, saying to him, "I explained everything to her several times already." He turned to her abruptly and told her, politely, to be quiet and go away, which she unwillingly did.

Then he said to me, "It was nice of you to make this request and to try to do everything correctly, but in fact it is not necessary. You can just move into your new room." I thanked him and asked if I need a signed paper. He said I don't. So then I asked if he would tell me his name so I could say he said so, if anyone asked. His name is Anh Đừng. I don't know his rank or who he is, but I'm going with this verdict. I realize now that we shouldn't have pursued this so hard for so long, or at all. Relieved, and declaring it over, I went home quickly on the bicycle.

At home I met Keith and Paul and Julie, who had just moved us out of our old place. They had had quite a time with the landlord—a dirty old dealer if ever there was one. Why isn't *his* house confiscated, but Anh Lòng's house is? He tried to cheat on the water and electricity bills up to the last minute. But we're out of there now, thank goodness.

We enjoyed sharing our stories of the morning's events with each other. Then from 2 to 4 p.m. we had a team meeting about budget. I proposed cutting our cook's salary in half. Half is still more than the cadres get, more than what a middle-level civil servant gets, and the Mennonite Central Committee's employees now get nothing.

After the meeting Keith and I went to the new flophouse to take over some bedding, and at 4:30 p.m. we went off on the bicycle, dressed up, me in an áo dài sitting side-saddle behind him, in the rain, under a big dirty poncho, on a forty-five-minute (bike!) ride to Anh Quang and Chị Tiến's house for dinner. The dinner was very delicious, a Cambodian dish of some red fruits and meat mixed together.

Anh Quang told us some of his relatives just came from Cambodia and said the new government is herding people, often at gunpoint, forcing them out of the cities en masse, whether they have somewhere to go or not. He said Vietnamese people, even if raised or even born in Cambodia, are being deported to Việt Nam. People are forced to leave all possessions behind. His relatives walked for a month to reach Sài Gòn.*

---

* When Khmer Rouge troops entered Phnom Penh in April 1975, the Khmer Communist Party leadership group under Pol Pot ordered the urban population to be relocated to rural areas. The objective was to create a primitive, cashless rural economy and a totalitarian society to prepare for a military confrontation with the Vietnamese, who were regarded officially as Cambodia's "hereditary enemies." The Pol Pot leadership ordered the expulsion of 200,000 ethnic Vietnamese who had been long-time residents of Cambodia, refused any negotiations on defining the border with Việt Nam, and launched artillery attacks on Vietnamese villages. The Vietnamese government

It was a stimulating evening, and when we got home we found three long letters from Tom, who has been in Đà Nẵng all this time. He says they have many other doctors there, and they pay him a small salary and give him room and board. He doesn't know when he might be able to travel to join us in Sài Gòn.

## SUNDAY, JUNE 1

It's June! We would have left Việt Nam already, been replaced, maybe been in Europe or Nepal relaxing and sightseeing. I'm getting a bit homesick, mostly due, I think, to a degree of boredom. Today we finished up our team meeting quickly. Good meeting. Budget created. As we're running out of money, our cook Bà Hai's salary will be lowered to 20,000 đồng. She was sad to hear it, of course, but then she saw that we too will be cutting our eating money, so she felt better.

We all now agree there's really no excuse for us to return to Quảng Ngãi. At this point we've been away a long time and our house is gone, so it's not "going home" and it's not really "business" or "visiting." So what would it be?

The high point of the day was going downtown on the bus to spend 250 đồng each to see an excellent film about Nguyễn Văn Trỗi and two short documentaries, one on the U.S. bombing of Hà Nội in 1972, the other on the fight for Quảng Trị, also in 1972. As usual, the footage was impressive and vivid, of U.S. bombers being shot down, and of dazed, wounded pilots being treated, then later brought in front of news cameras. Huge areas of housing in Hà Nội destroyed, and teams of people quickly cleaning up, rebuilding. Quảng Trị looked flattened. Then scenes of rebuilding Quảng Trị from scratch.

The Nguyễn Văn Trỗi film was with actors, not a documentary. Just as U.S. films about Vietnamese use Chinese or Japanese actors to play

---

invaded Cambodia in December 1978 to remove the Pol Pot regime, which was forced to flee from Phnom Penh in January 1979. Sources: Ben Kiernan, *How Pol Pot Came to Power* (London: Verso, 1985), 329–61; and Gareth Porter, "Vietnamese Policy and the Indochina Crisis," in David W. P. Elliott, ed., *The Third Indochina Crisis* (Boulder, Colorado: Westview Press), 93–110.

Vietnamese, this film had an East German playing the one American. He was terrible. Trỗi was an electrician and a revolutionary. His attempt to kill U.S. defense secretary Robert McNamara led to his fame and his death by execution. He planted explosives over the Công Lý bridge in Sài Gòn. He bicycled to the bridge with the explosives hidden in the bottom of a table fan and the fan in a radio case on his bike. Other electricians from his shop helped in the plot. But it was discovered, and he was arrested and beaten. He and his wife, Qùynh, had gotten married only nineteen days before he was arrested. She was imprisoned too for a time, and there she received her own political education and became radicalized. He would never admit to being guilty or a traitor.

In the movie, things I've read about and heard described were re-enacted. Tortures and beatings, prisoners in different cells calling to each other, sisterhood and revolutionary ideas created in prison. People just like I've met in the Quảng Ngãi Hospital women's prison ward who had wounds or seizures from torture. There have been hundreds, maybe thousands of individual firsthand reports of torture.

After some months in jail and a national furor over his arrest, the American and South Vietnamese authorities decided to kill Trỗi, despite even an offer from the Venezuelan guerrillas to release an American general if the U.S. would release Trỗi. In the end they killed him by firing squad, while he shouted, "Long live Việt Nam!" He was charismatic and is considered a "martyr of the revolution." He proclaimed himself a patriotic Vietnamese, for liberation of the country, for throwing off the Americans, and he is credited with speeding the end of the war by his actions and the publicity surrounding his arrest and execution.

*(See "Meeting General Giáp's Son" on page 238.)*

# 17

## "ROCKETS" AND NEWS

**MONDAY, JUNE 2**

This morning our friend Nayan Chanda was at our house early, taking notes for a story from Tom's letters. Great story, and a nice scoop for Nayan. He said UPI and AP will get "rockets" for this. Rockets, we learned, are what news agencies' home offices send their reporters when a rival agency, in Nayan's case Reuters, gets a story faster than they do. "Why didn't *you* send in that story?" say the editors back home. Nayan was very pleased we're letting him see Tom's letters for a story, and we are equally pleased to get Tom's news and information published through Nayan.

Next came our MCC friends Earl and Hiro and Max, just to visit, and also to find out if we have found a way of sending out cables. They're having the same problems we are. We let them read Tom's letters. When they left, I went over to our wonderfully close new flophouse to spend a half hour typing Tom's letters.

When I returned for lunch, Trần Văn An was there. What a surprise! He is from Quảng Ngãi and worked with AFSC before I got to Việt Nam. Keith knew him from then, and I know him through Keith. Trần Văn An has been living here in Sài Gòn for a while, but he didn't know we were here too, until recently. He thought we had left the country.

He's gone back to Quảng Ngãi for a brief visit since Liberation and visited with some of our staff members. Some still have hope the Quakers will return to "save" them, with money. Of course it doesn't look like that will happen, but hopefully the future will be brighter in other ways for them. At least they won't be drafted and they won't have to live in refugee housing, and hopefully they won't have to pay bribes.

Trần Văn An is studying for a degree in a medical field. At first he thought a degree wouldn't be needed in the new government, but he decided he was wrong, so he is enrolled in a program in Sài Gòn. When he finishes the program, the school will assign him where to work, where he's most needed. He says he understands that, but he doesn't like not being able to decide that for himself.

He said the bus trip north was exhilarating. Streets were crammed with buses, and buses were jammed with people. People in the buses were singing and clapping and laughing and gay. Unfortunately, he saw dead people on the way, some apparently accidentally hit by inattentive bus drivers, and others probably shot.

He said that at our rehab center, our close friend and receptionist Chị Mai is usually off at meetings, sometimes for several days. She's on the Central Province Committee, made up of only about seventeen people in the whole province. He said that Bích, our chief medical assistant practitioner, has been given a lower position at the center and seemed sad. I asked if there is a real danger of starvation in Quảng Ngãi now. He doesn't know, but while he was there a rice crop was being harvested.

Trần Văn An told us that for the last three years he has been learning about the Liberation cause but was too scared to actually act, even when a close friend of his went over. Now he's a founding member of a local People's Revolutionary Committee in his area here in Sài Gòn and works at a security office like the ones we've visited.

Meanwhile, no surprise that the cables we tried to send didn't get through. Apparently the post office workers have been told it's their responsibility to stop them and to not try to "sneak" them through. Funny, because we were sort of trying to sneak them through, I guess, and we got caught.

## TUESDAY, JUNE 3

Today I found Trần Văn An's house in Sài Gòn after a hot, tiring bike ride. I brought some letters to him and his wife, Vân, that we hope they can deliver to Quảng Ngãi for us if they go again. They had been planning to go back to live in their house there, but it was destroyed, dismantled actually. It happened three days *before* Liberation. A phế binh, or "war invalid," stood in front of it and sold it to the highest bidder, and for only 15,000 đồng. The buyer then took all the furniture, the roofing, everything he could—doors, windows—and disappeared to somewhere in the countryside. The neighbors did not intervene, because the phế binh was armed. The neighbors tried to get help, but the local police and ARVN soldiers were nowhere to be found, and they might not have helped anyway, since this was just three days before Liberation. At that point the old government was already in major disarray.

Meanwhile, Vân's parents had returned to Đà Nẵng, where they found people had stolen cement and lots of building materials from their store there. She strongly recommends that we foreigners not travel by road to Quảng Ngãi. She says there are a lot of very young guerrillas who haven't been in the revolution long and are exuberant and inadequately trained, who might just shoot an American.

She also told a strange story of three Westerners hiding in the jungles of Bình Tuy who refuse to come out and supposedly don't know what's going on outside their jungle hideout. She didn't know what nationality, just Westerners. She said officials know about them now and are urging them to come out.

We rarely hear airplanes, but rumor has it a plane is leaving Sài Gòn in two days. Some journalists are being requested to leave, apparently to thin out their ranks. We'll try to send some letters out with someone who is leaving.

## WEDNESDAY, JUNE 4

First thing in the morning I went down to the Ministry of Foreign Affairs to check for responses to our two requests, one about registering AFSC as an official organization, and the other about being able to send cables to the U.S., collect. A man in the outer office was very nice and concerned, but he said our RCS credit cards definitely have no value now, and we will have to pay cash to send cables. This of course was not the answer we hoped for, but it was clear he wished he could help. Then I asked him about registering our organization. He sent me to the consul room in the back. The door was closed and a sign said "Miễn mở cửa," which I misread as "You're invited to open the door," so I went in. But a man in the room looked surprised when I walked right in, and I realized I was thinking of "mời" ("You're welcome to"), not "miễn." A more accurate translation of the sign was more like "Kindly refrain from opening door" or "Request not open door." Whoops. But he just laughed as I apologized, so I laughed too.

Soon a different man, in dark-rimmed glasses, asked me in excellent English how he could help. I gave him my AFSC business card and he said, "Quakers. Aren't you the group Madame Bình invited to a reception? I received a lot of your literature when I was studying in New York. Aren't you an anti-war group?" Yes and yes. I never learned how he came to be studying in New York or how exactly he had heard of us.

He said he thought we, as a non-international organization (despite including volunteers from various countries), should register at the... Immigration Office. I said that the Immigration Office had told us to register here, at the Ministry of Foreign Affairs. I said we had already turned in our papers there but had had no success in getting registered. So he went to talk to his colleague in the outer office, who went into another office, presumably to look up our papers. They decided that since we were in their office now we could continue there, and they will look over our papers, and we should return in three days. Of course.

He said that if we need to meet with the Ministry of Health, to come to him first for an introduction to the minister of health. I apologized and said we'd already been to the Ministry of Health (perhaps against protocol), and he said it was okay, only to please give his office copies of whatever we gave them. We agreed.

I left and met up with Keith, and we went to the post office. We had learned that though we couldn't send a cable to the U.S., we could send one to Laos. So we cabled our friends and former AFSC Quảng Ngãi team members, Eryl and Lou Kubicka, who are working there in Laos, and asked them to forward our cable to the main office in Philadelphia.

Then I went to Nayan's office to read his story on Tom and to try to call the Associated Press office, but I couldn't get through on the phone. So I took the bicycle down to the AP office to see journalist George Esper, who is leaving the country soon. We chatted about him leaving. He seemed depressed, so much so that he surprised me. He said the government is making him leave and won't even let him delay for two weeks to get ready. I told him we will be leaving soon too, though we don't know when. In our conversation he learned for the first time that Quakers (AFSC) are not missionaries, and that AFSC has never planned to run our program in Quảng Ngãi forever. AFSC establishes programs around the world and then works to turn them over to local leadership and control.

He thought he was being kicked out because of some articles he wrote under the general heading "They've broken the spirit of Sài Gòn." I asked him what they were about. "Well," he said, "soldiers are sleeping in people's houses, on their floors. Would you like U.S. Marines sleeping on *your* floor? Wouldn't that break your spirit?" I could see how the government might not have liked those articles. As for me, I don't think I'd mind having PRG soldiers sleeping in my house, from what I've seen of them. They don't seem to need much attention. I told him stories of our Vietnamese friends who now have less money but actually seem happier, but he seems to have only met sad, rich people.

In the afternoon Yến's niece Thanh Bình came to visit and told us about an uncle, Yến's second-eldest brother, who just reappeared after being gone for the last thirty years. Thanh Bình, who is twenty, had never met him. In fact, Thanh Bình only met Yến herself for the first time in 1966, because until then Yến had spent twelve years in the north. I had no idea.

He is Thanh Bình's father's younger brother. Her father was the oldest and was tortured to death by the ARVN forces, who, she said, cut out his liver. She said Yến is child number six, so he is her older brother. I asked Thanh Bình if she was shy when she first met him, having never met her uncle before. She said no, not at all. Like Rip Van Winkle, he reappeared and picked up right where he left off, and she felt like she'd always known him.

Then the newly arrived brother himself walked in. He's about forty-five to fifty years old, a cadre officer. He came in and warmly shook my hand, then took off his sandals and pulled a pistol out of his belt and carefully put it on top of a high cabinet. He sat down next to me and said he'd heard of us Quakers and was happy to meet us. He's now working in Lộc Ninh but is trying to be moved closer to the ancestral family home of Biên Hòa, where Yến and their extended family live.

He asked me the name of the chairperson of AFSC. It took me a moment to remember Louis Schneider, which he quickly memorized and used a few minutes later in the conversation. Impressive. He asked if the Quakers have close connections with the American Communists. No. I said that the Quakers, AFSC, are neutral, anti-war, pro-peace, pro-humanity. He asked if Louis Schneider was a Republican or a Democrat. Well, I said, I didn't really know, but I would guess Democrat. He was warm and wonderful like the rest of the family. What a nice family!

## THURSDAY, JUNE 5

It's time to share something I've been worrying about. I've been thinking I might be pregnant again, and it would be awfully soon after my dangerous six-month miscarriage in late December. I was left with a uterine infection and very high titer levels for German measles. I don't know if I still have the infection, and I don't know if the high titer levels are good and protective for another pregnancy, or bad and dangerous. My guess is that pregnancy is not a good idea this soon.

So today I went downtown to the French Grall Hospital to find out about pregnancy tests and abortions. The receptionist said I'm a little too early and to come back on Monday. How can four days make a difference? Or is it just the "come back later" routine? I didn't ask her about abortions. I'll have to ask the doctor.

I went by the post office and bought two souvenir stamps, then saw the woman who used to send our telexes, Chị Phung, who is now operating telephones. I asked her if she is happy. She said, predictably of course, she is very happy. I asked if her family members are all well. (That's common courtesy and asked whenever you greet someone.) She told me she's getting 10,000 đồng a month, and she actually seemed to be grinning about that low salary for some reason. Then she added that she just got married on May 27.

She showed me photos of her wedding and said she and her husband are both thirty-six years old, he one month older. She said that being the same age is very good luck, because they'll either be very rich or very poor, but they'll be together. They met at the telex office, where he works at night. He is a teacher in the mornings. They had their engagement party a year ago, but waited for peace and for a particularly auspicious day for the wedding. In one photo she showed me two of her brothers, who just came back from the north after they went there thirty years ago. She said in all her life she never knew about them. Now they're over forty-five years old. They were welcomed back by her family as if they'd never left. Each one of these separation and reunion stories gives me goosebumps.

She has two big diamond rings and a simple gold band. The gold band is from the engagement party, is inexpensive, and she can never sell it, while the diamonds could be sold if necessary. Here's a woman I would have sworn would have left with the Americans, and look at her now! Reconciliation, peace, reuniting with relatives, one country.

In the afternoon I visited Phương-Hằng's sisters Thúy and Bình, and Thúy sounded very negative. She said the cadres in her neighborhood are rude and undisciplined, the newspapers too simplistic, and people don't have money to buy rice. Bình was in a better mood than Thúy, though she too has valid complaints. She says some less qualified people are being kept on at businesses rather than more qualified ones, apparently because they have friends in the right places.

In the evening we visited with Đoàn Mộng Ngô, husband of Xuân Lan, who worked with Keith when AFSC had a child daycare center in Quảng Ngãi in the old days. We chatted, and he said the PRG was caught a bit by surprise and hadn't actually wanted to take over the whole country at once. They wanted it bit by bit, province by province, as was happening at first, so they could do a good job of organizing in each area, each province. I remember my tutor Dung being shocked a few weeks before Liberation when people were predicting a revolution before the end of April. She said the PRG organization just wasn't ready yet; it couldn't go that fast. But then the old government abandoned city after city and province after province even before the National Liberation Front or the North Vietnamese Army had arrived, so they had to hurry to catch up.

Đoàn Mộng Ngô said no one in his family is working, and they plan to return to Huế, sending their two sons first to start a garden. The son of Đoàn Mộng Ngô's younger brother has married the daughter of Trường Chinh,* an important and well-known North Vietnamese Communist Party leader and philosopher. So now there's a very famous person in the family.

I'm in the newspaper today, in bold print, in the second issue of *Phụ Nữ* ("Woman"). It's an article about the photo display I attended on Tự Do Street, where I was asked to write in the guest book. They reprinted what I had written in English in that guest book, translated into Vietnamese, plus my signature. I had written that I was an American who was proud to be defeated so Việt Nam could have peace. I had also written, in Vietnamese, "Hoàn hô cách mạng muôn năm!" ("Hurray and long live the revolution!") This is rather embarrassing.

News is dribbling in that there's more trouble in Cambodia and that many more people are being forced to leave their homes and to leave the cities. Many are attempting to cross the border into Việt Nam for their own safety. The PRG is trying, in addition to its other responsibilities, to respond to the needs of all the Cambodian refugees flooding into Sài Gòn.

## FRIDAY, JUNE 6

It's the sixth anniversary of the establishment of the Provisional Revolutionary Government in 1969.† We spent the morning writing formal requests

---

* Trường Chinh held many government positions and was the Communist Party's general secretary from 1941 to 1956, when after the excesses of the Land Reform he was demoted to a Politburo member. He saw himself as the "builder and commander" of the party when it officially came out from underground in 1951. After 1956 he retained considerable political influence as a member of the party secretariat and head of the Nguyễn Ái Quốc Party School for a number of years. From 1981 to 1987 he was the third president of Việt Nam. President Hồ Chí Minh outranked him in the government structure, but Trường Chinh wielded considerable power.

† The Provisional Revolutionary Government was recognized as the government of South Việt Nam by most Communist countries even before it took control of South Việt

to submit today to the Ministry of Foreign Affairs. In the afternoon dear Yến came to visit and gave us four tickets to a cultural performance in the evening. She's tired and hoarse and beautiful. She's very busy working in the Quận 7 district office, in Gia Định. She sleeps there at the office, and she and the other cadres are often called upon to settle civil strife, like two wives of a husband fighting each other, or street fights. Many people won't let anyone but a real cadre decide their cases, she laughed. She is now thinking of putting her two older boys in a boarding school where they'll be taught "correctly," but the rest of the family objects. She said to come tell her before we leave the country, so we can have a day of fun at the house in Biên Hòa.

In the evening we went to the cultural performance, billed as a "comedy play," at the Trần Hưng Đạo Theater. It was a fun fantasy tale of a king who falls in love with a portrait of a woman and makes her become his wife. But she will never laugh, because she misses her peasant husband. Eventually, the peasant husband comes to see the king to beg for her return, and he brings huge onions as a gift. The peasant husband wins her back from the king, and the moral of the story seemed to be that onion sellers attract women more than kings.

The audience was bộ đội soldiers, and what looked to me like not rich people. My only gripe is Vietnamese audiences sit way forward in their seats, so I can never see well.

We turned in our requests for exit visas earlier today.

## SATURDAY, JUNE 7

Today Keith and Paul and I went to the Ministry of Foreign Affairs with all our đơn (forms, official requests). The ministry official assured us there will be continuing good relations between Việt Nam and AFSC.

Then to the post office to try to cable Philadelphia directly, despite the

---

Nam. It had signed the 1973 Paris Peace Agreement as an independent entity, separate from both North and South Việt Nam. It became the official provisional government of South Việt Nam, called the Republic of South Việt Nam, on April 30, 1975. On July 2, 1976, the Republic of South Việt Nam and the northern Democratic Republic of Việt Nam merged to form the Socialist Republic of Việt Nam.

price, which we expect to be 5,000 đồng. We feel we need to be in direct contact if at all possible, making this a priority even though we're running low on cash, so we hope this one cable helps clarify things. We're not sure the letters we gave George Esper made it out of the airport, where everyone is being checked. We were able to send that one cable to Laos, but we did not get acknowledgment of receipt at the other end.

This evening, at Mạnh Tường's request, I began working on correcting a Spanish version of a bulletin being produced by some local students. It had a lot of errors. I didn't know anyone here knew or studied Spanish, and I can't imagine who will be needing to read a document in Spanish, but I majored in Spanish literature in college and I'm happy to help.

Then Julie and Keith and Sophie and I went out for . . . beer! A special treat. We came back in the rain, happy and relaxed. Good night.

# 18

# A CULTURE OF VISITING

**SUNDAY, JUNE 8**

This afternoon, Sophie and I took the bicycle, Sophie pedaling and me in back, and we went to see the Mennonites. Earl is not ready to give up on his wish to return to Quảng Ngãi, hoping his wife, Pat, and their kids can join him. Max and Jim seem to agree with us that they have no more role here. I told them Keith and I have officially applied to leave. As we pedaled home, Sophie said she felt Max and Jim and maybe Earl would change their minds soon and also decide to leave. Keith and I haven't told anyone I might be pregnant, but for us that certainly factors into our decision to want to leave soon, with so many unknowns about the maybe pregnancy.

We had dinner and good conversation with Mạnh Tường and his friend Nghĩa. I told Mạnh Tường about the Spanish translation work and that the translator had not been quite up to the task. He said the translator had learned Spanish, or as much Spanish as he knew, in a seminary in Đà Lạt.

**MONDAY, JUNE 9**

This morning Keith and I passed the same display area where they had the women's photo series before. Now they have a display of a collection of artifacts from a museum in Hà Nội proving that Emperor Hùng Vương was real. It seems that previously they had only "traditional" proof, which I think means stories passed down, but now they have archaeological proof. A sign says this is a free exhibit "for the people."

We didn't go in, because we were on a quest. When we were at the Ministry of Foreign Affairs two days ago, we had run into Paul's friend Dr. Lộc, whom he'd met in Paris, and he had told us he knew of a place where we could get our Kodachrome color film processed in fresh, strong chemicals, so we followed up on that lead today. But despite our efforts, we failed.

I spent several hours at the Grall Hospital today again, trying unsuccessfully to get a pregnancy test. It wasn't clear why they wouldn't do it, while they did do some blood tests. It just felt like a runaround. I'm pretty sure I am pregnant. This is scary, so soon, even though of course I want to be, just not now. I don't want to lose another pregnancy to German measles or to the fact that I weigh ninety-eight pounds or less right now, or to typhoid fever or cholera or yellow fever or dengue or malaria or anything else. Well, the good part is it appears that I *can* get pregnant, despite what happened in December.

Phương-Hằng's sisters Bình and Thúy came to dinner. Thúy was full of stories and enthusiasm, much to our surprise. Some were bad stories. One was of a friend of hers in Tuy Hòa whose husband was a nice and honest policeman in the old government who, when they called for former police to step forward, did so fearlessly, knowing he had been honest and honorable. But he was arrested and killed.

She also told stories of the looting in Nha Trang before Liberation and what happened to an older sister in their family, who lives there. She had been at home when looters shot off the lock on the front door. She ran upstairs to hide. The first looters took the nicest things, and the next wave took the next-best things, and so on. For two full days she hid in the attic. She said some other people were able to give the looting ARVN soldiers money so they wouldn't take everything in their houses. But that only worked if it was a lot of money, and if there were men in the house who were more threatening to the looters than she could be. As a single woman, she felt she didn't dare come out from where she was hiding.

She said that looters burned to ashes the Nha Trang market, which had been one of the largest and most beautiful in the country. They shot into houses, murdered fleeing people for their money, destroyed buildings and vehicles. The ARVN soldiers and local police were fleeing (or doing the looting), so they weren't controlling the looting, and the PRG hadn't arrived yet. She said that when it was over, her sister owned nothing but a pair of flip-flops.

One funny story was about some Indians trying to leave Việt Nam on a boat to Phú Quốc before Liberation. They misheard an announcement. They thought the announcement said the boat was going ngoại quốc, meaning out of the country. They decided to throw their heavy bags of Vietnamese money into the water, believing they were leaving the country and that the money would have no value abroad. So when the boat landed at Phú Quốc (not ngoại quốc) they had no money and had to beg for food and housing.

She said many Indian storekeepers in Nha Trang lost everything before Liberation. One man has only his shorts and T-shirt, and is selling charcoal on the street. Many of these people were merchants and used to have a lot of money and lovely stores. She didn't know if they were targeted for being Indian, or if all store owners suffered similarly.

Thúy said the road from Sài Gòn to Nha Trang is still a mess and not totally safe from ex-ARVN bandits, but buses nonetheless run all night, a new freedom.

## TUESDAY, JUNE 10

Early in the morning I went back to the Grall Hospital to again try to find out if I'm pregnant. I was, predictably, told to come back later. Even though this hospital is run by the French, I guess it functions at typical Vietnamese bureaucratic speed. They did give me some test results from my last visit and a formal paper in stilted English about titer levels, and from reading it, it isn't clear at all what my situation is.

Next, another visit to the Ministry of Foreign Affairs. Last week we heard undeveloped film is being confiscated at the airport, so we came back here to find out if it's true and if it is, to see if we could get special permission to take ours out with us. We spoke to a woman there who said they'll try to help us, and then she, of course, told us to come back. So we're coming back today. We found the same woman and she told us the plan. She said we can give the ministry office our film and they will send it to Paris for developing, and then they'll give it back to us at the airport before we leave. She said that "anti-revolutionaries" have all their film thrown away, but we are not like those people, and they will do this favor for us. She said to bring in our film right away, and also our identity papers, and they'll approve them so we won't have any trouble at the airport.

Paul told us about something he witnessed on Sunday. Two guys on two motorcycles were yelling, asking some bộ đội soldiers to jump onto the back seats so they could chase a thief who had just stolen something and injured someone and was getting away on a Honda. The soldiers got on their motorcycles as requested, and two other Saigonese on their own motorcycles also went off chasing the thief. He didn't know if they caught him. It's just a great image, and impossible to imagine anyone taking old Sài Gòn police on their motorcycles like that, for that, or them being willing to get on at all.

We went home and went to bed late and had slept for about an hour when someone knocking at the door woke us up. Some other residents in the compound were asking us to help with the landlady, who was sick. We got up quickly and went to the door of her room to see what was going on. The people asked us to get a car and to contact the bộ đội soldiers for help. How were we supposed to get a car? How were we supposed to contact the soldiers? And why us? They're the Vietnamese! We were of no help. Is this the result of years of American colonialism having trained them to continue to look to Americans for solutions?

# 19

# YES, I AM

**WEDNESDAY, JUNE 11**

I slept late, feeling poorly after the episode with the sick landlady at midnight. At noon we were finally able to meet with the French doctor at Grall Hospital. Yes, I'm pregnant. Not intentionally. The bad news is that I still have a serious uterine infection, nearly six months later, and that's not good for this pregnancy. But he is hesitant to treat it with drugs because . . . I'm pregnant! I think this is called a lose/lose situation. He could not guarantee that this will be a healthy or even a full-term pregnancy.

Because of those worries, and my general lack of nutrition and my low weight, I asked for an abortion. He was utterly horrified. He told me off in French and very accented English. He almost kicked us out of the room. We left, and on the way out it dawned on us. The Grall Hospital is not just French but also Catholic, and that must be why he won't do an abortion. And we don't know of any other hospital or clinic we trust in Sài Gòn right now where I might get one.

The doctor did prescribe some tests, at a cost of 5,000 đồng, and he says the tests will surely indicate the need for antibiotics, and probably a stronger dose than I took right after the miscarriage, and he himself is "hesitant" to suggest I take them. So why have the tests done since no matter what they show, he won't let me get an abortion? What hubris, what arrogance, to put his opinion about abortion over the best medical treatment for me. Might I be able to get an abortion outside Việt Nam when we leave? Will it be in time? If not, is it better to have the infection, or the powerful antibiotics? I was miserable, angry, and scared as we left the doctor's office.

We learned that evening that the landlady's nephew is a doctor, and he came to see her. She apparently has high blood pressure but she is now fine.

## THURSDAY, JUNE 12

Not a very productive day. We went back to the Ministry of Foreign Affairs with our film, but the right people weren't there and we did not leave our undeveloped film rolls. We also didn't learn anything new about possible flights out of the country.

In the evening I went to visit Yến's nieces Hồng Vân and Hồng Quân. They told me that the other day Yến's son Em Tu, age seven, complained, "I want to go to boarding school where there's freedom. I don't like it at home where it's like American and puppet rule!" Their cousin Thắng, also seven years old, just arrived from Hà Nội by plane. His mother is Yến's older sister. He made a comment the other day too. He said something about such and such a situation was "like living with Nixon." How funny!

These kids' families have been involved in the political changes and have no doubt discussed politics at home. Of course that isn't true of all families. And all over the city, civil servants and former ARVN officers are beginning government-required re-education sessions. Some, the highest-level ones, go away together for a longer time. Lower ones just study during the day and go home at night, or work half a day and study half a day and go home at night. The newspaper is full of notices about studying, and loudspeaker trucks go around blaring out information.

This city now reminds me of a lot of other big cities, but not of old Sài Gòn. Now it's calm and it's quiet here. You can hear crickets and birds and voices. There are lots of bicycles but not many cars and motorcycles. You can ride a bike without having to breathe thick exhaust smoke from a vehicle in front of you.

Tom writes that the Đà Nẵng Hospital, which is an existing, pre-Liberation public civilian hospital, is much worse than the nice new medical centers cadres have recently set up. He said a doctor from the north walked into a pediatric ward in the Đà Nẵng Hospital and found three patients to a bed plus three relatives, and said, "Is this the best the Americans could do in thirty years?"

## FRIDAY, JUNE 13

This morning we went to ask about Bill at the security headquarters in Gia Định where we were interviewed. People there seemed to easily understand why we were asking, not just for ourselves, but that we feel knowing what's going on with Bill is our responsibility, especially to AFSC and to COR in the U.S. We made an appointment to come back tomorrow morning to see a cadre named Nam Thành, specifically about Bill. We used the Lambretta to get here, first time in a long time, and it was so much faster than a bike.

We had a special guest for lunch, our friend Anh Thứ from Quảng Ngãi. He's a cadre currently working in nearby Gia Định, coincidentally in the very same place as Anh Dũng, a neighbor in our old flophouse compound before Liberation.

I remember the night we met Anh Dũng, a very small man whose real name, Anh Thứ told us today, is Năm Hùng. We thought he was very anti-Communist, especially because he used terms like Việt Cộng. Now, it turns out, he is chairman and Anh Thứ is secretary of their local security station. Thứ said five of the leaders of their teaching group are from Quảng Ngãi. He joked that Quảng Ngãi is invading Sài Gòn.

Anh Thứ talked about his present work, learning and teaching the policies of the revolution. He said he loves to learn, and he is leading study practice sessions. Later on he wants to go to the countryside to teach people to read and write. His own mother is illiterate, and he wants to teach her. Right now two hundred former soldiers are studying at his center, and he leads a study group of about ten people. He said that he has learned not to lecture, but rather to let them talk and participate, because that's the only way they don't fall asleep.

Sometimes they tell him they don't like to be called "puppet soldiers," as they're called not only by the government but sometimes by their own families. He tells them that when they act like part of the revolution, people will stop calling them puppet soldiers.

He says that the former ARVN soldiers studying with him are beginning to see that the cadres suffer more than they do, and always have. He described a Sài Gòn woman he met who "demanded" the new government give her rice. She had a gold bracelet, a TV, car, electric fan, but no rice. He suggested she sell her bracelet before looking for handouts. Then she could do buying and selling in the market. She said she could never do that. With that attitude, he said, she should be forced to study more about the new society so she will learn how to participate.

He said the soldiers who were drafted (and that's most of his day students, who study during the day and go home at night) sometimes say they're guiltless, because they didn't choose to be soldiers. But, he says, they must study to learn about those who made them do it, and the effects of the war on their country. Some soldier students burst into tears when they learned about the history of the war. Many are uninformed and unaware, especially those whose families had paid bribes to get them safe posts in Sài Gòn.

Today's newspaper has three large photos of U.S. and ARVN treatment of prisoners. One is a man, Nguyễn Văn Lém, on the street with his hands tied behind his back, about to be shot in the head with a pistol, by South Vietnamese general Nguyễn Ngọc Loan.* Another is of a line of prisoners being led by ropes around their necks. The third is of a prisoner hanging upside down. These are familiar photos to us Americans, since they've been in the American press, but they've been mostly censored in South Việt Nam until now, so they are brand-new to most Saigonese.

Anh Thứ told a story about Bác Hồ ("Uncle" Hồ Chí Minh). At some point the General Assembly of North Việt Nam felt he was smoking

---

* The photograph of Nguyễn Văn Lém, on a Sài Gòn street with his hands tied behind his back, being shot in the head by South Vietnamese general Nguyễn Ngọc Loan, turned many Americans against the war in Việt Nam. The photo was taken by Eddie Adams of the Associated Press and was published in many newspapers, including the *New York Times*.

cigarettes too much, so they asked him to quit smoking. He complied, or tried to, but it soon became evident that his work was lower quality as a result, and his health even seemed to decline rather than improve. So the General Assembly asked him to ignore their previous plea and return to smoking. But he said the rescinding of such an order could only come from the people themselves, not the Assembly. The people must have agreed to rescind the order, because Hồ smoked like a chimney, I believe right until he died.

When we first met and were chatting with Nam Thành, the cadre we have an appointment with to find out about Bill, I asked him why he, a cadre, smoked so much. He asked me not to bring up so embarrassing a topic, so I tried to smooth it over by adding, "But Bác Hồ always smoked too, so this means you are like him." That saved face for both of us.

# 20

# CHỊ MAI, YẾN, AND DUNG

**SATURDAY, JUNE 14**

Early Saturday morning before we had a chance to go see cadre Nam Thành about Bill, Sophie came to our door with news of a very special visitor at the main house. Who? Chị Mai! We quickly went over to the main house. What a wonderful surprise! She came with five other people from Quảng Ngãi, only one of whom we know. They are an official delegation on a mission from Quảng Ngãi to Sài Gòn, to see us and to get that shipment of rehab center supplies to Quảng Ngãi.

After lots of hugs and happy tears, we got some tea for everyone and sat down and caught up. How she got here without legs is a story in itself. She's missing one leg above the knee and one below. Traveling by bus, or really by any vehicle, presents a serious bathroom problem in this country, and coming from Quảng Ngãi, some 330 miles away on bad roads, is a very long ride. If there were American-style toilets along the way that would be one thing, but there aren't, and there often aren't even squat toilets. In fact, she said there weren't any toilets at all on her bus trip. She said the bus stopped periodically, and the only option was to squat behind a tree or building, and if there's one thing Chị Mai cannot do, it's squat. To prevent this problem, she said she had not eaten or drunk anything at all for several days before the trip. And, she said, it worked.

It was very exciting and wonderful to see Chị Mai and everyone else. They had come to the house early, at about 7 a.m., and we talked together for a lively hour. Then Keith and I had to go off briefly to our appointment to ask about Bill. The visit didn't prove useful since we didn't learn anything new from Nam Thành, except that he promised that Bill would be released in the future. So we came right back to the house to be with our special visitors.

Anh Aí is the chairman, or "party officer," for the city of Quảng Ngãi. Anh Lùng is the cadre in charge of Thủ Lộ District. Chị Mai is the administrator at the rehab center, as we had hoped. We learned that Cảnh, our former employee who stole from us and whom Bill then hired, has come back to work at the rehab center, and Anh Lùng will have the task of dealing with him and his situation when he gets back to Quảng Ngãi after this trip. I wasn't clear why Cảnh hadn't been fired again already. Anh Lùng had been a public bus driver between Sài Gòn and Huệ for seven years, but also at the same time was secretly a Liberation soldier. Another member of the delegation, Anh Quang, told a bit of his own history, including how he argued with his only surviving sister, after two of their siblings had already been killed in the war, about which one of them should go off to be a soldier. He won, and she stayed home to help the family. When I asked Anh Quang why people want to be soldiers, especially in a family like his that has already lost so much, he was quiet. Finally, he said, "To defend our country of course."

I've been visiting a lot with Chị Mai and loving every minute of it. She has a very droll sense of humor and is almost always upbeat. *(For Chị Mai's story, see "My Story" on page 225.)* She's sharing information we never knew. We've learned from her that her real name is Khưu Thị Hồng. She also has another alias—Thủy. Is that why she named me Thu Thủy when I first came? She said her brother and her brother-in-law just got out of Côn Sơn Prison and are very weak. Two other brothers have been killed. Her father fought against the French and was later arrested and killed by the South Vietnamese government.

Chị Mai caught us up with life at the Trung Tâm Chỉnh Hình Quaker, the real name for our Quảng Ngãi physical rehabilitation center. Chị Mai says it's been announced that our TTCH workers, and regular hospital workers, will receive salaries, starting soon, of up to 40,000 đồng! I was astonished. Why so much? She doesn't understand it either, while cadres still receive no salaries. But of course it hasn't happened yet. She also says the TTCH will become a prosthetics training center. That's great, since we have excellent prosthetists there already.

Anh Quang told me that bộ đội soldiers in Quảng Ngãi used to receive only 350 đồng per month, enough to buy soap and toothpaste and not much else. Then it was 50 đồng per day plus rice. Then, just before Liberation, 75 đồng per day plus rice. Now 100 đồng per day plus rice, and he said if you eat collectively, that's enough for good food.

Some people who quit at our center during the panic right before Liberation now want to come back, but they're not being automatically allowed back by the new administrators. Apparently our physical therapy assistant Tuyết is being welcomed back because she had to quit because of her seven kids and her lazy husband, not because of politics. And our physical therapy assistant Nguyệt, Cảnh's wife, asked to return when no one was yet being paid, before news that there would be salaries, so she was accepted back.

Chị Bốn, another of our physical therapy assistants in Quảng Ngãi, is still very sick, not in body but in spirit. Chị Mai says she became hysterical on Liberation day in Quảng Ngãi, and cried about her missing leg when she saw the cadres walking along with packs on their backs. Now she's home with her family.

Chị Mai told us that our charming young friend Bùi Ngọc Hương, who lived in America for seven years, is dead. She said that on March 21 he went, at Bill's request, to Phú Thọ to get to Sài Gòn by boat, to bring back money for the COR children's program. He was not trying to flee. For three days he couldn't get on a boat. On March 23, Phú Thọ was liberated. Hương stood out, being tall from American milk and nutrition, and having long hair and wearing hippie American clothes. Children were screaming, "He's an American, an American!" He supposedly told them he was Vietnamese and that he worked for the Americans in Quảng Ngãi, probably thinking they'd know he meant the Quakers, not the American government. He couldn't speak clearly partly because of his rusty Vietnamese and partly because of the major facial deformity from the war injury that got him into COR's care in the first place. Chị Mai said she was told he had said he was injured by Communists, but more likely that was made up later by the embarrassed and ashamed local guerrillas who killed him. They shot him, saying he worked for the CIA. So horribly sad. The news hit me hard. I feel deeply sorry, and sorry for his U.S. foster family and his Quảng Ngãi grandmother, whom he had not been able to locate.

The COR program in Quảng Ngãi is now disbanded. Chị Mai told us that after Liberation, when food was hard to get, she helped by feeding the kids . . . Quaker Oats. That was her own joke, Quaker Oats! How she knows about Quaker Oats, I have no idea.

Our house was somewhat "pickpocketed," as she put it. A man we don't know was, for some reason, staying in our house. When he was there alone, young people would come by and say they knew Keith or another one of us, and that they had left something at the house. He would let them in, and then they would steal things.

Some other things in our house have been taken, even by our employees, but most of our and AFSC's possessions are still there. We discussed with Chị Mai how to distribute everything that is left. She said the landlord had publicly claimed that everything was his, which is of course a lie, so we wrote a statement about our belongings for Chị Mai to use as documentation. We asked her to not let the landlord have anything at all, not even our electrical fixtures. Similarly, Earl's and Pat's Quảng Ngãi landlord is in jail, and the landlady, his wife, is claiming all of Earl's and Pat's belongings.

The delegation's main mission here is to cut loose the shipment of supplies for the rehab center that we've been trying to get released. They got a lot done today, on a Saturday, more than we could ever hope to achieve any day. They are, after all, an official delegation. Keith and I went with them to the Ministry of Health, Ministry of the Interior, the Ban Quân Quản Military Administration office, Logistics, and more.

They went to several offices to negotiate to buy (cheap—150 đồng per liter as opposed to 1,000 đồng) government gas, and succeeded even though the appropriate authorities were already off work for the day.

Keith and I asked Bà Hai if we could invite the whole delegation of six to dinner tonight. As expected, she said it would be no problem at all, so we invited them, and then we left briefly to check in with Yến about her invitation to visit with her and her family tomorrow in Biên Hòa.

In the evening Bà Hai made quite a feast for our guests and us, and it was, as always, delicious. We had a moment tonight just like when Yến told Bà Hai of her true political leanings. This time it was Chị Mai telling Bà Hai that she, Chị Mai, has actually secretly been with the PRG for a long time. Bà Hai reacted well, used to this sort of revelation by now of course. Then they had a great idea. They borrowed a couple of helmets from the cadres in the delegation and we took their picture to create a nice souvenir.

## SUNDAY, JUNE 15

We went to Yến's office at 6:30 a.m. to travel to her home together, but she wasn't there. We were told by someone in her office that she had gone to Biên Hòa already. That was surprising, but we accepted it and went to Biên Hòa by ourselves. At 10 a.m. we were at her house when we learned she was waiting for us back at her office in Sài Gòn. The person who had told us she was gone had been completely wrong. Another visit with Yến at her lovely home in Biên Hòa cut short! We didn't see her until 1 p.m., when she came out by bus. It was very disappointing because soon after that we had to leave. I was sad to have so little time with her, and thought about how we had missed her husband's death day anniversary entirely, though of course not intentionally. This visit wasn't intentionally short either, of course.

We enjoyed the time we had though, and I learned to make fried noodles. I also learned that the crispy rice that sticks to the bottom of the pan is the kids' favorite part of the rice. It's a bit like toast, since it's toasted rice. Their family has an electric rice cooker.

While there, we took a walk with Yến's three adorable boys and the young nephew who had recently arrived from the north. We got stopped in the next ấp or local checkpoint and questioned. Who were we, what were we doing, who were the kids? What were they doing with us? It was a tiny office in the countryside with nice but very cautious and diligent local officials. They took notes from Keith's ID paper, and then gave us a pass to travel in their hamlet. We didn't mind it. Better careful than not, surely, from their point of view.

We returned to Sài Gòn and went to Dung's and Ba Minh's house for dinner. What a feast! What a great food day! Dung made us a meal that was fabulous, plentiful, amazing. We all sat on the floor around carefully arranged newspaper pages that served as a long tablecloth. Guests included all of us, Mạnh Tường, Nghĩa, and Mennonites Earl, Max, Jim, and Hiro. There was a sort of crab salad first, and it was out of this world delicious. Then a second course of a chicken and bean casserole and hunks of pork and rice. Then papayas. Then cigarettes (which Julie and Keith took, to be polite) and of course tea. And there were toothpicks at the end of the meal, as there always are. After dinner Dung and Ba Minh recited poetry and sang, and we each took our turn singing songs. It was a lovely evening, memorable, heart-warming, intimate, lighthearted and also at times somber and serious. Lots of emotions, and such delicious food.

Unfortunately, I needed to use the bathroom while we were there. I don't remember this ever happening to me before, since I, like everyone else, always do everything I can to avoid it. But I was getting uncomfortable, so with embarrassment I asked Dung to let me use their bathroom, using the most vague word I could think of for "bathroom." She led me to it. The room was the size of a fairly large closet, with a tile floor and a shower head and a drain. Nothing else. Luckily, that worked for me. It did leave me wondering where other needs are met, though. As I said, we never use a bathroom at a private home. Just don't.

## MONDAY, JUNE 16

Today was spent largely trying, one more time, to free up our shipment. It seems so sensible that they should release it, but no, at least not yet. We tried, the delegation tried, but it's still stuck at the docks.

We've heard that Bill is okay and will probably remain detained for a while, but then will be released. No details. Similarly, we've heard Duy is finally back in Quảng Ngãi, but we don't have any updates on how he is faring. We didn't see him before he left, but that's fine.

## TUESDAY, JUNE 17

Disappointing day. In the morning we went to Logistics yet again and saw the truck our Quảng Ngãi delegation already rented, with tractor attached, parked in the big warehouse building, ready and waiting, but they still wouldn't release the shipment to them. The Logistics political officer asked Anh Ái to go with him to the Ministry of Health to discuss it. Yesterday, he and we met only a lower official, who thought it could be released but didn't have the authority to make it happen. So this was a second try, an attempt to see a higher official. But it ended up that a committee at the Ministry of Health had already met for two hours, without Anh Ái or any of us present to plead our case, and they had decided their verdict is still no.

Their principle, they explained to Anh Ái later, was to have a committee do a survey of *all* the rehab centers in the country and their needs, and then to divide the goods fairly. Anh Ái answered that many of the goods in our shipment are only usable in Quảng Ngãi, like the special material for our head prosthetist Quy's rubber experiments to improve crutch tips. Quy has been trying for a while to find a way to make crutch tips that will last as long as ones we regularly imported from Hong Kong. Anh Ái and we pointed out that this delegation had spent a lot of money and effort coming down to Sài Gòn, and they had already rented the truck. But the answer is still NO. We went home very depressed, met Chị Mai there, who was determined to try yet again.

# 21

# THE FUTURE

**WEDNESDAY, JUNE 18**

It's my birthday. I'm twenty-seven today. This morning we magically received two cables from Philadelphia. One read: "Psipsi (numbering system for our cables) received your omicron (number again) agree Team return Phila stop Team set date for departure stop AFSC continues to feel direct return States important please acknowledge." This was in response to Keith's and my request to not go straight back to the U.S. and to instead return via Nepal. So the answer is no.

The other cable asked us to sign contracts with the Vietnamese government and to send an AFSC shopping list to the Goulds in Hong Kong. The Goulds would have replaced us in March as directors if they had been able to get visas and if other things hadn't interrupted the plan. As for us somehow convincing the government to sign contracts, well, reality keeps interfering.

I wonder if they're actually sending the Goulds to Hong Kong just to do a buying trip. That doesn't make sense since we have no permission to import anything, and of course we can't even get our big shipment that's already in the country released and sent north. We're obviously not getting the message through to our home office.

We cabled back the shortest answer we could come up with: "Teitel pipi received psipsi team." That was the minimum length for a cable, and the minimum price.

We've just been told that the shipment was supposedly held up by just one man who wouldn't agree to send it, but we don't know who he is or why he would do this. How can this possibly be true in this world of committees being formed to consider everything and anything, where everyone has to come to agreement? I guess he couldn't be convinced.

I spent the morning writing letters, waiting for Chị Mai and Anh Ái and the others to appear. We were beginning to think they weren't coming when they finally showed up at about 10:30 a.m. Their spirits were improved, despite being unable to take *any* of the shipment supplies with them. Even Chị Mai had not been able to persuade the people at the dock. In fact, we learned that the delegation sent the truck with the tractor to Quảng Ngãi already. They've decided to collect cars instead of the supplies in the shipment, the Mennonites' Toyota and our Subaru, which we just gave them, though unfortunately it needs work. Better than going back completely empty-handed.

After lunch we bade farewell and watched their attempts to get our Subaru going, and eventually they towed it. Then we headed home and were greeted with a fine surprise. There was a fantastic birthday dinner the others had prepared, of roast chicken! Delicious! Julie had tried to buy me a new gecko, but the store had closed down. So sweet of her to remember I wished I had grabbed my small ceramic gecko and had put it in my pocket when we left Quảng Ngãi with almost nothing at all. That gecko reminded me of the little live ones that were always on our walls and ceilings and were hugely entertaining and cute.

Paul had tried to buy wine for our little party, but that store was also closed. Keith bought me a Pilot Pen tip and a new Liberation (black-and-white checkered) scarf. Then we all went out for beer, and it's been way too much food and drink, and I'm sleepy. Happy birthday to me.

Yesterday I visited the nearby Tan Định medical clinic to give its staff some photos I took of people who work there who we met when they were giving immunization injections on the street. I talked a few minutes with a man who was in the photos and who has worked there for quite a few years. He said the Tân Định clinic will become a hospital, and other nearby clinics will handle lighter medical problems. He said, to my surprise, there's no lack of doctors, there are even extra doctors. They have two or three doctors at their clinic twenty-four hours a day. Most of their doctors come from the nearby neighborhood, and one is from the north, newly arrived to help. Most of the newly arrived PRG doctors aren't assigned to specific medical clinics now; they move around. He doesn't know if that will change.

Right now the government is selling their clinic the medicines it needs at a very low price, and patients in turn pay the clinic a low price for these medicines. In future, he says, medicine as well as medical care will all be free. He's very excited about the changes. All their staff members are receiving salaries of up to 30,000 đồng. Compared to before, the lower-paid staff now receive more, and the highest-paid receive less.

Phương-Hằng's sister Bình visited yesterday and as usual had some interesting tales to tell. She'll be doing three days of study and practice (re-education). She says the longest anyone in Sài Gòn is doing it seems to be one month, as opposed to three months in Quảng Ngãi and Tuy Hòa. Apparently it's up to local authorities to decide. She and other journalist friends have some serious criticisms of the new Sài Gòn newspaper. The headlines are dull, the articles are backwards (names, details first, substance later), and the photos aren't very good. She has an advanced journalism degree. In fact, she was in the first graduating class of a four-year journalism program at Vạn Hạnh University. I hope her own talents can be incorporated into the new journalism to improve it, but she may well not want to put up with how amateur it is. Right now they have, for some reason, hired four times as many new journalists as there used to be, which, she said, helps explain the low quality.

She told us a story of two Vietnamese who became refugees on Guam. This was before Liberation. One was her eighteen-year-old female cousin, the other a twenty-five-year-old man. The two arrived separately on Guam, where they said they encountered extreme hostility from the U.S. soldiers, who called her a whore, spat on him, and had no sympathy for either of them. And they found the prices of everything there impossible. They didn't like the housing or anything else about the situation, and somehow they both managed to get back to Sài Gòn on a plane that had brought refugees there and was returning to Sài Gòn to evacuate more people. They told Bình that the U.S. soldiers had said that the Vietnamese who left in the evacuation were the corrupt ones, and they didn't like them. I doubt that opinion was widespread, but that was their experience.

Today our saga of the Kodachrome film almost came to an end. I again went to the Ministry of Foreign Affairs to find Paul's friend Dr. Lộc, who had tried to direct us to a good place to develop our film in Sài Gòn. He wasn't there, but Anh Cương, the cadre who had studied in New York, greeted us and said, "Are you here about your film?" "Yes."

He said, "Well then, would you like to talk to Anh Đòi? He's the head of the consulate." I said yes. In seconds a man walked in from another room and said one sentence to me, in Vietnamese: "When the plane goes, you can take it." I was so surprised, I thought he must be referring to something else. But no, apparently he wasn't. He said, "Since you were willing to let us have the film to be developed in France, we trust you and will let you take it with you." I thanked him and we shook hands.

We chatted a bit more, and then before leaving I asked him if he would be kind enough to put the permission in writing, so I could hand someone at the airport a document in case I wasn't believed. He said he will notify the airport when the time comes for our flight. I really feel the need to get something in writing, and I don't know why he (politely) refused, but even just having a decision feels good. Now I can stop coming here, for one thing. We have to hope it really works out.

Nayan Chanda told us he has been asked by the government to stay, which he is pleased about. I read his Reuters clip, which reported about a meeting between government officials and representatives of various Catholic organizations. The goal of the meeting was to promote a spirit of unity, and for the government to confirm that it guarantees religious freedom.

The Việt Nam National Bank is now open, stating it is eager to help establish a strong economy that can export. It welcomes foreign money and aid that will help agriculture and industry and will enable the use of the country's raw materials.

The re-education program is continuing. The government is still lenient toward soldiers who haven't reported in yet. Sound trucks around the city urge them to report. Checkpoints on streets check papers. At completion of re-education, participants receive a certificate. They study four main topics: One, "Why the American war?" Second, "Role and responsibilities of the Vietnamese puppets." Third, "The future: Soldiers should show good faith by now going home and helping the country produce." And fourth, "Reassurance of absolutely no revenge."

## MONDAY, JUNE 23

Yesterday morning we went to the PRG bookshop around the corner for an hour or so. When I came home I read magazines, ate lunch, and slept in the hot afternoon. Then Dick Hughes, founder of the Shoeshine Boys Project for street children, dropped in to visit. Dick asked us to contact the Christopher Reynolds Foundation in New York City, as well as his own foundation in the U.S., when we leave, to explain the situation here and to tell them not to be upset if their aid isn't a top priority for the PRG. We of course are familiar with that issue!*

This morning I took lots of pictures, out on the Lambretta. I went to an excellent exhibit in the Cercle Sportif, formerly a very exclusive foreigners'

---

* The Shoeshine Boys Project, founded by American Dick Hughes in 1968, helped Vietnamese children who lived on the streets and survived by shining shoes, guarding motorbikes, selling lottery tickets, and similar activities. After the first home for them was established at Phạm Ngũ Lão Street, Hughes turned the effort over to a group of Vietnamese students who opened additional homes and created a volunteer management committee, while he focused on fundraising. Funded almost exclusively by donations from media interviews Hughes did, the Shoeshine Boys Project also received some grants from Oxfam-England and the Christopher Reynolds Foundation. The project had eight homes, six in Sài Gòn and two in Đà Nẵng, and included two farms and a technical training center, rendering assistance to some 2,500 children by the war's end. Hughes remained in South Việt Nam for fifteen months after reunification on April 30, 1975, during which time some of the children were reunited with their families, others went into centers for street children set up by the new government, and a number returned to the streets. Hughes returned home in August 1976 and has stayed involved in postwar healing efforts, including participation in a small nonprofit addressing the issue of victims of Agent Orange (www.loosecannons.us). See also Gloria Emerson,

club near the Presidential Palace, famous for its pool, horseback riding, tennis, and fencing events. Now the pool and tennis courts don't seem to be in use and there are no horses, and the inside of the building has been turned into a beautiful exhibition hall. Many of the paintings are the works of soldiers who have been in battles and have lived in liberated areas for a long time. Many are patriotic posters in strong colors, and all the pictures are scenes of reality, nothing abstract.

In the afternoon I felt pretty bad. "Afternoon sickness," I guess. I stayed in bed. I worried. I worry that this pregnancy will end badly like the last one. I worry that the infection will do this baby harm if it is born full-term. And worse, what if it isn't born full-term? When I have time to worry, that's what I do now.

No recent news from Tom. No answer yet to our latest avalanche of in-country cables. It's getting worrisome now. Is he okay? *(See "Letter from Đà Nẵng" on page 227.)*

We've been going to the Foreign Office every day to check the passenger list. We went today, and it hasn't changed from yesterday. Our names are still on what it refers to as "the third flight." Since enough passengers are posted to fill the seats on two planes already, we assume the very next flight list will contain our names. So, we're beginning to think we will soon be leaving.

### TUESDAY, JUNE 24

Today is our third wedding anniversary. We decided to change our daily schedule, not that there's really much of a daily schedule. Instead of eating lunch at home, we took a bus downtown and walked around. I hate to admit that I'm having trouble with some foods, even with the delicious food Bà Hai makes, and I don't want her to know that. So instead of eating, we strolled around in the hot sun. Lots of people are selling things right on

---

"Until They Found Shelter, Their Home Was Danang's Streets," *New York Times*, August 4, 1970; Richard Hughes, "Learning from the Vietnamese—and Giving," *New York Times*, December 4, 1976.

the streets, but we don't see a lot of people buying. Of course we're not the only ones running low on money.

A new service industry we noticed today on the sidewalk is wristwatch polishing. This is done with a little machine with little wheels and cleaning fluid and costs 100 đồng. People seem to be getting watches polished and are then trying to sell them. I wonder if there are any soldiers and cadres left who have not already bought themselves new watches.

It started to rain as we were walking around, which was a relief but also quite a downpour, so we went into a movie theater (as usual) to wait out the rain. We were watching the movie, Keith eating a snack, when he felt what he thought was a little cat nuzzling under his arm. He tried to pet it but it left. Then it came back, and this time he realized it was actually a rat. That was a new experience! We changed seats. I don't remember the movie.

## WEDNESDAY, JUNE 25

We cabled Philly, via the Kubickas in Laos, saying we are on a passenger list to get on an Air France flight out of the country, but we don't yet know exactly when we can leave, and that our inability to leave right away is involuntary. We also wrote, "Quảng Ngãi delegation including Chị Mai specific purpose release stored shipment completely unsuccessful," so they'll know we've been trying, and failing, to get the shipment released.

Julie got news from Tom that he hopes to stay and work in Đà Nẵng for six months. This makes her own decision about leaving or staying more difficult. In the evening we visited at our house with Mạnh Tường and his girlfriend, the ballerina Quỳnh Chi, along with Dung and Ba Minh. I love visiting with them and will miss them all very much.

Mạnh Tường told us a story of a historic figure whose name I didn't catch, who was so opposed to the French occupation that he said he wouldn't even walk on the French-built streets of Sài Gòn. He was an important and influential man, so the French tried to bribe him to change his attitude. The French governor general of Sài Gòn visited him with a large sum of money and praised and tried to flatter him, saying that in his own country, France, they had a custom of giving prizes to people of merit or talent. He said this as he tried to hand him the money. The historic figure, so the story goes, responded by saying thank you, but in his country, in Việt Nam, they also had a custom, which was "People with self-respect do not take money from people like you."

## THURSDAY, JUNE 26

Today we got a new message from Tom. He is applying for immediate departure, to join Julie. A change of plan. Then another cable came from him saying he'd just gotten six cables from Julie alone, plus cables from us, and was overwhelmed, I hope in a good way, and would leave there as soon as he could. Julie cheered up immediately.

About a week ago I went ahead and, with a high degree of embarrassment, told the rest of the team that I am pregnant. Again. And yes, we had used birth control and we hadn't planned this. We told them the rest of the details about the infection, all of it making me feel uncomfortable and anxious. We told them about the horrible doctor at the Grall Hospital and all he had said to us. Our teammates were sympathetic and supportive, which I greatly appreciate.

## FRIDAY, JUNE 27

Today's newspaper says foreigners and Vietnamese working for foreign organizations must re-register at 107 Nguyễn Du Street. Re-register? Julie is checking on this. We don't especially mind doing it, but it's just more bureaucracy. While Julie went there, Keith and I went to see a new doctor, not affiliated with Grall Hospital. She's a woman gynecologist, recommended to us by Dung. This doctor gave us some good news. She said the infection seems to be gone (and the Grall doctor was wrong), but I'm "weak" and I'm supposed to get lots of rest. That's rather funny to me, the suggestion to get lots of rest. It's a huge relief about the infection. She said I should try to gain weight, but that in general the pregnancy is going well. WELL!

We feel pressure to see everyone and tie up loose ends because one plane of foreigners is scheduled to leave this morning, so probably our names will soon appear on a new list.

## SATURDAY, JUNE 28

The first planeload of foreigners did finally leave yesterday. There's a posted passenger list for the next two flights, scheduled for June 30 and July 1, with about fifty names listed. Our names are not on the new list at all. Keith went to send AFSC Philly a short cable telling them we still don't know when we'll be leaving. No way of knowing if it got through.

Some good news for our cook Bà Hai. Her son, Anh Ba, has returned home safe and sound from the Delta, where he was an ARVN soldier. Our diet these weeks has been quite simple, rice with a vegetable and a very small amount of fish or shrimp and occasionally a soup in addition. Bà Hai, with such a small group to cook for, is at loose ends, and with such a low food budget she's got even less to do. Of course, cooking on charcoal as she now has to do does take more time.

We've noticed another new industry on the streets in addition to watch polishing. It is making "Liberation sandals" like ours, from truck tires, and selling them. We saw people buying them, too. Actually they're not as well made as ours, because they have thin soles while ours have thick ones. But they look good. How funny that they're now in style, sort of, on the streets of Sài Gòn, while before they aroused suspicion and sometimes people wearing them were actually arrested just for that.

Even though we're not on the current passenger list, Keith and I assume we will be leaving soon, in a few days. Sophie and Paul are requesting exit visas for a flight in one or two weeks. Julie is waiting for Tom to arrive, and that timing is unknown.

## SUNDAY, JUNE 29

We continue to enjoy a most delicious bowl of phở bắc for breakfast at a noodle stand we found over a month ago. Since we come every morning, they've given us a special low price. One thing I know for sure is that I could eat this phở bắc for breakfast every morning for the rest of my life, especially if I could eat a mango with it.

We had visitors today as usual, including Maurice, a technician from the Adventist hospital in Sài Gòn, and others including Dung's little sister

Em Thu and Chị Yến herself, with a bộ đội man friend and another woman. I wonder how the Vietnamese who went to America will survive without all the visiting, without the social circles of life in Việt Nam. I will definitely miss all the people dropping in, us dropping in on them, all the visiting with each other.

Keith went to the Foreign Office and saw that a new passenger list had been posted, but we still weren't on it. It's odd, since we were once on a list. While he was there, Earl appeared and said that he, too, is now thinking we foreigners ought to be leaving soon. An official he had been talking with said we could come back as visitors, but it wasn't a good idea to stay as residents.

# 22

# WE'RE LEAVING

**MONDAY, JUNE 30**

We got up early and went again to the Foreign Office because we'd been told to apply for new visas. Oh, bureaucracy! We have been told there will be flights all week, so we also wanted to check on our status since our names still aren't on the current posted list. Anh Cương, the man we usually see there, who studied in New York and had known about AFSC, looked through papers on his desk but couldn't find our names on any flight list at all. We told him we had seen our names there several days ago. He said that our names from that first list somehow were dropped and didn't make it to the next list. We should write a request to have this error corrected. Wasn't our being there and asking him enough of a request that it be corrected? But of course we complied and put our request in writing.

We also tried to confirm again, just to be sure, that we will have permission at the airport, whenever we get onto a flight, to take our photos and undeveloped film with us, as promised. We said that since we had written a request to correct the error of our names being dropped from the list, could he please write a document we can show to prove we have permission to leave with our film canisters? He responded nicely, politely, and said there is an "in principle" agreement with the security force at the airport to let us board the plane with them. But he still won't write it on a piece of paper. We don't know why. He was somewhat reassuring, but it leaves room for doubt.

We submitted our new request to get our names on a passenger list to someone else in the office, jumped through some other hoops, and magically, on the same day, saw our names on the passenger list for Thursday's flight to Vientiane, Laos. That's just when we would like to leave. The flight is not going directly to Hong Kong, which is fine, and we will probably go from Vientiane to Hong Kong to fly home.

Now that we have an actual date, we feel rushed to do last-minute things and especially to say goodbye to all of our friends. We went to see Phương-Hằng's sisters, but only Thúy was home, with adorable little Cún. Thúy was unhappy, very depressed about the situation for herself and for Cún. She feels afraid to let Cún go to school, because she believes the newly retrained teachers tell the children to hate Americans and America, and that those attitudes will endanger a half-American child like Cún. She wants her child to grow up without having to face these issues, so she plans to teach her at home.

At noon we had a very unusual adventure. As we were at home eating lunch, Bà Hai glanced out the front window and cried, "Thieves!!" We all poured out after her into the alley. There were two thin, dirty men, attempting to look menacing, one on foot and the other one a double-leg amputee sitting in a wheelchair. A towel from our alley clothesline lay bunched on the ground under the next-door window, and a sheet was half off the line. They had been trying to steal them. We, especially Bà Hai, yelled at them, saying we would report them, and shame on them.

The wheelchair thief was obnoxious and belligerent, calling us motherf—ers, in Vietnamese of course. He just stayed there looking at us, making no effort to leave. The one on foot started to leave but I followed him around the corner. It wasn't hard to follow him because he walked rather than ran, probably because he didn't want to be seen running while someone was yelling that he was a thief. Meanwhile, the wheelchair amputee actually climbed out of his chair and got himself down on the ground.

I found some soldiers on the main street, briefly explained the situation, and asked them to come into the alley. I asked them to bring the would-be thief I'd been following, and they complied. He came back with them willingly. There was no sense of urgency to any of this. I found myself smiling that here I was, an American, doing what I thought I'd never do, asking Liberation soldiers to help us foreigners with Vietnamese who were breaking the law. It felt to me more like we were in a performance.

In fact, when I got back to the alley I saw an enthusiastic audience of all of our neighbors, who had come out of their houses to watch our little drama. One of the soldiers went off to get a more official cadre. The two would-be thieves just stayed put. When the cadre came he asked them their story, and the amputee said Keith had dumped him out of his wheelchair, had ruined the chair, and had stolen his rice. He said Keith had knocked him to the ground where he had fallen on the hard stones.

They helped him back into his wheelchair and escorted the two of them, along with us and Bà Hai, to the closest administrative office. There they separated them to ask them questions, and they got different answers from each, since they hadn't coordinated their stories. It didn't take long. They asked for their identification papers, which they didn't have.

Bà Hai and we had to give depositions. Keith said in his statement that we had reported them because that was our duty. That satisfied the officials and we were free to go. They kept the two guys, calling them "hoodlums." They especially seemed to care not that they had attempted to steal laundry, but that they had no registration papers. The adventure for us ended there, and we felt justified in having turned them in.

## TUESDAY, JULY 1

We're told Keith and I will be the first American non-journalists to leave the country since Liberation. And we have the approval of the Foreign Ministry. I would imagine we do by now.

We had a long visit with our Mennonite friends, Earl, Hiro, Max, and Jim. They offered us the use of a car to get ourselves to the airport on Thursday. We went to say goodbye to dear Huỳnh Liên at the monastery. She expressed concern at the bad behavior of some low-level cadres in their area, and wondered how the government will get better control over crime. We told her about how we bravely "captured" two thieves! She of course greatly enjoyed the story.

Julie received a telegram from Tom saying he doesn't have the money necessary for the flight to Sài Gòn. Julie and Sophie have been trying to get money in U.S. dollars from the International Red Cross to help Tom, and for a while it seemed hopeful, but apparently it didn't work. Keith and I will only take enough dollars with us to pay for our plane tickets. Air France is insisting on payment in cash, so the others will need the rest of the money for their own flights, and hopefully there's enough to cover everyone, including Tom.

## WEDNESDAY, JULY 2

Guests at the house all day! One was Anh Thứ from Quảng Ngãi, who arrived with our tape recorder and a few other items to return to us. But we don't need them, so we told him to keep them. He reported that our little green Subaru had not made it back to Quảng Ngãi. Partway there it had already had three flats, so they left it with a friend, to be retrieved later.

We did our daily trek at 2:30 p.m. to the Foreign Office to see if our names were on the actual posted list, and no, they were not there anymore. We returned to look at 4 p.m., and this time our names were on the list for tomorrow, numbers 21 and 22. Actually not our names. The list says, in Vietnamese, "Directors, Quaker Medical Organization."

Then we went to the Mennonites to set up borrowing their car for the trip to the airport. We arranged to meet at our house at 11 a.m. tomorrow, to be at the airport by noon. I said we would provide lunch for all. We went to say goodbye to Mạnh Tường, and that was especially difficult and sad. We gave him a small gift of a Cross pen and told him that the next time we see him we will bring refills for it. But who knows when we'll see each other again.

Earl is scheduled to fly out a week from now, and Sophie and Paul in two weeks.

## THURSDAY, JULY 3

We moved out of our room and paid the last three days' rent. At the house we had a team meeting and discussed what was important to tell AFSC Philly and the news media after we leave. At 11 a.m. we sat around eating the delicious sandwiches Bà Hai had prepared. Then we said goodbye to the Mennonites and off we, including Bà Hai, went to the airport.

At the gatehouse at the airport entrance we were told only one person could go in with us to drive the car back out. Julie volunteered. We hugged and said goodbye to Sophie and Paul and Bà Hai, and Julie and Keith and I went on in. We saw parts of the airport that had been completely destroyed by fire. Julie waited while Keith and I went into the little terminal, got in line, paid $120 U.S. each, and were handed airplane tickets.

We started through customs and my luggage was searched carefully. We were still worried about our precious undeveloped film. An inexperienced cadre found and removed the film, along with letters I had in my bag. He took them to an office. This was going to be a delay, so I quickly went back outside and told Julie what was happening, and that we had our tickets and she might as well leave. We said a quick goodbye. I went back in the terminal, and we watched her start to drive out of the airport and stop almost immediately. The Mennonite's VW van's clutch cable broke right then, we learned later.

Back in line to check in, we had some good luck. Our French reporter friend Jean-Claude Labbé was on our flight. He introduced us to the chief of airport security, whom he somehow knew. Almost at the same time, I managed to locate Nguyễn Như Đoi, the government consul officer. Between the two officials, we got our letters and our rolls of films returned to us. Relief! I quickly wrote a note to Julie, and the consul himself offered to take it to her. She was still outside with the broken-down van. This was it. We were leaving. Hopefully Julie was going to be able to leave the airport soon, too.

We found seats on a plastic bench and sat down to wait. After an hour and a half, there was an announcement that there would be no flight today because of bad weather, and we should all leave the airport and return tomorrow. The announcement was, of course, in Vietnamese, which most of the foreign passengers didn't understand. I translated it into English for everyone, and Keith translated it into French. People crowded at the ticket counter and a general groan went up as they learned that the luggage, which was already checked, was being returned to everyone. Keith and I had only hand luggage.

Julie and the car weren't there when we came out of the terminal to find her, so somehow she had managed to leave. We walked out of the airport, not sure where to go. The airport officials had been unclear about whether or not our one-day Laos visas would work the next day, so we decided to see if our friend Thérèse, a French teacher, might be able to help us. We knew she had contacts at the Laos Embassy. So we took a bus to La Rainière, the French apartment complex where she lives. She was home, so we asked her if she might go to the embassy with us to find out if we need new visas or not. She said it closed on June 26, after being open for a while after Liberation. So we went instead to a nearby administrative office to find out if anyone there knew about Laos visas. They did. They said we do not need visas at all, that we can get seven-day visas on arrival in Laos.

So that was taken care of, and we went back to Thérèse's apartment to visit. She invited us to spend the night there, and we gratefully accepted. After all, we didn't have the flophouse anymore, the main house was a bit crowded and not near the airport, and of course we had already said goodbye to everyone!

It was definitely anti-climactic to still be in Sài Gòn. We bought some vegetables and helped make dinner, and we were chatting and eating when there was a knock on the door. Thérèse opened it, and of all people, Đoàn Mộng Ngô was standing there, smiling broadly. He introduced himself to Thérèse and she invited him in. He had come to say goodbye to us. We could not imagine how he'd found out where we were, and he wouldn't tell us how he knew. He just grinned at our astonishment at seeing him. He joined us for dinner, and we were able to ask him to say goodbye to Xuân Lan and the rest of the family for us, something we hadn't managed to do this busy week.

## FRIDAY, JULY 4

It's the 4th of July, and if the flight goes and if we're on it, this will be our last day in Việt Nam. This morning we thanked Thérèse, said goodbye, and took a bus back to the airport. We were again worried about the six rolls of Kodachrome film and the sixty issues of the newspaper *Sài Gòn Giải Phóng* that we were carrying. We hoped today would go as well as yesterday, but there were new people at the airport, and two of them wanted to take the newspapers from us. We told them we had permission to take them, but they just looked at us suspiciously. Then, luckily, someone from yesterday saw us and confirmed our story.

It wasn't as if we were trying to smuggle out anything they wouldn't have approved of anyway. It was just pictures from before and after Liberation, and copies of their own published newspapers. Of course it's unfortunate that they are censoring what leaves the country, but based on past history, it's pretty easy to understand their sensitivity.

While we were in line waiting to go through customs again, we chatted with a bộ đội soldier from Nghĩa Hành, in Quảng Ngãi Province. When he learned who we were, he told us that he knew of the delegation from the north, way up north, from Hà Nội, that had come to visit the Quakers in Quảng Ngãi right after the city was liberated. He said they specifically came to our house to meet us, and were disappointed that we weren't there. He thought that meant we had left the country with the American evacuation, and yet here we were.

The plane took off smoothly. It wasn't a DC-3. It was bigger and nicer, and it had no flames or smoke coming from its engines. As we rose in the air I saw the greenery of the Sài Gòn area, the palm trees, the rice fields, and I didn't see any bomb craters.

We always saw bomb craters from the air on flights to and from Quảng Ngãi. And now I've seen, from documentaries, vivid scenes of what it's like to be on the receiving end of the bombs and the violence my own country exploded onto these people for so many years.

## TUESDAY, JULY 8

We had a few days in Laos and then flew to Hong Kong, and from there straight back, if you call a forty-hour trip "straight back," to the U.S. Before we left Sài Gòn, when the five of us were all together, the others threw us a farewell dinner party and gave us a wonderful gift. It was a set of three cassettes called *The Songs of Liberation*. They're very powerful, and easy to sing (or march) along with. Two songs in particular make me cry. One is sung by a young woman who had been with the NLF and was killed just before Liberation. The other is "Liberate the South," which Yến had taught me to sing when she told me her husband had died, when she was pregnant with their third child. When we got back to the U.S. and got a tape player, we played those cassettes over and over again.

I think of all the incendiary propaganda, the widespread warnings about what would happen when Sài Gòn "fell" to the Communists. If you say it often enough, and if there are no witnesses who say otherwise, it becomes fact, it becomes history. But Việt Nam did not fall off the face of the earth when the American government withdrew. It's still there, with its long sense of history and its resilient people, some of whom still suffer from the effects of Agent Orange, from having lost legs or arms, from the risk of stepping on still-buried landmines, and from other remnants of the American War.

# EPILOGUE

When we got back to Philadelphia we found a doctor and received welcome reassurance. I was three and a half months pregnant and the outlook for a successful full-term pregnancy was good, although I was supposed to gain weight. That wasn't difficult to do with ample American food.

We were back in America, away from war, and abruptly disconnected from our lives in Việt Nam. Keith and I went on a speaking tour around the country for AFSC. We still lived simply, staying at the homes of local Quakers before driving to the next event. The war seemed to be quickly becoming ancient history, except that now there were many Vietnamese in America. They were opening Vietnamese restaurants and flying old South Vietnamese flags. We wondered what their circumstances had been back home that made them leave, and who they had left behind.

As my pregnancy progressed, we ended our speaking tour and rented an unheated two-room carriage house over a garage outside downtown Philadelphia. We had been thinking about baby names for months, and our plan was that if we had a girl, her name would be an anglicized variation of the Vietnamese word Ái, or "love," plus "ry," to make Airy. By complete coincidence, our carriage house was in a suburb named Mount Airy.

In January 1976 our beautiful baby girl was born. The first thing I did was check that she wasn't deaf or blind from German measles, and that she had all her fingers and toes. Airy was indeed exquisitely perfect.

Communication channels between the U.S. and Việt Nam were closed for many years. We did not know of any way to send letters, packages, or telegrams to Việt Nam, because of the American embargo. There also, of course, was no internet. Even if there had been a way to make calls, and even if our friends had acquired telephones, we did not know the phone numbers. We lost touch with everyone. No one there knew about our baby Airy or her two sisters, Sophia and Vivian, born a few years later. Chị Mai, of course, found herself in the same situation and could not tell us she also had a daughter, named Thúy, born just a few months after Airy.

Việt Nam suffered many years of hunger and deprivation after the initial euphoria of the end of the war. A country that once exported rice now had to import it, and people could not afford to buy it. American economic support had ended abruptly, helping to collapse the already weak Vietnamese economy. In the ensuing years, hundreds of thousands of Vietnamese "boat people" fled from Việt Nam, and most of them eventually made their way to the United States as refugees. We in America knew little about what was happening inside Việt Nam for many years, except from newspaper interviews with boat people.* The American embargo was not lifted until 1994, and relations were not normalized between the two countries until the following year, twenty years after I left. In 2023 political relations were officially elevated between the two countries as part of a political coalition against China.

---

* Boat people was a term used to refer to Vietnamese who fled from Việt Nam by boat during the years after the end of the war in 1975. This migration of hundreds of thousands of people was at its highest in 1978 and 1979 and continued through the early 1990s. Economic sanctions, the legacy of destruction left by the war, policies of the Vietnamese government, and conflicts with neighboring countries caused an international humanitarian crisis. Many boat people died at sea, and many who survived the journey spent years in refugee camps before finally being settled in, usually, a Western country. UNHCR, *The State of the World's Refugees 2000: Fifty Years of Humanitarian Action* (Oxford: Oxford University Press, 2000).

Imagine if we had simply had good relations with Việt Nam from 1954 on. Imagine if there had been no war. Imagine if no Vietnamese had ended up far away from their families. All these decades later American veterans, and children of boat people, are visiting Việt Nam as tourists, and Vietnamese students are studying abroad in America.

In 2004 we went back to Việt Nam for the first time. Our rehabilitation center still had quite a few of the same skilled staff from when we had left, though it had been moved to nearby Qui Nhơn. We had a tearful reunion with Chị Mai and stayed in her modest two-room house in Tam Kỳ. We slept on a thin straw mat on her wooden platform bed, and she slept on the wooden kitchen table. She joked that it gave her more than enough leg room. We met her daughter and son-in-law and their eighteen-month-old baby girl, and we visited with several of our former staff members and friends.

In Hồ Chí Minh City (Sài Gòn) we saw Dung and her husband, and their two teenage children. As in 1975, Hồ Chí Minh City was a much more sophisticated place than the "country town" where Mai and her family lived. Dung told us they were pessimistic about the state of the country. Their children were very Westernized, in dress and interests. We could not find my other language tutor, Yến.

In 2010 we and other AFSC teammates who had worked with Chị Mai organized a reunion and brought her and her daughter to the U.S. for two weeks. Chị Mai was astounded at the ease with which someone in a wheelchair could get around. She could hardly believe that the tram operators at South Lake Tahoe would stop the machinery to install a special ramp just so she could go to the top to see the scenery.

I went back again in 2017, and it was easy to see that things had improved for everyone. I saw no beggars and no homeless people. Children were in school, not following us around. Chị Mai's daughter and son-in-law had built a spacious new house and a lovely small house a few feet away on property in Tam Kỳ. Chị Mai lives in the small house, and her daughter and son-in-law live in the larger house, which they share with their two children and Mai's son-in-law's parents. Mai's grandchildren are traditionally respectful, studious, and polite, and speak remarkably good English. When

I was there, a documentary was being filmed about Chị Mai's life and her sacrifices for the revolution. They asked if they could interview me, and I was honored to participate.

In February 2023 Keith and I returned again to Việt Nam and visited Chị Mai and other family members and friends in both Tam Kỳ and Hà Nội. In Hà Nội we visited the Vietnamese Women's Museum, where we had been on previous visits, but this time Keith looked at an exhibit and exclaimed with astonishment, "It's Chị Mai!" The exhibit was called "Twelve false identity cards used by the female revolutionaries," and one item in the display case was Chị Mai's false identity card with her photo. Also on display was a lacquer box captioned in English "Jewellery box used to conceal documents by Khưu Thị Hồng." And that of course was her real name, though the exhibit did not say that the name on the identity card and the name on the box were the same person. Chị Mai and her family had not known about this exhibit until we told them, though Chị Mai remembered someone many years ago asking her for her identity card.

During my 2017 trip to Việt Nam I was honored to be invited to attend a special event called "Finding Memories" at the old "Hanoi Hilton" prison, now the Hỏa Lò Museum, in Hà Nội. It was held on November 29, 2017, to commemorate the forty-fifth anniversary of the release of American POWs, including my friend Bob Chenoweth, who was a prisoner of war for five years and a featured speaker.

This special event was to honor and in some cases reunite American POWs and their Vietnamese captors, guards, and interpreters. Of course many could not attend or were no longer alive, although some relatives of both the Americans and the Vietnamese who couldn't attend were there. On this day, after so many years, I looked around at all the old people, many in their uniforms adorned with medals, and at all the young people, very respectful of their elders and of the occasion. I could not hold back my tears as I joined a somber procession walking slowly toward the grand and beautifully decorated shrine at the famous old prison, honoring all who were lost, all that was lost, during that war so long ago. Like the others, I held a stick of incense between my palms, and when I reached the shrine I stood facing it, hands held out in front of me with my incense offering, and bowed.

Phương-Hằng Phan and her husband live in Washington. In the 1980s, sponsored by Phương-Hằng's father-in-law, her sisters Bình and Thúy, and little Cún, moved to Germany.

Bill Cooper was released after a few months and spent some time in Hồ Chí Minh City (Sài Gòn) before returning to the U.S.

Mạnh Tường and his girlfriend, ballet dancer Quỳnh Chi, married and divorced. Later, disillusioned with the new government, he moved with his second wife to Canada, where he died in the early 2000s.

Dung and Ba Minh live in Hồ Chí Minh City.

We could not find Yến but assume her family is still in Biên Hòa.

Cảnh and Nguyệt stayed in Quảng Ngãi, and Cảnh died at a young age of high blood pressure.

On each visit with Chị Mai's family, we also connected with several other former AFSC Vietnamese staff members and friends. We learned that Duy (not his real name) recovered and has lived happily near Quảng Ngãi in the years since we saw him in 1975.

The Quaker Rehabilitation Center continues to serve patients in Qui Nhơn.

Sophie Quinn-Judge and Paul Quinn-Judge live in France.

Julie Forsythe and Tom Hoskins live in Vermont.

Heidi Kuglin lives in New Zealand.

My husband, Keith Brinton, and I live in California.

# ACKNOWLEDGMENTS

I have many people to thank for their help and encouragement. I thank my AFSC teammates who experienced this with me, and all former AFSC Việt Nam teammates and colleagues. Thank you to AFSC itself and especially to archivist Don Davis. I thank Gareth Porter and the other contributors whose valuable essays are in the appendix: Nguyễn Thị Mai (Khưu Thị Hồng), Tom Hoskins, Phương-Hằng Phan, the late Paul N. "Pete" McCloskey Jr. and his wife Helen McCloskey, the late Don Luce and his husband Mark Bonacci, Bob Chenoweth, Max Ediger, Beryl Nelson and his late sister Marjorie Nelson, and Craig McNamara.

I am very grateful to my wonderful UVA Press editors Nadine Zimmerli and Ellen Satrom, and to UVA publisher Eric Brandt for being interested in the first place. Thank you to Sophie Quinn-Judge, Diane Jones, and Earl Martin for their contributions. Special thanks to Beth Taylor for her long-term support and to Ron Milam for his. Thank you to Dick Hughes, Mireille Yanow, Nayan Chanda, Frances Fitzgerald, W. D. Ehrhart, Doug Hostetter, Michael Ann Strange, Charles Postel, Andrés Resendez, and many others. Thank you to Bob Chenoweth and Jane Griffith for inviting me to join them for the Finding Memories event in Hà Nội, and thank you to my friends, Chị Mai's family members Trần Hoàng Thúy, Võ Phước Long, Võ Thị Ngân, Ngô Văn Quốc, Võ Ngân Giang, and Mai Tuân Hải.

I love and thank my supportive family cheering squad, daughter Airy

Krich-Brinton and Simon Pitfield and their amazing children Peter and Corin, daughter Sophia Krich-Brinton and Jon Cotton and their fabulous children Hazel and Rory, daughter Vivian Krich-Brinton and her exceptional cat GreyGrey, and my helpful and loving husband, Keith Brinton.

Thank you to *Ms. Magazine* for publishing an excerpt from my Việt Nam diary in their July 1976 issue. At the end of the article I wrote, "Claudia Krich is working on a book-length version of her journal."

# APPENDIX

# HISTORICAL CONTEXT

## My Story

*Nguyễn Thị Mai (Khưu Thị Hồng)*

I was born in 1938 in Xã Tam Thái commune, district of Phú Ninh. I am the youngest in a family of seven children. At the age of twenty-two I joined the revolutionary forces, and I worked with them for ten years. The area where I lived and worked in the mountains was run by the North Vietnamese government. I was a reporter, and my job was to gather information about battles and find out when, where, how many casualties there were, and who won.

My family didn't like the South Vietnamese government, which controlled where we lived. They beat many people in my family. My father and third brother were arrested and shot dead. My mother stayed at home, then died of old age. My fifth sister died from American bombs, died on the spot. Việt Nam is a country of Vietnamese people, so why did Americans go there? War is very inhumane. In my view, the Americans killed and persecuted the Vietnamese.

When I joined the resistance, many people in Quảng Ngãi and in Việt

Nam preferred the Communist side because the South Vietnamese government didn't care about the people and only cared about American money. My mother approved of me joining the resistance, because if I had stayed I probably would have been killed. I left home around 1960 and didn't see my mother again until 1975.

Before going to the mountains I worked as a nurse in an enemy area. When I first went to the mountains I taught farmers to read and write. I felt free and unafraid. It was a safe area. In the mountains we had a government from the north.

One day after about ten years of working in the mountains, I was collecting information in the mountains of Quế Sơn when I saw a red dot in the bushes—a Claymore mine. The American soldiers detonated the landmine and I heard a loud noise and fell unconscious. I was carrying my notebook, documents, and some gold. Gold was like money. It was to buy food. Families exchanged livestock for gold because of the war. I had two gold threads (cây vàng) with me when I was injured.

When I woke up I saw many Americans around me. I was in Chu Lai, in a field hospital. I was afraid the Americans would execute me. They had an interpreter who asked me questions. They asked me what my name was, what I was doing, where my house was, my occupation. I was barely conscious and yet they kept asking questions, but I wouldn't answer anything. Later, when I became conscious enough, I answered their questions. But I said my name was Nguyễn Thị Mai and I was a farmer, just walking on the path. I never said I was with the revolutionary forces. They took me in a helicopter to the hospital in Quảng Ngãi. They had put a piece of tape on my forehead that said "VC," but I took it off before we arrived.

They amputated both of my legs, one above the knee and one below. When I recovered enough, they took me to the American Quaker Rehabilitation Center in Quảng Ngãi, where they gave me prosthetic legs and crutches and taught me how to walk on them. For many years I still dreamed I had legs, and sometimes I got out of bed and fell down. At the rehabilitation center I met kind Americans who encouraged me to recover. As I got better, I learned that there was a vacancy for a position at the rehabilitation center, and Mr. Bích, who worked there, recommended me for the job and I got it. I became the receptionist. Part of my job was to screen patients to make sure they were civilians, not military, and that no one brought in weapons. There were rumors that I was a Communist, because I had no family and no visitors. Mr. Bích defended me and said, "She's not a Communist." I was happy to work with the Quakers, and they are still my dear friends after all these years.

Written in March 2023 in Vietnamese and translated into English.

## Letter from Đà Nẵng

### Tom Hoskins, M.D.

The changeover in Đà Nẵng was peaceful. However, just before, on March 27 and 28, there was fear, anarchy, looting, and shooting in the streets. The police left their posts and abandoned any effort to maintain the appearance of order. The remnants of Thiệu's army ranged up and down the city streets, discharging their M16s at any available target. Later I was to meet several hundred people in the hospital who had been wounded by the guns and grenades of routed ARVN soldiers. As one Vietnamese said in broken English, "The streets are the Wild West." How true: Different gangs of ARVN soldiers were shooting it out with each other from one street corner to the next.

I was listening to a patient's chest about noontime, March 29, when I removed the stethoscope from my ears and sensed a difference in the street noise. The rifle fire had stopped. It was quiet. By one o'clock many more patients were coming in. By two and three o'clock nurses, doctors, and volunteers began to pitch in. By five o'clock there were groups of students organized about the city to bring in the wounded and the sick. By this time there were first aid squads and operating units at work in both the hospitals.

I left the hospital at 8 p.m., having been so engrossed all day in patching up and bandaging that I never even asked what was happening outside. I found the streets rapidly returning to normal, no gunfire or warfare anywhere. All of the Sài Gòn red and yellow flags were gone. There were flags of the Buddhist Pagoda everywhere. I climbed into a jeep with people returning to the pagoda, and suddenly there was a huge ARVN tank making straight toward us. But the tank was covered with cheering schoolchildren and decked out in Buddhist flags.

Then a jeep full of civilians passed us bearing the red, blue, and gold Liberation flag. And then the flags of Liberation, the Provisional Revolutionary Government, were everywhere. Đà Nẵng had been liberated while I had been busy in the hospital. And yet as I thought back on it, I had seen the process happening during the day as I was working. The cessation of bloodshed, the citizens returning to their tasks, the working together for the care of the people.

When we arrived at the pagoda I saw an arsenal of weapons in the courtyard. Men and women came carrying armaments. Students brought in rocket launchers and discarded M16s, M79s, rockets, and mines. Students disarmed the guns and mines, and the pile grew larger.

This letter was written to the AFSC about what happened in March 1975 in Đà Nẵng.

## How I Came to Live in America

*Phương-Hằng Phan*

On April 30, 1975, I was alone in my room at my host family's house in Lansdale, Pennsylvania, when I heard the news of the fall of Sài Gòn on the radio. I was petrified about what was happening in Việt Nam. I was in America in an MCC-sponsored exchange visitor program, feeling so lost and lonely and homesick. I was worried about my family, and I was worried about how dangerous it would be to escape if they tried to. I had no idea what they were doing or thinking or if they were still alive. There was no communication out of Việt Nam as of that day. All I read in the U.S. papers was about the evacuations. It seemed scary, dangerous, and totally chaotic to me. But at the same time, I was very glad the war was finally over. I tried to imagine how excited my father must be about that. I wanted to go home, but there was no way to. My passport was no longer valid because it was issued by a country that no longer existed. I immediately became a refugee in this country. I did not hear from my family for over a year after that day, but when I did, my father wrote to say I must remain in the U.S. and not go back.

How did I end up here? I was going to college in Sài Gòn, and I also worked at the MCC headquarters in Sài Gòn as a secretary. I was born during the war, grew up while the war was going on. There was never a time I knew peace. I had often wondered what it would be like living in peace. The MCC director in Việt Nam wrote to MCC in the U.S. to apply for me to participate in a one-year program. I would live with an American family and work as a volunteer with MCC programs during this one-year stay, starting in July. I did not get my visa until December 12, 1974, when my planned year in America was already half over. At the time, I was living in Sài Gòn, and since I would be joining the program already six months late, I left directly from Sài Gòn without a chance to return home to Tuy Hòa to say goodbye to my parents. I wished I could see them before I left but I thought I would be back in six months, when I would see them.

On December 19, 1974, I left Việt Nam with a small suitcase, a small plastic carry-on bag, and a single piece of my favorite jewelry—a pendant imprinted with the words "War is not healthy for children and other living things." As I excitedly boarded the plane, little did I know that April 30, 1975, would change my life forever.

I came in December, and when I arrived it was snowing. I had only a pair of open-toe sandals. But I loved the snow. I wrote the names of my friends in the snow and took pictures to send to them. Christmas was coming, so most of the houses in Lansdale had wreaths on the front doors and some had decorations on the front lawns. All looked like those beautiful pictures on recycled Christmas cards donated to Protestant churches I used to see in Việt Nam at Christmastime. Here it was so peaceful. I thought I should be happy, yet I felt very lonely because I was homesick.

I used some money from my $30 monthly stipend to make an extravagant purchase: a small radio so I could listen to the news about what was happening in Việt Nam. My host family went to church three times a week: Sunday morning, Sunday evening, and Bible study on Thursday evening. I was supposed to participate in the activities of my host family so I went along. In church, they prayed for the American government. The war had intensified in Việt Nam. Nobody talked about the war. My host mother asked me if people wore shoes in Việt Nam. I had the choice of staying with one family the entire time, but I asked MCC to move me. I was assigned to the Mennonite camp, Camp Deerpark, in Westbrookville, New York, for the remaining time of my experience. At Camp Deerpark I used to take walks when I was not working with the summer camp kids. Near the camp lived a gentle elderly Jewish couple, and we became good friends. They asked me about the war, and we talked about our experiences.

In July 1975, MCC sent me to New York City to work at Friendshipment,* helping with office work. I spent much of that winter after work sitting in a small room in a small apartment in Greenwich Village listening to Joni Mitchell's *Blue* album. By spring of 1976, MCC helped me find a job at the Lancaster School District (Intermediate Unit 13), helping the influx of Vietnamese refugees find jobs and get settled. During this time, I started the paperwork to sponsor some of my family to leave Việt Nam. My parents and my two oldest sisters had chosen to stay in Việt Nam.

In 1993 I finally was able to return to Việt Nam. My father had passed away nine years earlier. My mother was living with one of my sisters at the house my father had built in Tuy Hòa. Our mother's hair was all white and she could no longer see due to cataract conditions left untreated in both eyes. She was very thin, and yet when she put her arms around me she worried about me not eating enough. Having become a mother myself, I realized how heartbroken my mother must have been when her children left, knowing she might never see them again. Her heart was shattered once again when we left this time. Two years later, she died. I returned to Việt Nam several times to visit my two sisters there. They have since passed away. I have no one in Việt Nam anymore, though Việt Nam is still my other home.

Written in May 2022.

---

\* Friendshipment was an American organization founded by peace and justice activist Cora Weiss. It was a coalition of approximately thirty-six political, religious, and community organizations. Weiss established it in the 1970s to provide humanitarian relief to Việt Nam and to help Việt Nam rebuild through people-to-people aid.

# My Congressional Delegation Trip to Việt Nam

*Paul N. "Pete" McCloskey Jr.*

I visited Việt Nam four times, including in February/March 1975 as a member of the U.S. Congress. On that fourth visit I broke away from the eight-member delegation and flew to Đà Nẵng to get the advice of the I Corps commander, General Thi, who a former U.S. marine had told me was one of the few reliable South Vietnamese generals. The rest of the delegation never got to Đà Nẵng and mostly stayed in Sài Gòn.

General Thi showed me his map that showed his one and a half divisions of ARVN surrounded to the north and west by an arc of two and a half full-strength NVA divisions. He said that Nguyễn Văn Thiệu had taken south both the marine and paratroop divisions to defend Sài Gòn. General Thi told me that if the North Vietnamese attacked through II Corps, he was powerless to stop them and they would reach the coast in two weeks or less. Congressman Tip O'Neill and I had led a successful vote on June 25, 1973, to take away from the president the power to order the bombing in Southeast Asia that had stopped the NVA in 1972.

When we got back to D.C. in early March 1975, Gerry Ford asked me and Senator Dewey Bartlett to come to the Oval Office and tell him what we had seen and learned in South Việt Nam and at our brief stopover in Phnom Penh. Present were only the president, Dick Cheney, Henry Kissinger, and Bartlett, who didn't say anything. I told Ford about the military situation in the north and relayed the statement that the NVA would cut South Việt Nam in half in two weeks if they attacked. Kissinger said the south had thirteen and a half times more artillery ammunition than the NVA.

On that brief visit to Sài Gòn, Bartlett and I met with CIA chief of station Thomas Polgar, who echoed Ambassador Ellsworth Bunker's rosy picture that we were winning in South Việt Nam, and that there was no danger. I think Bunker, and perhaps Thiệu, really believed this fantasy, but Polgar knew the danger and simply lied to echo Bunker's position. I thought Thiệu was moving in a dream world, fostered by Bunker's obsession.

We had severely cut back funding, but not completely ended it. Within a few days after the meeting in the White House, the NVA attacked and the ARVN collapsed. I believe Phnom Penh fell on April 15 and Sài Gòn on the 30th.

Bob Tunnell, the commander of the 2nd Battalion, 9th Marines, had landed in Đà Nẵng, and in October 1965 he lost a leg to a buried 105 shell while watching his troops attack a village from which mortars and rockets had destroyed some South Vietnamese planes. He described the problem: when a burst of fire hit the marines, they responded with fire that killed a few women and children and then held Zippo lighters up to the thatched roofs of the village. He said that there was no way we were going to win the minds and hearts of the Vietnamese peasantry, as we had trained to do at Camp Pendleton together in the summer of 1964. He was convinced we could not win the war.

From an interview with Claudia Krich, June 2021.

## I Helped Find the Tiger Cages

### Don Luce

In 1970, President Nixon sent a delegation of ten members of Congress to Việt Nam to investigate pacification. A part of their mandate included a visit to a prison in South Việt Nam as a way to be allowed to visit a prison in the north where U.S. POWs were being held.

Tom Harkin, an aide to the congressional group and later a U.S. senator from Iowa, convinced two of the congressmen to investigate stories of torture in the "Tiger Cages" off the coast of Việt Nam. (The French built the cages in 1939 to hold political opponents; similar ones in French Guinea became famous in the movie *Papillon*, starring Steve McQueen and Dustin Hoffman.) The congressman requisitioned a plane for the 200-mile trip to Côn Sơn Island. I was asked to go as an interpreter and specialist in Vietnamese prisons. At that time I was working for the World Council of Churches.

On the way out, Frank Walton, the U.S. prison advisor, described Côn

Sơn as being like "a Boy Scout recreational camp." It was, he said, "the largest prison in the Free World."

We saw a very different scene when we got to the prison. Using maps drawn by a former tiger cage prisoner, we diverted from the planned tour and hurried down an alleyway between two prison buildings. We found the tiny door that led to the cages between the prison walls. A guard inside heard the commotion outside and opened the door. We walked in.

The faces of the prisoners in the cages below are still etched indelibly in my mind: the man with three fingers cut off; the man (soon to die) from Quảng Trị Province whose skull was split open; and the Buddhist monk from Huế who spoke intensely about the repression of the Buddhists. I remember clearly the terrible stench from diarrhea and the open sores where shackles cut into the prisoners' ankles. "Donnez-moi de l'eau" ("Give me water"), they begged. They sent us scurrying between cells to check on other prisoners' health and continued to ask for water.

The photos that Harkin took were printed in the July 17, 1970, issue of *Life* magazine. The international protest that resulted brought about the transfer of the 180 men and 300 women from the cages. Some were sent to other prisons. Some were sent to mental institutions.

Today, behind the five-by-nine-foot cages is a cemetery for the 20,000 people who died in Côn Sơn Prison. Most graves are unmarked. The prisoners at Côn Sơn didn't even have numbers. When the survivors return, they bring flowers, pray, and softly sing the songs that were whispered in the cages.

Excerpted with permission from Don Luce, *We've Been Here Before: The Tiger Cages of Vietnam.* https://historynewsnetwork.org/article/11001.

## I Was a Prisoner of War

### Bob Chenoweth

I was the crew chief (SP-5) on a UH-1D helicopter. We were a crew of four, with a gunner and two pilots. We had two passengers, a lieutenant colonel and a SP-4. On February 8, 1968, we were shot down near Quảng Trị City during the Tết Offensive by a local NLF militia group of men and women. One of the pilots and the SP-4 were seriously injured. We were taken to the same village we had walked through earlier that day, where we had seen no one. Now the villagers appeared and gave us tea. We moved by boat after dark, and by the end of the evening we were in the mountains. We fell asleep in a dried-up creek bed.

We stayed in a mountain camp for about a month and then began moving north up the Hồ Chí Minh Trail, traveling on foot and by truck. Our first camp was in Nghệ An Province, in a village made up of three or four hamlets. We came there in April and left in November, moving north and staying at a camp in Hà Tây Province, southwest of Hà Nội. We were there from November 1968 to November 20, 1970. Then we moved to 17 Lý Nam Đế Street, "the Plantation," in downtown Hà Nội. We stayed at the Plantation until December 27, 1972. That night we moved into Hỏa Lò Prison, the "Hanoi Hilton," during the Christmas Bombing. We saw a B-52 explode and come crashing down through the clouds. We thought that one landed in the lake. I was in the Hanoi Hilton until my release on March 15, 1973.

Our living conditions, especially in the mountains and while traveling the Hồ Chí Minh Trail, were very spartan. It was a harsh environment, and there was always the danger of being bombed. In Nghệ An we lived in a village and were surrounded by the local residents. We worked to repair bomb shelters, raised crops and pigs, and sometimes went out at night to carry supplies from other villages to ours. Sometimes the goods were going farther along, but mostly we carried rice, sugar, cooking pots, blankets, and other items needed for our own camp and the village. In Hà Tây we were confined in our camp, which had a bamboo mat fence around it. We had wells and gardens inside the camp. We knew from those experiences that we ate what the soldiers ate. I would say we ate a little more than they did.

In Hà Nội we were confined in an old French military compound. On rare occasions, usually in the evening, we went out on organized field trips. We went to the National Museum, the Museum of the Revolution, and a performance of traditional music at the opera house. We went to see the One Pillar Pagoda and walked around Hoàn Kiếm Lake and had coffee at a garden shop that had topiary animals. It is still there, and I have had coffee there several times since then.

I think most of us in our group liked the countryside better than the city. When we lived in Nghệ An we often got peanuts, pineapples, and other fruits from the villagers walking in from the fields. We had squash and beans too. In Hà Nội there was no chance of getting those little treats. We did have beer a few times, and that was a welcome "city treat." We would tie all the bottles together and sink them in the well for a couple of hours. They got pretty cold. I worked with a friendly English-speaking official named Mr. Khai to produce the camp radio program. It played in the evening at about seven o'clock with news and music we put together. Lots of guys made radio programs for the camp, and I did it quite a bit.

Another group of POWs held in the south in a camp around Huế joined us in 1971. The group included twenty-some Americans and two German nurses, a man and a woman, from the West German hospital ship *Helgoland*. It also included James A. Daly, who later became part of the peace committee. They had been in a lot of danger in the south, and their camp was even attacked by the Americans. After Daly's group arrived and settled into the Plantation, we were able to set up a basketball court and have games. In the evening the guards played volleyball and we sometimes joined in if we were out. They were much better at it, but we had fun.

We were released in accord with the Paris Peace Agreement, which stated that each side had ninety days to return all the captives they had. I was in the fifth or sixth release group of twenty to thirty persons.

Written in July 2022.

## At a Demonstration Led by Buddhist Nuns

*Max Ediger*

From 1971 to April 1976 I worked in Sài Gòn with the Mennonite Central Committee program in Việt Nam. We provided medical care in two hospitals in Sài Gòn, helped refugees, and documented all aspects of the war, especially its effects on rural villagers.

Before May 1975, we were documenting the protests taking place around the country calling for the resignation of President Thiệu, the end of the war, and the withdrawal of all U.S. troops. In the months leading up to the war's end on April 30, 1975, demonstrations around the country against the war increased. Many Buddhist monks and nuns played an important role in these demonstrations. One group of Buddhist nuns, led by Most Venerable head nun Bhikkhuni Hùynh Liên, maintained a pagoda not far from our office. We would see them drive by in their Lambro 550 on their way to the city center, large anti-war banners strapped to the sides of the vehicle. As soon as we saw them pass the office we knew another demonstration was taking place, so we jumped on our Hondas and followed them.

Hundreds of people lined the streets to observe the demonstrations. The nuns would unroll their banners and walk along chanting anti-war slogans. Soon others would join them, and the streets would quickly fill up with demonstrators. Groups of students would show up, as would well-known leaders of the anti-war movement. We documented these demonstrations and interviewed as many people as we could.

During one demonstration, the nuns began their march near the front of the parliament building. A contingent of police blocked their way. As the nuns walked down the street followed by hundreds of supporters, they showed no hesitation when confronted by the line of baton-swinging police. The nuns and the police stood face-to-face in confrontation. Suddenly one of the police officers kicked at a nun's shin. In Việt Nam, Buddhist monks and nuns are highly respected and are not to be harmed. When the watching crowd saw this, they surged forward. The police quickly fled the scene. Hundreds of people then stopped just observing and joined the protest.

Written in July 2022.

# I Sailed on the *Phoenix*

## Beryl Nelson

The *Phoenix of Hiroshima* was a fifty-foot sailboat built in Hiroshima, Japan, for anthropologist Earle Reynolds, who was under contract with the U.S. government to study the long-term health effects of the nuclear bombing on civilians. In 1958 Earle and his family left Japan to circumnavigate the world. Near the end of the voyage, they stopped in Hawaii and visited Quakers in jail who had been arrested on board the *Golden Rule* sailboat while protesting U.S. nuclear testing. Earle and his family were inspired to sail the *Phoenix* into the Bikini atoll test area to carry on the interrupted Quaker protest voyage.

During their jail visit they had met George Willoughby, who was a crew member on the *Golden Rule*. In 1967 George, along with Larry Scott and George Lakey, was organizing protests against the Việt Nam war. They contacted Earle Reynolds and asked if he and the *Phoenix* were available to help deliver a shipment of medical supplies to North Việt Nam. Reynolds agreed, and on March 22, 1967, the *Phoenix* set sail. They arrived in North Việt Nam five days later, where the crew successfully delivered the medical supplies to the North Vietnamese Red Cross to help civilians injured by the American bombing.

Shortly after this, I was in Philadelphia visiting my sister, Marjorie Nelson, M.D., and she took me to a presentation by A Quaker Action Group (AQAG) where I learned details about the *Phoenix*'s protest/humanitarian assistance voyage. Quakers are pacifists, opposed to war, but are not passive. They engage in nonviolent direct action such as this trip.

The American war in Việt Nam was a life-changing time for many, including for my sister and myself. As U.S. Quakers we were both led to undertake personal action in the war zone. She served in Việt Nam with the American Friends Service Committee, and I joined AQAG, volunteering as a crew member on the second and third *Phoenix* voyages to Việt Nam.

I flew to Japan and joined the *Phoenix* as first mate under captain Bob Eaton, who had been the youngest crew member on the first voyage to

Việt Nam. Bob's passport was revoked due to his role in that first voyage. He said, "The U.S. government also retaliated against our efforts by freezing our bank accounts and threatening us with long prison sentences for aiding the enemy." After the completion of the *Phoenix* voyages, Bob was convicted of draft evasion and served several years in U.S. federal prison.

During my time aboard the *Phoenix* we made a trip to Đà Nẵng attempting to deliver medical supplies to the South Vietnamese Red Cross and a Buddhist organization. However, the South Vietnamese and U.S. governments did not allow the *Phoenix* to enter South Việt Nam, so we returned to Hong Kong and had the supplies shipped to South Việt Nam. We then sailed to Hải Phòng in North Việt Nam with medical equipment and supplies, timing our arrival to occur during the U.S. bombing pause in February 1968, at the time of the Tết holiday and what turned out to be the Tết Offensive.

Bob Eaton flew back to the U.S. in late February, and I took over as captain of the *Phoenix* to supervise maintenance in Hong Kong and deliver the boat back to Hiroshima. My time on the *Phoenix,* which included a trip to the Hiroshima Memorial Peace Museum in Hiroshima, altered my life to the extent that in 1973, when I was twenty-nine, I emigrated out of the United States.

Written in January 2023. Beryl Nelson's sister, Marjorie E. Nelson, published a detailed account of his time on the *Phoenix* and her experiences as a physician and prisoner of the NLF in Việt Nam. He highly recommends her book, *To Live in Peace in Midst of the Vietnam War* (2019), which is available on Amazon and for Kindle.

## Meeting General Giáp's Son

### *Craig McNamara*

On the morning we met Võ Hồng Nam in Hà Nội in 2017, at 4 a.m. the traffic was just beginning as we made our way to Hà Nội's largest flower market. I picked out four dozen of the freshest long-stemmed roses. Each tiny rosebud was wrapped in tissue paper. At first I thought this was a waste of someone's labor; later I appreciated it as we sped through Hà Nội on motor scooters, with the wind jostling forty-eight rosebuds held tightly in my arms.

When we arrived at the house, we were met by Nam and his wife, Rose. They asked us to join them in the garden. They had a peaceful patio behind one of the oldest residences in Hà Nội, originally occupied by the French governor Henri Hoppenot. It was a stucco villa, faded yellow with green shutters. Hồ Chí Minh had given this home to General Giáp after he defeated the French at the battle of Điện Biên Phủ.

Nam is the youngest son of General Võ Nguyên Giáp. He and I are two sons of two fathers involved in the same struggle. His father came to be revered; mine came to be hated.* He was in Việt Nam for the American War. I was in America during the Việt Nam War.

The garden was welcoming, with the general's koi pond at its center. Surrounding the pond a tall trellis supported baskets of deep green ferns and climbing roses. Nam explained to me that the gray canisters supporting the trellis were casings from U.S. bombs dropped on Hà Nội. I didn't ask whether the bombs had struck close to the home where he now lived.

Together, we squatted on our haunches on the patio tile, trimming rose stems and placing them in large brass urns. Our conversation was that of new acquaintances, curious about the past and present, filled with kindness and respect. Had the roles been reversed, with Nam and Rose arriving at our farm in California on a summer day, I could envision us greeting each other in the same way, peacefully accepting a gift.

I followed Nam and Rose up the steps into a room of their home that housed the shrine of his father. As we entered the shrine, we removed our shoes and lit incense, placing it on the altar adorned with fresh fruit. We placed our roses on the altar. Nam took my hand. Together, we bowed in silence. On the wall behind me was a large portrait of the general in uniform, a warm smile on his face, made from a collage of over 3,000 smaller photos of him.

We then crossed the patio to the general's formal meeting room. The walls, bookshelves, and tables—every square inch—were covered with

---

* Robert S. McNamara was the U.S. secretary of defense from 1961 to 1968 and played a major role in the U.S. military involvement in the Việt Nam War.

photos, statues, medals, banners, plaques, and memorabilia from the general's long life. In this room, Võ Nguyên Giáp had met with hundreds of leaders from around the world. I saw statues of Uncle Hồ and Chairman Mao, as well as photos of Fidel Castro, Leonid Brezhnev, Chilean president Michelle Bachelet, Brazilian president Lula da Silva, Jacques Chirac, and so many more.

As we sat and talked, Nam presented me with a recently released book celebrating his father's life. As we leafed through the pages, I found on page 165 a photo of General Giáp and my father taken on November 9, 1993. The caption read: "The most brilliant Vietnamese general was the Vietnamese people, the Vietnamese nation. The Americans were defeated by Việt Nam because they did not yet understand that general."

My father was synonymous with the war in the minds of Americans. I mentioned this to Nam. He replied, "I think that when my father met your father, he said, 'Americans didn't understand Vietnamese culture and history.' And he was so right."

From Craig McNamara, *Because Our Fathers Lied: A Memoir of Truth and Family, from Vietnam to Today* (Boston: Little, Brown, and Company, 2022), 240–43. Reprinted by permission of the author.

## Why So Many South Vietnamese Feared a Bloodbath

### Gareth Porter

The chaotic scenes of panicked South Vietnamese desperately trying to get on American helicopters at the U.S. Embassy in Sài Gòn and American ships offshore dramatized the extreme fear of Communist postwar reprisals that had permeated the minds of those who worked for the U.S. or South Vietnamese military or government, as well as citizens without such connections.

It is no wonder that the fear of postwar revenge killings had become so extreme by the end of the war. The Sài Gòn and U.S. governments had worked hard to establish that idea in the minds of both South Vietnamese and Americans beginning early in the U.S. war in Việt Nam. One such effort was to make an alleged defector, Lê Xuân Chuyển—who claimed to have been a lieutenant colonel in the Việt Nam People's Army before defecting in August 1966—available for interviews with correspondents for two U.S. newspapers. He informed one reporter that the Communists had a so-called "blood debt" list that included some five million South Vietnamese, and told another reporter that there were three million on the list, and that 10 to 15 percent of them would be killed.*

But even the official U.S. interrogators of Lê Xuân Chuyển were doubtful about his claim to be a senior officer, pointedly putting question marks after the rank and past assignments he claimed to have had in the Việt Nam People's Army. Furthermore, Lê Xuân Chuyển had immediately volunteered to work for either the Americans or the Sài Gòn government, and within only a few months he was named director of the government's Chiêu Hồi ("Open Arms") [Rallier] Program for Sài Gòn—the position he held when his testimony was being offered as authoritative evidence of North Vietnamese intentions to carry out bloody postwar reprisals.†

A second Communist defector, Colonel Trần Văn Đắc, made an even more important contribution to the fear of a postwar bloodbath. The leading U.S. propagandist on the issue, Douglas Pike of the U.S. Information Agency, wrote a tract released by the U.S. government operations in Sài Gòn in 1970 that quoted a statement by Colonel Trần Văn Đắc that "there are 3 million South Vietnamese on the blood debt list." His claim was then published in the *Washington Post* and in an op-ed in the *New York Times* by British counterinsurgency specialist Sir Robert Thompson in 1972.

But Trần Văn Đắc's statement had no credibility either, since at that time he was working as planning adviser to the General Directorate of Political Warfare of the Sài Gòn Army and thus represented the interest of the military regime.‡

Furthermore, this writer obtained the full text of the series of U.S.

---

\* *Daily News Washington*, November 5, 1969; *Los Angeles Times*, November 20, 1969.

† U.S. State Department, *Captured Documents and Interrogation Reports* (1968), item no. 55, "Interrogation of Lê Xuân Chuyển."

‡ Gareth Porter, "The 1968 'Hue Massacre,'" *Indochina Chronicle*, no. 33 (June 24, 1974). https://msuweb.montclair.edu/~furrg/porterhue1.html.

interviews with Trần Văn Đắc from the Joint U.S. Public Affairs Office in 1971 and found that he had said nothing to suggest the existence of any blood debt list or Communist policy of reprisals against military or civilian personnel of the Sài Gòn government in the time before going to work for the government. Instead he said that those who had collaborated with the Sài Gòn regime would be subject to "re-education."

What Trần Văn Đắc had claimed did not happen after the war, as was acknowledged by journalists and scholars who confirmed that the dreaded postwar killings had not happened.* Nevertheless, two authors, Jacqueline Desbarats and Karl D. Jackson (who later served as deputy assistant secretary of defense for East Asia and the Pacific and as special assistant to the president and senior director for Asia at the National Security Council), claimed that as many as 65,000 Vietnamese had been executed by the Vietnamese authorities in the early postwar years.

But they arrived at that sensational conclusion only by using a methodology that was so fundamentally flawed that it rendered their estimate meaningless. From interviews with Vietnamese refugee networks in Chicago and California in the early 1980s, Desbarats and Jackson had collected forty-seven stories of individuals said to have been killed for political reasons after the war. But of those forty-seven stories, sixteen—one-third of the total—were duplicates. Therefore there were only thirty-one unique names, from which they extrapolated without correcting for the problem of duplications, to arrive at their 65,000 estimate.

If they had used statistically valid methodology for estimating how many names would have been produced by interviewing comparable networks worldwide—a methodology called sampling with replacement—along with the computer program necessary to simulate the necessary number of such random samples, they would have found that the 34 percent duplication rate in their very small sample of forty-seven names was so high that it indicated that the total number of unique names worldwide would have

---

* See Elizabeth Becker, "Vietnam: The Faltering Revolution," *Washington Post*, September 23, 1979; William Duiker, *Vietnam since the Fall of Saigon* (Athens: Ohio University Monographs in International Studies, Southeast Asia Series, no. 56, revised edition, 1985), 10–13.

been only fifty-two. What the authors actually confirmed by that exercise, therefore, was that there was, in fact, no postwar killing of people for their wartime roles.*

Written in 2022.

## War Crimes against Vietnamese Civilians
### Gareth Porter

The American military forces in Việt Nam inflicted war crimes against Vietnamese civilians both on the ground and from the air. The U.S. carried out indiscriminate air and artillery strikes on hamlets that had been identified as "Việt Cộng–controlled," killing a massive number of civilians. Those attacks were justified by the creation of "free fire zones," which effectively treated civilians as legitimate military targets and were violations of the laws of war, but they were approved by Secretary of Defense Robert S. McNamara as helpful to the war effort.[†]

American troops also used napalm in flamethrowers against tunnels and other shelters in villages where they believed what they referred to as the Việt Cộng were hiding. That meant that many Vietnamese civilians in shelters were killed by napalm, a sticky, gel-like firebomb. Napalm generates eight to twelve times more heat than is required to boil water and kills by both burns and asphyxiation, by generating carbon monoxide while removing oxygen from the air. This was especially effective in a confined space. Use of napalm generated anti-war protests and the demand for a boycott against the manufacturer, the Dow Chemical Company.

The most widely known war crime was the cold-blooded killings on March 16, 1968, of more than five hundred old men, women, and children

---

[*] Gareth Porter and James Roberts, "Creating a Bloodbath by Statistical Manipulation," *Pacific Affairs*, vol. 61, no. 2 (Summer 1988), 303–10.

[†] Gareth Porter, "My Lai and the American Way of War Crimes," in *The United States, Southeast Asia, and Historical Memory*, ed. Mark Pavlick with Carolyn Luft (Chicago: Haymarket Books, 2019), 98–100.

in Mỹ Lai and Mỹ Khê, two hamlets of Sơn Mỹ village in Quảng Ngãi Province. This became generally known only because of a story filed by then independent journalist Seymour Hersh through the virtually unknown Dispatch News Service.

A military commission led by General William Peers conducted an investigation into how and why the atrocities were carried out, but that investigation stopped short of asking what responsibility the commander of U.S. forces in Việt Nam, General William Westmoreland, had for the killings.* The Peers Commission report explained that company commanders in charge of the operation in the two hamlets had been instructed by the commander of the task force to which the company belonged that Mỹ Lai was considered to be what it referred to as a Việt Cộng stronghold, and that "only the enemy remained in the operational area and that the enemy was to be destroyed."

It would have been an explicit and punishable war crime to order troops to kill innocent civilians, in this case women and children and old people. But the Peers Commission learned that this order had been couched in indirect terms that clearly implied but did not state flatly that civilians were to be killed. Instead, the commission described the policy directives from Westmoreland's command approvingly as "adhering to the human standard of protecting the civilians within the combat zone," citing in particular the 1965 command directive that it described as forbidding "indiscriminate fire" in populated zones.

But the Peers Commission deliberately covered up the truth, which was that the directive clearly stated that prohibitions on indiscriminate fire against civilians did not apply to National Liberation Front base areas where the insurgents had exercised long-term control. The commission had carried out a carefully calculated cover-up of the military command's responsibility for the slaughter of innocent civilians. That fact should not be surprising, because by the time the Peers Commission began its investigation, General Westmoreland was the chief of staff of the U.S. Army and Peers was therefore part of his chain of command, meaning that Peers could

---

* Porter, "My Lai and the American Way of War Crimes," 90–97.

not and did not carry out a truly independent and honest investigation of Mỹ Lai.

Americans were not the only foreign troops that committed mass civilian atrocities during the war. South Korean troops were operating in Việt Nam in return for full payment of all their expenses and extremely lucrative contracts for South Korean construction firms and exporters for the war.* Residents of hamlets within the areas in which South Korean troops were carrying out military operations provided detailed testimony that there were many incidents of deliberate mass killings of Vietnamese civilians by South Korean troops. AFSC staff members Diane Jones and Michael Jones collected the testimonies of survivors of those atrocities over several months in 1972. In a detailed report of what they learned from survivors in forty-five hamlets in different provinces of northern South Việt Nam, twenty-two of which were in two districts of Quảng Ngãi Province, they reported the cold-blooded killing of between 1,720 and 2,220 civilians.†

These South Korean atrocities had been brought to the attention of the U.S. military as early as 1966, after a Pentagon-supported team of Vietnamese interviewers was told by hundreds of village residents about incidents in which the Korean troops had lined up women, men, and children and shot them in cold blood in retribution after having taken sniper fire somewhere near a hamlet. Terry Rambo, the American director of the research, told the U.S officer assigned to monitor the project about his findings, and he was summoned to Sài Gòn to brief a group of senior U.S. officers. Soon after that meeting, Rambo was ordered by his liaison officer to stop investigating the South Koreans and to not mention the reported atrocities in his written report.‡

---

* Frank Baldwin, "The American Utilization of South Korean Troops in Vietnam," in *America's Rented Troops: South Koreans in Vietnam* (Philadelphia: American Friends Service Committee, 1974), 1–16.

† Diane Jones and Michael Jones, "Allies Called Koreans—A Report from Vietnam," in *America's Rented Troops: South Koreans in Vietnam* (Philadelphia: American Friends Service Committee, 1974), 17–45.

‡ Robert M. Smith, "Vietnam Killings Laid to Koreans," *New York Times*, January 10, 1970.

The U.S. military sought to keep the atrocities of its Korean allies secret because the Pentagon was dependent on the South Koreans to maintain control of the northern provinces. The United States pressured the South Korean government to keep troops there, especially after President Nixon began withdrawing U.S. troops. No South Korean troops were withdrawn from South Việt Nam until after the Paris Peace Agreement was signed in January 1973.*

Written in 2022.

## Agent Orange and Birth Defects

### Gareth Porter

Between 1962 and 1971, U.S. forces sprayed some 19.5 million gallons of highly toxic chemical defoliants—including approximately 12 million gallons of Agent Orange—onto nearly 4 million acres in South Việt Nam in a campaign named Operation Ranch Hand. It has been estimated that at least 2.1 million people living in 3,181 hamlets were sprayed, and the true number is probably more than twice that many. Scientists who learned that those defoliants contained dioxins, which are highly toxic and extremely persistent environmental pollutants, lobbied against the policy. The result was a study contracted by the U.S. government in the mid-1960s that concluded that the dioxin known as TCDD in Agent Orange caused increased stillbirths and birth defects in pregnant rats exposed to it.†

By the 1970s the incidence of Vietnamese children born with horrible deformities, as well as deformed fetuses of stillborn babies, was extremely widespread, and over the intervening decades the effects of Agent Orange have afflicted later generations. *Wall Street Journal* reporter Peter Waldman

---

* Benjamin A. Engel, "Viewing Seoul from Saigon: Withdrawal from the Vietnam War and the Yushin Regime," *Journal of Northeast Asian History*, vol. 13, no. 1 (Summer 2016): 77–106.

† Jesse King and Cecilia Chou, "Agent Orange Birth Defects," The Embryo Project Encyclopedia. https://embryo.asu.edu/pages/agent-orange-birth-defects.

wrote in 1997 about the nursery in Hồ Chí Minh City's Từ Dũ Hospital, where he saw babies with toes where legs should be, arms that ended above the elbow, and a partial torso and a head. Even more gruesome were aborted and stillborn fetuses in glass jars. They included "giant heads with tiny bodies, faces without features," and "partly formed fetuses ravaged by grape-like tumors" from their own placentas. This writer had been shown similar deformed fetuses displayed in the laboratory of Dr. Nguyễn Thị Ngọc Phượng, the leading researcher on the effects of Agent Orange on children in Việt Nam, during a visit to Từ Dũ Hospital in 1982.

U.S. service members, especially those who worked around those bases where Agent Orange was stored and who operated in rivers whose banks were heavily sprayed, were also exposed to the dioxins, causing a wide range of serious illnesses. More than 650,000 veterans have been granted disability benefits for diseases related to their Agent Orange exposure, according to Department of Veterans Affairs estimates.* In 1996 Veterans Affairs finally acknowledged an association between male veterans' exposure to Agent Orange and spina bifida neural defects by adding that condition to the official list of diseases recognized as connected to such exposure, although they refused to include other defects of the brain, spine, and spinal cord.†

But the U.S. government has resisted taking responsibility for Vietnamese birth defects and other serious disabilities caused by Agent Orange exposure, denying that it had reliable evidence of a link between them and exposure to dioxin. The U.S. ambassador to Việt Nam, Michael W. Marine, declared in 2007, "[W]e just don't have the scientific evidence to make that statement [that birth defects are linked to dioxin exposure] with certainty."‡

The U.S. Congress has appropriated $266 million on environmental remediation of the Đà Nẵng and Biên Hòa airbases, the two main sites for storing the herbicides, and $94.4 million on programs designated for

---

* Charles Ornstein, "Agent Orange Act Was Supposed to Help Vietnam Veterans—But Many Still Don't Qualify," *ProPublica*, July 17, 2015. https://www.propublica.org/article/agent-orange-act-was-supposed-to-help-vietnam-veterans-but-many-still-dont-.

† King and Chou, "Agent Orange Birth Defects," The Embryo Project Encyclopedia.

‡ Michael F. Martin, "Vietnam Victims of Agent Orange and U.S.-Vietnam Relations," *Congressional Research Service*, August 29, 2012, 7. https://fas.org/sgp/crs/row/RL34761.pdf.

disability and health in those locations where the herbicides were sprayed and are regarded as Agent Orange hotspots. But the Congressional Research Service pointed out that the U.S. Agency for International Development spent less than two-thirds of the funds Congress had appropriated from FY 2011 through FY 2017 for health-related projects in those areas. Little of the money that was spent, moreover, went to assist individuals with severe mobility impairment in areas known to be contaminated by dioxins, despite the explicit directive of Senate Appropriations Committee chairman Patrick Leahy. The explanation for these anomalies, as CRS specialist Michael Martin explained, is that the State Department was determined to avoid any implication of legal liability for the human costs of Agent Orange by steering clear of any right to medical benefits from the United States.*

Written in 2022.

## The Third Force

### Gareth Porter

The Third Force in South Việt Nam during the Việt Nam War was not a specific political organization. Rather, it was a political tendency toward neutralism and an end to the war through a peaceful settlement that influenced the North Vietnamese leadership to include a "third segment" in its proposal for an ultimate political settlement, in addition to the PRG (Provisional Revolutionary Government) and the military-dominated Thiệu government.[†]

---

* Congressional Research Service, "U.S. Agent Orange/Dioxin Assistance to Vietnam," updated February 10, 2021. https://crsreports.congress.gov/product/pdf/R/R44268/26; Amruta Byatnal, "USAID Begins New Round of Agent Orange Cleanup in Vietnam," *Devex Inside Development/Global Health*, January 8, 2020. https://www.devex.com/news/usaid-begins-new-round-of-agent-orange-cleanup-in vietnam-96222#:~:text=More%20on%20USAID%3A&text=The%20operation%20follows%20a%20similar,took%20six%20years%20to%20complete.

† For a full-length study of the Third Force, see Sophie Quinn-Judge, *The Third Force in the Vietnam War: The Elusive Search for Peace, 1954–75* (London: I. B. Tauris, 2017).

In contrast to the 1966 struggle movements, the Third Force was neither a mass movement nor an organization with a formal structure. It was a grouping of political figures in South Việt Nam's cities who were adamantly opposed to the military government and advocated an end to the war, but who were not part of the Communist-controlled political organization in the south.

Those who associated themselves with the Third Force were prominent lawyers (Trần Ngọc Liếng and Columbia University–trained Ngô Bá Thành), National Assembly members (Ngô Công Đức, Lý Quí Chung, and Hồ Ngọc Nhuận), Catholic priests (Nguyễn Ngọc Lan and Chân Tín), the Buddhist clergy (Mendicant nun Huỳnh Liên), university professors (Châu Tâm Luân), and student leaders (Huỳnh Tấn Mẫm, chairman of the Sài Gòn–Gia Định Student Union). It reflected common demands from urban strata for peace and independence from the overweening U.S. influence and against the imposition of military rule on South Việt Nam.

This new political force emerged after the tumultuous events of the 1966–68 period of the war. Mass struggle movements broke out in Sài Gòn and central Việt Nam in defiance of the U.S.-supported military government. They took control in Đà Nẵng and Huế but were ultimately broken up by police and government troops.* The result was that militant mass protests and defiance ended, with most of the militants joining the Communist forces or going into hiding. Then the ultimate failure of the Communist 1968 Tết Offensive, which was launched in the hope that popular uprisings would be triggered in the cities, forced a fundamental re-evaluation of Hà Nội's war strategy.

In 1969 the Democratic Republic of Việt Nam decided on a prolonged lull in offensive military action in the south and began to revise its diplomatic strategy to put new emphasis on the Third Force. In September 1970, the DRV and NLF proposed for the first time a provisional coalition government with three distinct segments: one representing the PRG; one

---

* James R. Bullington, "The Impolite American Consul: A Memoir of the 1966 Buddhist Struggle Movement in Huế," *American Diplomacy* (August 2020). https://americandiplomacy.web.unc.edu/2020/08/the-impolite-american-consul-a-memoir-of-the-1966-buddhist-struggle-movement-in-hue/.

representing the Sài Gòn administration, excluding Thiệu, Nguyễn Cao Kỳ, and Prime Minister Trần Thiện Khiêm; and one representing "persons of various political and religious forces and tendencies standing for peace, independence, neutrality and democracy." In the negotiations between North Việt Nam and Henry Kissinger in 1972 and early 1973, the proposed tripartite governing structure became the National Council of Reconciliation and Concord, responsible for overseeing national elections in which the Third Force would be represented in one of the segments. But although that structure became part of the agreement, the National Council was never formed, because Thiệu's resistance prevented the Paris Peace Agreement from being carried out.*

After the Communist victory in 1975, some in the Third Force joined the victorious regime while others sought to remain completely independent. Ngô Bá Thành became a member of the National Assembly in Hà Nội, where she exercised independent judgment as part of the committee that wrote an entirely new penal code. Ngô Công Đức continued to publish *Tin Sáng* as a newspaper independent of the government from 1975 to 1981, but it was then closed down by the authorities in order to achieve "complete unity of will and voice."†

Redemptorist priest Chân Tín ran afoul of the authorities by criticizing the arrest of political dissidents and was accused of "alienating believers and the clergy from the people and the regime." He was exiled to a remote parish from 1990 to 1993 before finally being released and allowed to return to Hồ Chí Minh City.‡

Written in 2022.

---

* Gareth Porter, *A Peace Denied: The United States, Vietnam, and the Paris Agreement* (Bloomington: Indiana University Press, 1975), 92–95, 97–98, 167.

† Gareth Porter, *Vietnam: The Politics of Bureaucratic Socialism* (Ithaca: Cornell University Press, 1993), 74, 167.

‡ "Father Chân Tín Has Been Unconditionally Released," *Tin Nha* (Paris), May 13, 1993. http://www.iath.virginia.edu/sixties/HTML_docs/Texts/Scholarly/Tuong_Chan_Tin_release.html.

# Re-education Camps

*Gareth Porter*

The new government in South Việt Nam after the Communist victory in 1975 was confronted with a sociopolitical problem of massive proportions: the defeated Army of the Republic of Việt Nam, generally known as ARVN, numbered more than a million men by 1972, with more than 400,000 regulars and some 500,00 territorial militias, making it the fourth-largest army in the world.* Along with the South Vietnamese police and civilian intelligence organizations and anti-Communist political parties, it constituted a political security nightmare for the Communists.

The approach of the Communist Party leadership in Hà Nội to the problem was similar to the one carried out in North Việt Nam after the 1954 victory over the French forces: a large-scale system of re-education camps for a selected portion of the total population that had been associated with the regime's political-military effort. As many as one million people were ordered to attend local re-education sessions in Sài Gòn and other cities and released after a few days. But somewhere between 200,000 and 300,000 South Vietnamese soldiers, security personnel, and higher-level bureaucrats and leaders of political parties that supported the war were sent to twenty-one such camps in the first few years.†

At first those re-education camps appeared to be striving to change the political attitudes of these anti-Communist officials and activists through a process of "confessions" and collective discussions of their "crimes." But

---

* "Republic of Vietnam Armed Forces (RVNAF) Strength," GlobalSecurity.org. https://www.globalsecurity.org/military/world/vietnam/rvn-af-strength.htm.

† In 1976, the vice chairman of the Hồ Chí Minh City administration said the number of people sent to re-education camps was more than 200,000, whereas former PRG minister of justice Trương Như Tảng, who later wrote a memoir critical of the Communist regime, put the number at 300,000. Nayan Chanda, "Opening Day for a New Class of Generals," *Far Eastern Economic Review* (May 14, 1976), 20; Trương Như Tảng, *A Vietcong Memoir: An Inside Account of the Vietnam War and Its Aftermath* (New York: Knopf Doubleday, 1986), 282.

after the rise of what party officials regarded as more serious security threats from China, along with severe economic problems beginning in 1978, the camps apparently became more a way to isolate those presumed security risks from active illegal opposition groups, and their detention was prolonged indefinitely.*

Living conditions in the camps were not uniform, and there were reports of beatings for violating camp rules. In some cases food and medical supplies were inadequate, causing the deaths of some inmates. There were instances of prisoners being executed for trying to escape from the camps.†

In 1984 the National Assembly of the Socialist Republic of Việt Nam passed legislation eliminating re-education as a form of punishment, replacing it with "residence under surveillance"—that is, surveillance in place. But the security apparatus in South Việt Nam had acquired the power to get around even such fundamental legal requirements. In 1987 the Peoples Committee of Hồ Chí Minh City adopted regulations providing for "concentrated re-education" for those who "refuse to be re-educated." It was not until 1988 that nearly all the original camp inmates were finally released.‡

Written in 2022.

## Việt Nam's Religions

### Gareth Porter

Before and during the Việt Nam conflict, most Vietnamese did not follow either of the two dominant organized religions in the country, Buddhism and Catholicism. Instead, they integrated Mahayana Buddhist teachings, Daoist beliefs, and Confucianism—a combination called tam giáo ("the

---

\* For testimony of a former camp inmate, see *Christian Science Monitor,* November 2, 1987.

† Ginetta Sagan and Stephen Denney, *Violations of Human Rights in the Socialist Republic of Vietnam, April 30, 1975–April 30, 1983* (Atherton, California: Aurora Foundation, 1983), 18–33.

‡ Gareth Porter, *Vietnam: The Politics of Bureaucratic Socialism* (Ithaca: Cornell University Press, 1993), 175–76.

three religions"). Most villagers in South Việt Nam attended Buddhist pagodas on holidays but were more likely to identify their religion as "ancestor worship" rather than Buddhism.

Many Buddhist monks, however, became discontent with Catholic president Ngô Đình Diệm's favoritism toward Catholics, and this sparked protests in spring and summer 1963. The protests culminated in Buddhist monk Thích Quảng Đức immolating himself, leading to the political crisis and overthrow of the regime.

In March 1966, Buddhist activists against President Diệm's regime launched what they called the Struggle Movement and, with the support of troops loyal to the Buddhist South Vietnamese Army Corps commander for the region, took control of Đà Nẵng and Huế, the two largest cities in central Việt Nam. The military regime was not able to regain control of Đà Nẵng until late May and Huế until mid-June, and even though it had to go underground, the political influence of the Struggle Movement lingered in both cities and reverberated in Sài Gòn itself.

Vietnamese Catholics were concentrated mainly in North Việt Nam, and they organized communities over which priests presided. Most Catholic communities were organized by the Catholic hierarchy to resist the Việt Minh forces, but many Catholics did support the Việt Minh war against the French. In 1954, more than 600,000 Catholics took advantage of the 1954 Geneva Agreement to move from Communist-led North Việt Nam to South Việt Nam, which was already under a Catholic regime. The move was carried out on U.S. Navy ships under the leadership of 350 anti-Communist North Vietnamese parish priests and ten of the twelve Vietnamese bishops in all of North Việt Nam. In the south, the parish priests continued to act as the Catholic community's political as well as spiritual guides. Later, a number of Catholic priests turned against the American war and became part of the Third Force.

A much smaller community of Vietnamese Protestants, 200,000 in South Việt Nam, was affiliated with the Protestant Evangelical Church of Việt Nam. The church's officials and clergy were highly critical of the new regime in the south and had significant membership among the ethnic minorities of the Central Highlands of South Việt Nam, many of whom fought with the United Front for the Liberation of Oppressed Races

(FULRO) against both the Sài Gòn regime and the Communist forces during the war. Acute conflict between these ethnic minority Protestants and the Communist regime led to armed resistance in the postwar period, which had died down by the early 1980s.* The Protestant Evangelical Church also gained a large following among young urban professionals.

The Hòa Hảo Buddhist sect arose in the Seven Mountains area of South Việt Nam near the Cambodian border, where its founder, Hùynh Phú Sổ, was regarded as a Buddhist prophet and mystic who encouraged simple Buddhist worship. He gained as many as two million followers in the western Mekong Delta region in the 1930s, and after the Japanese occupation forces armed the Hòa Hảo, the sect established political and military control over the region. He refused to form a united front with the Communist-led Việt Minh against the French, and instead allied the sect with the French. The Việt Minh then executed Sổ on charges of treason. The Hòa Hảo conflict with the Communist-led forces continued through the entire Việt Minh War and again during the U.S. war.

The Cao Đài sect prominent in the Mekong Delta region of South Việt Nam blends the tam giáo religious tradition with the hierarchy of the Catholic Church. It was started by educated Vietnamese landowners and also recruited hundreds of thousands of landless peasants. Its colorful Holy See temple headquarters in Tây Ninh is a cross between a Buddhist pagoda and a Catholic cathedral. Once estimated to have 900,000 followers, the sect was initially armed by the Japanese occupation forces in the early 1940s and allied with the French against the Việt Minh. It remained anti-Communist through the Việt Nam War and was reduced to a fraction of that number after the Communist victory.

Written in 2022. Based on Gareth Porter, *Vietnam: The Politics of Bureaucratic Socialism* (Ithaca: Cornell University Press, 1993), 13, 37–42, except where indicated.

---

* Reg Reimer, "Evangelicals in Vietnam: We Are Living by Faith," *Indochina Issues* (April 1987), 8–9. Interview with a member of the Evangelical Church of Vietnam living in the United States, January 18, 1988; *Montagnard Christians in Vietnam: A Case Study in Religious Repression*. Human Rights Watch, 2011. http://www.hrw.org/sites/default/files/reports/vietnam0311Web.pdf.

# The Paris Peace Agreement

*Gareth Porter*

The Paris Peace Agreement, signed on January 27, 1973, was supposed to end the war in Việt Nam with a U.S. withdrawal and a ceasefire. It did accomplish the U.S. troop withdrawal but failed to end the war between the regime of Nguyễn Văn Thiệu and the Communist-led forces opposing it, because of the policy of the Richard M. Nixon administration to continue to maintain its client regime in Sài Gòn under President Nguyễn Văn Thiệu.

Signatories to the agreement were the Government of the Republic of Việt Nam (South), the Democratic Republic of Việt Nam (North), the Provisional Revolutionary Government (South), and the United States of America. The signing of the Paris Agreement was the direct result of a major North Vietnamese offensive in spring 1972 that broke a four-year stalemate in U.S.–North Vietnamese peace talks in Paris and resulted in agreement in October 1972 on most of a complete text, but with crucial issues still outstanding. Nixon then ordered the bombing of civilian targets in the northern cities of Hà Nội and Hải Phòng by B-52 bombers, an attack that later became known as the Christmas Bombing because it began December 18 and continued until December 29. Nixon's objective in carrying out the bombing was to wrest further concessions from the North Vietnamese in a final round of negotiations in Paris in January 1973. South Vietnamese president Thiệu wanted more concessions, but he was compelled to sign what the U.S. had agreed to.

However, in the final January 1973 negotiations, North Vietnamese negotiators obtained what they regarded as critical concessions from Secretary of State Henry Kissinger on the most crucial issues remaining: the principal of unity of Việt Nam, the status of North Vietnamese troops in the south, and the characterization of a National Council of Reconciliation and Concord, representing the core of a political settlement process in South Việt Nam. The North Vietnamese negotiators were able to win those concessions because they were ultimately more important to the North Vietnamese side than to the American side, and the Americans believed they could not get a settlement without making them.

The result was the Agreement on Ending the War and Restoring Peace in Việt Nam, under which U.S. forces were finally completely withdrawn from Việt Nam but North Vietnamese forces remained in the south in support of southerners under Communist command fighting the Thiệu regime. Thiệu, who had opposed the negotiation of any such agreement from the beginning as a threat to his power, sought to nullify it, but Hà Nội and its supporters in the south sought to use it to further weaken the legitimacy of the U.S.-backed regime. Nixon and Kissinger wanted the agreement to affirm the demarcation line between North and South Việt Nam as a permanent legal reality. But one of the primary objectives of the Vietnamese negotiators in Paris was to deny the permanent legal status of that demarcation line. The 1954 Geneva Accords had established the demarcation line to divide the northern and southern parts of Việt Nam only temporarily, until a scheduled vote could take place in 1956 to reunify the country under one government. That vote did not happen, however, because the United States encouraged the South Vietnamese regime of Ngô Đình Diệm to refuse to cooperate in carrying out such an election, almost certain that it would be won by Hồ Chí Minh's Communist government.

The agreement also established the National Council of Reconciliation and Concord, which had as a key function promoting implementation of the agreement and achievement of national reconciliation and democratic liberties. The agreement further required freedom of movement of people displaced by war, which represented a threat to the Thiệu regime of a potential loss of hundreds of thousands of people who had fled from bombing and artillery operations against the Communist-controlled areas and now wished to return to their homes in the PRG zones of control. Zones of control were never officially demarcated; they simply reflected the territory in which the military forces of the two sides were stationed at the time of the ceasefire.

The agreement called for a standstill ceasefire to go into effect on January 27—the same day the peace agreement was signed. But the ceasefire was doomed from the start by Nixon's policy of bolstering Thiệu militarily and assuring him that the U.S.–Sài Gòn patron-client relationship would continue as before. Even just before the agreement was signed, the United

States had delivered an additional $1.2 billion in new armaments to the Thiệu regime. In private letters in November and again in January, Nixon assured Thiệu that the U.S. would respond "with full force" to any North Vietnamese violation of the agreement. Finally, just as the last U.S. troops were leaving the country, the Pentagon secretly sent a new corps of several thousand civilian military specialists working for twenty-three military contractors to continue work in maintaining Thiệu's air force. That was an obvious violation of Article 4 of the agreement, under which the United States pledged that it "would not continue its military involvement or intervene in the internal affairs of South Việt Nam."

Instead of observing a ceasefire, Thiệu carried out a nationwide counter-offensive after the ceasefire to recapture territory that had been seized by Communist-led forces just prior to the ceasefire. Journalists for *Newsweek*, the *Manchester Guardian*, and the *Times of London* were in PRG-controlled villages during the first few days of the ceasefire and reported Thiệu-government shelling and bombing attacks on those villages.

Communist-led forces in the south, calling themselves the People's Liberation Armed Forces (PLAF) did not respond militarily to the Thiệu regime's violations of the ceasefire agreement with counterattacks on the Sài Gòn zone for eight months. But in October 1973 the PRG issued a public order to main-force units to counterattack in any area attacked by the Thiệu regime forces if they continued their offensive strikes. Over the next two months the anti-Thiệu forces regained territory in several provinces. Thiệu then declared that the Third Indochina War had begun. He ordered heavy bombing raids on Lộc Ninh and other towns controlled by the PRG in Tây Ninh Province, and sent twenty-one battalions to push the PLAF out of their main areas of control in the northern Mekong Delta. U.S. officials estimated Sài Gòn had regained control of an estimated one million people through the new offensive operations in the PRG zone there.

But Thiệu was counting on Nixon's threat to resume the bombing of North Việt Nam to force the PLAF to avoid an all-out counter-offensive. Instead, Nixon's cover-up of his role in the Watergate break-in began to unravel at the end of April, and on July 31 the U.S. House of Representatives voted to end the bombing in Cambodia and to prohibit any further

U.S. military activity in Indochina without congressional authorization.*
The PLAF launched a new phase of offensive operations aimed at regaining territory recently taken in ARVN operations. The party leadership in Hà Nội decided in October that the opportune moment had finally arrived for a decisive offensive in 1975 to defeat the Thiệu regime's army and finally end the war in Việt Nam.

Written in 2022 and based on Gareth Porter, *A Peace Denied: The United States, Vietnam, and the Paris Agreement* (Bloomington: Indiana University Press, 1975).

---

* Indochina, also called the Indochinese Peninsula, was the name given by Europeans in the early 1800s to the region east of India and south of China, comprised generally of the land of the current countries of Việt Nam, Laos, and Kampuchea (French Indochina), and also Malaysia, Myanmar, and Thailand.

# INDEX

*Vietnamese names are alphabetized as in Vietnamese (family name first, then middle, then first), but because people are often referred to only by their first names (for example, Nguyễn Văn Thiệu is referred to as Thiệu), a cross-reference is also given at the first name for more famous people.*

Abzug, Bella (member of Congress), 19
Adams, Eddie (photographer), 190
AFSC. *See* American Friends Service Committee
Agent Orange, 12, 101, 203, 216, 246, 247, 248
Agreement on Ending the War and Restoring Peace in Việt Nam, 256
Air America airline, 7, 26, 46
Air Việt Nam airline (Air Vietnam), 7, 8, 46
American Friends Service Committee (AFSC), x, xv, 1, 6, 7, 10, 11, 15, 19, 21, 22, 23, 29, 36, 42, 94, 101, 107, 122, 137, 140, 145, 152, 166, 175, 177, 178, 179, 199, 217, 228, 237, 245. *See also* Quakers
ancestor worship, Vietnamese belief, 9, 253. *See also* religions
Anh Duy, 110, 111, 121, 134, 135, 142
Army of the Republic of (South) Việt Nam (ARVN), xv, 21, 22, 23, 24, 26, 27, 29, 31, 34, 39, 40, 41, 47, 48, 50, 53, 55, 56, 57, 58, 59, 60, 62, 65, 67, 71, 72, 73, 98, 118, 135, 136, 140, 144, 175, 184, 185, 188, 190, 227, 231, 232, 251, 258
Arnett, Peter, 43

ARVN. *See* Army of the Republic of (South) Việt Nam
Associated Press, 43, 69, 177, 190

Bà Hai (cook), 47, 48, 73, 74, 83, 94, 96, 124, 133, 171, 196, 207, 210–11, 213
Baldwin, Frank, 245
Ba Minh (Dung's husband), 73, 146, 197
Ban Mê Thuột (city), 24
Barclay Quakers, 46, 160
Barsky Hospital (Barsky Unit), 45, 46, 128, 142
Bartlett, Dewey (U.S. senator), 19–20, 231
BBC (British Broadcasting Corporation), 8, 20, 29, 37, 48, 50, 51, 52, 59, 68, 100, 150
*Because Our Fathers Lied* (McNamara), 238–40
begging nuns. *See* Mendicant nuns
B-52 bombers, 11, 38, 69, 85, 255
Biên Hòa (city), 36, 39, 42, 47–48, 51, 52, 77, 91, 196
Biên Hòa airbase, 42, 247
"Big" Minh. *See* Dương Văn Minh (Duong Van Minh)

# INDEX

Bình, Nguyễn Thị. *See* Nguyễn Thị Bình
Bình Dân (Binh Dan) Hospital, 127
Bình Thủy (Binh Thuy) airbase, 44
birth defects, 101, 246–48. *See also* Agent Orange
black market, 29, 46, 81, 139
bloodbath, fears of, ix, 20, 44, 240–43
blood debt lists, ix, 242
boat people, 218–19. *See also* refugees
Brinton, Keith, 1, 5, 6, 10–13, 18, 19, 58, 60, 93, 104, 105, 136, 142, 179, 217, 220, 221
*Brother Enemy* (Chanda), 112
Buddhism, 33, 41, 73, 78, 88, 141, 147, 148, 233, 235–36, 249, 252–54
Bunker, Ellsworth (admiral), 231
Bửu Chi (Buu Chi), 65

Cambodia, 12, 110, 111, 113, 114, 116, 163, 167, 170, 171, 180, 257
Cần Thơ (city), 36, 50, 147
Cao Đài (Cao Dai) sect, 38, 254
Catholicism (Catholic), 77, 87, 151, 187, 249, 252–54
CBU55 bomb, 41, 101
Central Intelligence Agency (CIA), x, 7, 19, 25, 138, 231
Chanda, Nayan, 89, 112, 162, 163, 164, 167, 173, 202, 251
Chân Tín (Chan Tin), 87, 150, 151, 155, 167, 250
Châu Tâm Luân (Chau Tam Luan), 249
Cheney, Dick, 231
Chenoweth, Bob, 220, 233–35
Chez Albert Restaurant, 46
Chiêu Hồi (Chieu Hoi) Program, 135, 241
Chị Mai (Chi Mai), 71, 72, 146, 174, 192, 192–96, 200, 205, 218, 219, 220, 221
Chinh, Trường. *See* Trường Chinh
Christmas Bombing, 11, 12, 85, 234, 255
CIA. *See* Central Intelligence Agency

Committee of Responsibility (COR), xv, 45, 92, 93, 94, 189, 194, 195
Congressional Research Service, 248
Cooper, Bill, 45, 92–95, 101, 110, 189, 193, 194, 197, 221
"cowboys," 68, 98, 99, 101, 107, 137, 153
curfew, 24, 27, 38, 49, 50, 52, 60, 76, 100, 131

*Decent Interval* (Snepp), x
Democratic Republic of Việt Nam, xv, 34, 70, 104, 181, 249, 255
Desbarats, Jacqueline, 242
Diệm, Ngô Đình. *See* Ngô Đình Diệm
Điện Biên Phủ (Dien Bien Phu; city), 70, 88, 124, 239
*Điện Tín* (newspaper), 51
Đình, Nguyễn Thị. *See* Nguyễn Thị Đình
dioxins, 246–48
Dispatch News Service, xvii, 244
divestiture program, 153
Đoàn Mộng Ngô, 179, 180, 214
Đồng, Phạm Văn. *See* Phạm Văn Đồng
Dow Chemical Company, 243
Đức, Ngô Công. *See* Ngô Công Đức
Dung, 13, 73, 83, 99, 107, 146, 192, 219
Dương Văn Minh (Duong Van Minh), 37, 40, 45, 47, 48, 51, 55, 59, 66
Duy. *See* Anh Duy

Eaton, Bob, 237–38
Ediger, Max, 44, 72, 144, 173, 183, 197, 211, 235–36
ethnic minorities, 253–54

Fonda, Jane, 145
Ford, Gerald (president), 19, 52, 110, 231
Forsythe, Julie, 11, 12, 17, 18, 27, 28, 85, 105, 107, 111, 147, 166, 206, 212, 213, 221
free fire zones, 243

Friendshipment, 230
*Friends Journal* (magazine), 105

Garrison, Mary Lee (vice consul), 35
Geneva Accords (agreement), 70, 88, 253, 256
German Hospital, 3, 4, 28, 235
*Giai Phong* (Terzani), 41
Giáp, Võ Nguyên. *See* Võ Nguyên Giáp
Giau, Lê Công. *See* Lê Công Giau
*Golden Rule* (sailboat), 237
Government of the Republic of Việt Nam (GRVN), xv, 34, 35, 37, 42, 66, 78, 98, 112, 135, 251, 255
Grall Hospital, 178, 184, 185, 187, 206
GRVN. *See* Government of the Republic of Việt Nam

Hải Phòng (city), 11, 238, 255
Hà Nội (city), 11, 79, 81, 84, 85, 104, 109, 117, 145, 171, 220, 233–35, 238–40, 251, 255
Hanoi Hilton (Hoả Lò; Hoa Lo), 220, 234
Harkin, Tom, 232
Hayden, Tom, 145
Hersh, Seymour, 244
Hoà Hảo (Hoa Hao) Buddhist sect, 254
Hoả Lò (Hoa Lo) Prison. *See* Hanoi Hilton
Hoàng Lộc (Hoang Loc), 96, 97, 99, 103, 112, 123, 128, 145
Hồ Chí Minh (Ho Chi Minh), 70, 102, 103, 239, 247
Hồ Chí Minh City. *See* Sài Gòn
Hồ Chí Minh (Ho Chi Minh) Trail, 87, 234
*Ho Chi Minh: The Missing Years* (Quinn-Judge), 70
Holt Adoption Agency, 37
Hồ Ngọc Nhuận (Ho Ngoc Nhuan), 40, 42, 249
Hồng Quân, 97, 118, 132, 188
Hồng Vân, 97, 118, 132, 160, 188

Hoskins, Tom, 8, 11, 12, 17, 18, 92, 173, 189, 204, 221, 227–28
Hostetter, Pat, 25, 183, 195
Hotel Caravelle, 38
Hotel Continental, 163
*How Pol Pot Came to Power* (Kiernan), 171
Hughes, Richard "Dick," 33, 203. *See also* Shoeshine Boys
Hùynh Liên (Huynh Lien), 33, 73, 78, 87, 125, 141, 147, 148, 211, 236, 249. *See also* Mendicant nuns
Hùynh Tấn Mẫm (Huynh Tan Mam), 44, 52, 66
Hùynh Tấn Phát (Huynh Tan Phat), 66, 111, 112, 115

Ichikawa, Hiro Yoshihiro (Hiro), 71, 72, 105, 173, 211
"I'm Dreaming of a White Christmas," 32
Indochina, 70, 84, 98, 114, 145, 171, 241, 257, 258
Indochina Peace Campaign, 145
International Social Services, 37

Jackson, Karl D., 242
Japanese occupation, 254
Jenkins, Loren, 45
Joint Military Commission, 34
Jones, Diane, xii, 21, 22, 245
Jones, Michael, xii, 245

Khmer Rouge, 111, 170
Khưu Thị Hồng. *See* Chị Mai
King, Jesse, 246
Kissinger, Henry, x, xi, 94, 115, 231, 250, 255, 256
Klassen, Jim, 72
Kontum (city), 24, 151
Kubicka, Eryl, 177, 205
Kubicka, Lou, 177, 205

# INDEX

Kuglin, Heidi, 8, 11, 12, 17, 25, 221
Kỳ, Nguyễn Cao. *See* Nguyễn Cao Kỳ

Lakey, George, 237
Lan, Nguyễn Ngọc. *See* Nguyễn Ngọc Lan
landmines, 2, 5, 21, 25, 72, 122, 216, 226
Land to the Tiller program, 153
language tutors. *See* Dung; Yến
Lao Động (Lao Dong) Party, x
Leahy, Patrick, 248
Lê Công Giàu (Le Cong Giau), 65, 66
Lê Đức Thọ (Le Duc Tho), xi, 115
Lê Xuân Chuyển (Le Xuan Chuyen), 241
"Liberate the South" (national anthem), 64, 89, 216
*Life* magazine, 233
Loan, Nguyễn Ngọc. *See* Nguyễn Ngọc Loan
Lộc Ninh (city), 45, 178, 257
looting, 50, 51, 56, 58, 59, 65, 69, 144, 184, 185, 227
Luce, Don, 154, 232–33
Lý Qúi Chung (Ly Quy Chung), 249

Mai. *See* Chị Mai
Mạnh Tường (Manh Tuong), 54–55, 56, 58, 66, 73, 74, 82, 89, 123, 124, 132, 182, 183, 205, 212, 221
Martin, Earl, 25, 27, 71, 72, 105, 139, 157, 173, 183, 195, 208, 212
Martin, Graham, x
Martin, Luke, 25, 34
*Mayaguez* (ship) "incident," 111, 114
MCC. *See* Mennonite Central Committee
McCloskey, Paul N. "Pete," Jr., 19, 20, 231–32
McNamara, Craig, 172, 238–40
McNamara, Robert, 138, 172, 239, 243
Mekong Delta, 38, 254, 257
Mendicant nuns, 33, 41, 141

Mennonite Central Committee (MCC), xv, 25, 34, 72, 76, 228–30
*Military Half, The* (Schell), xii
Minh, Đương Văn. *See* Đương Văn Minh
Ministry of Foreign Affairs, 88, 100, 104, 105, 175, 176, 181, 185, 188, 202
Montagnard, 254
Mỹ Khê hamlet, 244
Mỹ Lại, xii, 20, 21, 94, 244, 245
Mỹ Lại (My Lai) massacre. *See* Mỹ Lại

napalm, 5, 12, 101, 243
National Council of Reconciliation and Concord, 256
National Liberation Front (NLF), xi, xv, 1, 3, 15, 18, 20–24, 27, 29, 42, 64, 74, 83, 89, 115, 138, 153, 244
Nelson, Beryl, 237–38
Nelson, Marjorie, 238
Ngô Bá Thanh (Ngo Ba Thanh), 98, 99, 147, 148, 249, 250
Ngô Công Đức (Ngo Cong Duc), 249, 250
Ngô Đình Diệm (Ngo Dinh Diem), 66, 70, 253
Nguyễn Ái Quốc (Nguyen Ai Quoc). *See* Hồ Chí Minh (Ho Chi Minh)
Nguyễn Cao Kỳ (Nguyen Cao Ky), 47, 151, 250
Nguyễn Hữu Thái (Nguyen Huu Thai), 51, 65
Nguyễn Hữu Thọ (Nguyen Huu Tho), 111, 112, 115, 116
Nguyễn Ngọc Lan (Nguyen Ngoc Lan), 249
Nguyễn Ngọc Loan (Nguyen Ngoc Loan), 190
Nguyễn Thành Trung (Nguyen Thanh Trung), 31
Nguyễn Thị Bình (Nguyen Thi Binh), 111, 115, 118, 159
Nguyễn Thị Định (Nguyen Thi Dinh), 115
Nguyễn Thị Mai. *See* Chị Mai

Nguyễn Thị Ngọc Phượng (Nguyen Thi Ngoc Phuong), 247
Nguyễn Văn Lém (Nguyen Van Lem), 190
Nguyễn Văn Thiệu (Nguyen Van Thieu), 13, 19, 31, 36, 37, 38, 39, 40, 41, 44, 47, 66, 83, 87, 116, 119, 141, 151, 231, 236, 248, 250, 255–58
Nguyễn Văn Trỗi (Nguyen Van Troi), 138, 171
*Nhân Dân* (newspaper), 102
Nixon, Richard, 14, 19, 232, 246, 255–57
NLF. *See* National Liberation Front
Nobel Peace Prize, xv, 11, 115
northern doctors, 3, 108
northern medicine, 108, 166
North Vietnamese Army (NVA), xv, 18, 23, 25, 27, 82, 180
NVA. *See* North Vietnamese Army

Open Arms Program, 241
Operation Ranch Hand, 246

pacification, 24, 232
Paris Peace Agreement, 11, 12, 22, 34, 38, 40, 42, 44, 51, 112, 115, 181, 235, 246, 250, 255–58
*Peace Denied, A* (Porter), 250
Peers, William (general), 244
Peers Commission, 244
Phạm Văn Đồng (Pham Van Dong), 88, 104, 124, 132
Phạm Văn Lương (doctor), 4
Phan Thị Quyên (Phan Thi Quyen), 138
Phnom Penh, 47, 111, 170, 171, 232
*Phoenix of Hiroshima* (boat), 237–38
*Phụ Nữ Giải Phóng* (newspaper), 130, 180
Phương-Hằng Phan (Phuong-Hang Phan), 76, 143, 221, 228–30
Pike, Douglas, 241
Pilger, John, 45
Plantation, the, 234, 235

Pleiku, 24, 60
Pol Pot, 170, 171
Porter, Gareth, ix–xiii, 34, 171
POWs. *See* prisoners of war
Presidential Palace, 31, 47, 59, 63, 69, 70, 89, 96, 97, 115
PRG. *See* Provisional Revolutionary Government
prisoners of war (POWs), 220, 233–35
propaganda, ix, xi, xii, 41, 42, 55, 78, 80, 88
prosthetists, 5, 6, 8, 24, 194, 198
Protestant Evangelical Church of Việt Nam, 253, 254
Provisional Revolutionary Government (PRG), xvi, 27, 34, 52, 66, 85, 112, 115, 148, 159, 180, 248, 255

Quakers, 2, 5, 9, 10, 12, 46, 106, 177, 178, 221, 237. *See also* American Friends Service Committee
Quảng Đức (Quang Duc). *See* Thích Quảng Đức
Quảng Ngãi (city), xi, xii, 1, 4, 5, 7, 8, 11, 14–17, 19, 22, 25, 27, 58, 71–72, 108, 145, 172, 192, 193
Quinn-Judge, Paul, 11, 12, 21–23, 25, 28, 38, 39, 48, 58, 98, 105, 118, 159, 207, 221
Quinn-Judge, Sophie, 11, 12, 21–23, 25, 39, 44, 48, 70, 104, 105, 142, 166, 207, 221
Quỳnh Chi, 132, 172, 205, 221

Race, Jeffrey, 153
Rallier Program, 241
Rambo, Terry, 245
Rangers, 98
Red Cross, 45, 238
refugees, 1, 15, 110, 121, 138, 152, 157, 180, 218, 230, 235
rehabilitation center, 2, 4, 5, 19, 26, 27, 35, 71, 92, 111, 166, 174, 198, 219, 221, 226

religions, 38, 252–54. *See also* ancestor worship
Reynolds, Earle, 237

Sài Gòn (Saigon; Hồ Chí Minh City), 250, 251, 252
*Sài Gòn Giải Phóng* (newspaper), 143, 214
*Saigon Post* (newspaper), 37
sandals, 58, 61, 125, 135, 136, 140, 207
Sáu Xiân Tín (Sau Xian Tin), 158, 160, 161
Schell, Jonathan, xii
Schneider, Louis, 178
Scott, Larry, 237
secret police, 82, 88, 99, 151, 153
Self-Defense Forces, 24, 57, 68, 79, 98, 106, 144
Seven Mountains, 254
Seventh Day Adventist Hospital, 4, 207
Shoeshine Boys Project, 33, 203. *See also* Hughes, Richard "Dick"
Smith, Robert M., 245
Socialist Republic of Việt Nam, xvi, 115, 181, 252
Sơn Mỹ village, 244
Struggle Movements, 249, 253
Student Association Revolutionary Committee, 51, 65

Tam Giáo three religions, 252, 254
Tân Sơn Nhứt Airport, 28, 34, 45, 50, 53, 55, 64, 150
Taylor, Elizabeth "Beth," 10
Tây Ninh (city, province), 254, 257
Terzani, Tiziano, 41, 108
Tết Offensive, 18, 24, 234, 238, 249
*Tet with the Provisional Revolutionary Government* (Jones), 22
Thái, Nguyễn Hữ. *See* Nguyễn Hữ Thái
Thailand, 39, 59, 69, 111, 113, 116, 153, 258
Thanh, Ngô Bá. *See* Ngô Bá Thanh

Thanh Bình (Yến's niece), 47, 48, 51, 53, 177
*Thanh Niên* (newspaper), 45
Thích Quảng Đức (Thich Quang Duc), 253
Thiệu, Nguyễn Văn. *See* Nguyễn Văn Thiệu
Third Force (Third Segment), xvi, 33, 40, 73, 87, 98, 99, 141, 147, 148, 150, 248–50, 253
Thọ, Lê Đức. *See* Lê Đức Thọ (Le Duc Tho)
Thọ, Nguyễn Hưu. *See* Nguyễn Hưu Thọ
Thompson, Richard "Rick," 5, 8, 10, 11
Tiger Cages, 150, 154, 156, 232–33
*Tin Sáng* (newspaper), 250
torture, 5, 44, 66, 122, 155
Trần Hưu Thanh (Tran Huu Thanh), 150, 151
Trần Ngọc Liễng (Tran Ngoc Lieng), 249
Trần Thiện Khiêm (Tran Thien Khiem), 250
Trần Văn An (Tran Van An), 173, 174, 175
Trần Văn Đắc (Tran Van Dac), 241, 242
Trần Văn Hương (Tran Van Huong), 37, 39, 45, 47
Trỗi, Nguyễn Văn. *See* Nguyễn Văn Trỗi
Trung, Nguyễn Thành. *See* Nguyễn Thành Trung
Trường Chinh (Truong Chinh), 180
Trương Như Tảng (Truong Nhu Tang), 251
Tunnell, Bob, 232

UNICEF, 159
United Front for the Liberation of Oppressed Races (FULRO), 254
USAID, 3, 19, 25, 26, 50, 138, 153, 167, 248
U.S. Embassy, ix, 4, 32, 35, 36, 39, 43, 45, 54, 59, 240

Vạn Hạnh University, 56, 57, 88, 201
VC. *See* Việt Cong
Việt Cong (Viet Cong; VC), 43, 52, 71, 85, 118, 226, 251
Việt Minh, 253, 254

Việt Mỹ Organization, 145
Vietnamese Women's Museum, 220
Võ Hồng Nam (Vo Hong Nam), 238
Voice of America Radio, 52
Võ Nguyên Giáp (Vo Nguyen Giap), 239–40
Vũng Tàu (city), 127, 156
Vũ Văm Mẫu (Vu Van Mau), 66

Waldman, Peter, 246–47
Walton, Frank, 232–33
Watergate, 257

Weiss, Cora, 230
Westmoreland, William (general), xi, 244
white phosphorus, 5, 101
Wiles, Peter, 139
Willoughby, George, 237
World Council of Churches, 232

Xuân Lan (Xuan Lan), 179

Yến (Yen), 13, 35, 39, 42, 51, 64, 73, 74, 77–80, 83, 97, 98, 99, 109, 177, 196, 216, 219